What people are sa

Silver Butterfly Wings

Silver Butterfly Wings perfectly captures the confusion, half-understood conversations, and conflicting emotions of early grief. The narrative moves with ease from the distractions of the concrete practicalities that accompany death to a quiet Otherworldly divine place of "pure, radiant Love". Willow's honest and skillful storytelling immediately pulled me into the narrative, and I stayed with her, coffee cup in hand, throughout this beautifully-told sacred story. A must-read for anyone who has lost a loved one and knows intuitively that Love endures."
Kim Harrison, PhD, writer, poet, and author of *Just Write Poetry: 3 Weeks of Prompts to Establish a Daily Writing Practice, Silence Your Inner Critic & Learn To Trust Your Unique Poetic Voice*. www.RubyRiddlestein.com

A beautifully written, powerful and sensual account of personal loss and transformation that sweeps the reader from the cruel reality of physical death to the strength of pure and enduring love, heralded by signs and messages of life after life. I felt myself wince, smile, chuckle and hold my breath but I couldn't stop reading!
Constance C.F. Golden, PhD, author of *Healing Roots* and *Leaves of the Heart*

Previous Book

Reading Between The Lines
A Peek into the Secret World of a Palm Reader
ISBN: 978 1 84694 672 1

Silver Butterfly Wings

Signs From the Other Side Offering
Comfort and Hope After Death of a
Loved One

Silver Butterfly Wings

Signs From the Other Side Offering
Comfort and Hope After Death of a
Loved One

Wendy Willow

BOOKS

Winchester, UK
Washington, USA

JOHN HUNT PUBLISHING

First published by O-Books, 2022
O-Books is an imprint of John Hunt Publishing Ltd., 3 East St., Alresford,
Hampshire SO24 9EE, UK
office@jhpbooks.com
www.johnhuntpublishing.com
www.o-books.com

For distributor details and how to order please visit the 'Ordering' section on our website.

Text copyright: Wendy Willow 2021

ISBN: 978 1 78904 900 8
978 1 78904 901 5 (ebook)
Library of Congress Control Number: 2021913722

Design: Stuart Davies

UK: Printed and bound by CPI Group (UK) Ltd, Croydon, CR0 4YY
Printed in North America by CPI GPS partners

We operate a distinctive and ethical publishing philosophy in
all areas of our business, from our global network of authors to
production and worldwide distribution.

Contents

Book I: Silver Butterfly Wings   **1**

Chapter 1: July 3, 2010 – Mount Sinai Hospital, Montreal   3

Chapter 2: Early Days   15
- The Gathering   28

Chapter 3: Scattering of the Ashes   32

Chapter 4: Missing Him   39

Chapter 5: Slipping Away   48

Chapter 6: Difficult Days   58

Chapter 7: I'm Not Ready   76

Chapter 8: The Diagnosis   88

Chapter 9: Turning Point   97

Chapter 10: The Lines Between Us Are Blurry   117

Chapter 11: Hospital Madness   121

Chapter 12: The Transfer   138

Chapter 13: Palliative Care   148

Chapter 14: November   158

Chapter 15: Where Are You?   169

Chapter 16: Christmas   174

Chapter 17: The New Car   179

Chapter 18: January   185

Chapter 19: February   192
   - Do Spirits Cry?
   - Where Are The Birds?   193

Chapter 20: Valentine's Day   206
   - A Dinner To Remember   209

Chapter 21: March   216

Chapter 22: April   225
   - Caravan Day   232

Chapter 23: Changes   238

Chapter 24: May   243

Chapter 25: Transitioning   268

Chapter 26: Walking His Last Days   275

Book II: Silver Dragonfly Wings   **307**

Part I
Chapter 1: Year Two   309

Chapter 2: Autumn   321

Chapter 3: Winter   325

Chapter 4: Spring 2012   338

Chapter 5: Summer 2012   348

Chapter 6: Year Three   352

Part II
Chapter 1: Moving On   369

Chapter 2: Testing My Wings   385

Chapter 3: Full Circle   399

Author Biography   400

Previous Title   401

Note to Reader   403

This book is dedicated to all those grieving souls who have lost someone very dear to them. May you find hope and encouragement within these pages as you share in my journey from overwhelming heartache and loss to a place of comfort, strength and peace.

Hope is like the sun, which, as we journey toward it, casts the shadow of our burden behind us.

– Samuel Smiles

Book I

Silver Butterfly Wings

Chapter 1

July 3, 2010 – Mount Sinai Hospital, Montreal

"He's gone."

I felt nothing. My daughter's words meant nothing.

Gone? What did that even mean? Gone where?

My husband appeared to be sleeping peacefully on white hospital sheets. I waited expectantly for his chest to rise.

Nothing.

My eyes flew to my daughter's face seeking reassurance. There was none. Profound sadness, a twist of pain and something soft like compassion flowed from her eyes into mine.

I felt hollow. David couldn't be dead, could he? He was breathing a moment ago. I saw him. I heard him.

"He's gone, Mom," Brenda repeated.

She gently removed her hands from David's chest and eased back in her chair. Mine still held fast, yearning for the echo of his last heartbeat.

I could not let go. His body was still warm.

"Mom, he's gone."

Tears streamed down my cheeks. I was not ready to give him up. I wanted to catch the last rays of his life as they slipped through my fingers.

"I love you."

I kissed him gently, caressing his face with my own, knowing we would never have this time again.

I smoothed back his hair, and whispered loving words into his still ears. Could he hear me? Was he watching us somehow, from some other place?

The room was quiet; miraculously, no one had intruded during these last sacred moments of my husband's life. Late afternoon sunlight filtering through the windowsill garden, brought life and a slice of home to this sick room.

Time swirled around us, its calm softness meaning nothing.

"I want to wash his face."

Brenda looked up, eyes searching my face. Concerned. A flicker of something, then it was gone.

What? Did I say something wrong? I sucked in a breath and held it, waiting. But then her face softened and she smiled, speaking softly to me as if to a child.

"All right, we'll do that."

She rose briskly from her chair, gave my hand an encouraging squeeze, then left the room to locate the linen cart.

While she was gone, I eased back the bedcovers and slipped in beside my husband, snuggling him close. I gathered his lifeless body into my arms wanting to give comfort, and at the same time needing to suffuse my soul with whatever was left of his life force. How odd, this final exchange, how strange to not feel his warm embrace in return.

The swish of a curtain being pulled back signaled Brenda's return, arms laden with fresh towels.

As a registered nurse, she was quite comfortable with caring for a person whose life had just come to an end. I could hear a fraction of hesitation in her step, a pause, then tiptoeing footsteps as she made her way around the bed. She settled into her chair to wait, to give us time, as if watching her mother cradle a body was the most natural thing in the world. When I was ready, she handed me a facecloth.

I walked over to the tiny sink by the bed, rinsed the cloth in warm water and lovingly washed away the last remnants of my husband's illness.

Then I sat back down and just looked at him. I could not go. Could not leave him here. I wanted to do more.

Brenda, picking up on my feelings or sensing my uncertainty asked, "Do you want to wash the rest of him?"

4

"Oh yes," I replied. How did she know? That's exactly what I wanted.

"And we'll dress him in nice clothes too," she soothed.

Yes, I thought. That's just what I want to do.

The adjoining bathroom was only a few steps away. I went right in and turned on the taps to fill a basin with warm water. Just then the doctor arrived. I could hear him talking to my daughter in the room, but their voices were not clear. They were discussing the actual *time of death*, but I didn't know that.

"Four o'clock?" asked Doctor.

"Not quite," said Brenda.

I heard, "Not yet."

"Not yet?" I repeated in confusion, coming out of the bathroom, the basin of wash water in my hands. "You mean he's not dead yet?" My heart quickened in that instant and a wild surge of hope swept over me.

Brenda and Doctor looked blankly at one another. Then she understood.

"Yes he is, Mom," she said in a patient and gentle tone, sounding more like the mother and I the daughter. "He's gone."

Doctor left to start the paperwork. He popped back in a few minutes later.

"Where do you want your husband's remains sent?"

I just stared. What was he talking about?

"What funeral home?" he prompted.

"I have no idea." I truly didn't. You would think having my husband in Palliative Care meant we were "prepared" for this, but I wasn't. I could not think past this moment. Could not grasp that my dearly beloved had really died. After all, he was alive only a few moments ago.

"We'll call and let you know." My daughter seemed so wise. She knew how to do this. I did not. Doctor nodded and left the room.

Brenda turned to the clothes closet, opened the door and

5

took out a couple of shirts, holding them up for me to see.

"What do you think, the blue or the beige?"

"Neither. David likes purple – let's find his nice purple shirt."

Lovingly and tenderly we washed my dear husband, in a ritual as ancient as time itself. I made sure to cover up the body parts that were not being washed as we went along. I wanted to preserve his dignity, but also to keep him warm. I had cared for him faithfully throughout his illness and could not just stop because his life was over. That caring instinct is so strong, so protective. Letting go makes as much sense as holding back the tides.

Once we were done washing and dressing him, I gazed at his dear face; it was as if he was sleeping peacefully. The oxygen mask was finally gone and I could see him more clearly. He looked almost like the old David, the one I knew well before lung disease had stepped in to claim him. In death, he looked better than he had in sickness – almost. His face was relaxed, anxiety lines smoothed away, yet those impish sparkly eyes of his were closed forever.

I still could not leave.

"I'm going to wash his hair."

Brenda did not look surprised. She was accustomed to guiding families through the dying process. Care and ritual given to a loved one at the end-of-life and afterwards was part of that process.

I picked up a bottle of "no rinse shampoo" that was sitting on a shelf beside my husband's bed and proceeded to pour some of the liquid into my hands. As I rubbed shampoo into David's hair I wondered why he had to die so young. At 67 his hair was only partially grey, not completely, and it had grown over the weeks of his hospital stay.

Taking a fresh towel from the nightstand, I carefully dried his hair, making sure to lift his head from the pillow so the back was done too. Then I combed it all nice and neat.

"Oh, I know what you're thinking," I said to David. "Stop fussing over me, sweetheart!" Not that he would ever say that out loud; he was a gentle and sensitive soul and would probably have kept that thought to himself. Except that now he can't think.

He's dead.

But was he watching and listening to us as we lovingly cared for his inert body?

"I'm going home now, Mom," said Brenda gathering up her things. "When you're ready, come on over. You can stay with us as long as you like."

I nodded and watched her go. I don't know how much longer I stayed at David's bedside. It could have been minutes, it could have been days.

You will know when it's time to leave, echoed a voice in my head. I had read those words on a pamphlet I'd picked up at the nursing station a few weeks earlier. It was full of information meant to guide and support families through the painful process of watching a loved one die.

I took one last look at my husband's sweet, familiar, loving face, as he lay there peacefully amidst the starkness of white hospital sheets, and slipped quietly out the door. I could not face anyone, so kept my eyes to the floor as I walked swiftly away from that room. I did not thank or even acknowledge the nursing staff on my way out.

I just left.

For the last time, I thought, with a pang in my heart as the automatic glass doors of Mount Sinai Hospital swooshed open before me. Stepping out into the warm summer sunshine, I let out a sigh of relief as some of the heaviness slipped from my shoulders.

Relief?

Where had that come from? What was wrong with me? How

7

could I feel even a tiny measure of relief? My husband had just died and I'm feeling relief?

He's not sick anymore, my rational brain tried to tell me. He's safe... somewhere.

Safe? my emotions screamed back.

He's dead, how could he be safe? My broken heart could not comprehend, could not cope with the agony of such a total and final loss.

Somehow I found myself standing in front of my car in the parking lot. My body knew where it was going, knew what to do, but my mind was still with David in his hospital room.

But then in an instant everything changed. Conflicting emotions spun me around. I wanted to stay. No, I wanted to leave.

I couldn't wait to get out of there, couldn't wait to go somewhere, anywhere. I wanted to erase those thoughts, those pictures in my mind of David on his deathbed. I wanted to flee, to run from the pain.

And yet, how could I leave? How could I leave my husband behind?

Frantically I searched my mind for a solution. Somehow, I had to get him out of there. I had to find a way to bring him back home. This whole nightmare had to have been some horrible mistake.

Taking a deep breath, I forced myself to calm down.

I had to face reality.

I could not bring him home, not now, not ever. There was no mistake.

He was gone and I had to learn to accept that. I hoped, I prayed that he was in a higher place, a better place, somewhere other than where he had been for the past three months, tied to that hospital bed by an oxygen hose, struggling to breathe.

My car knew the way to the nearest Tim Hortons coffee shop. I was very much in need of the soothing reassurance a simple cup of coffee would provide. I gave my order to the server, but could not bring myself to ask for only one cup. I had to order two; one for David and one for me. Just like we always did.

By the time I arrived at my daughter's home in Lachine, the street was deserted. Nobody was about and I assumed people were in their backyards where trees and patio umbrellas provided welcome shade.

I parked the car on the street and just sat for a while. There was no hurry, no one to rush home to. The frantic pace I'd kept up with while David was in hospital was slowly ebbing away, and a quiet, unhurried protective fog of shock settled over me like a cloud drifting over a meadow, softening the landscape.

I needed a minute to shift gears, to comprehend...

Comprehend what?

Something, I don't know. And anyway, what was I going to do with David's coffee?

I looked around at the neighbors' homes: lawns green and tidy or sprinkled with dandelions, roses and peonies heavy with fragrance, pansies, snapdragons, marigolds spilling out of gardens or obediently lining a walkway, sidewalk chalk abandoned on the road.

Was it really summer?

Why would David choose to die in this warm and glorious season? Summer is the best time of year in my opinion.

Protectively clutching our take-out coffee, I angled my way out of the car, slammed the door with my foot, and drifted towards Brenda's front yard.

An enormous maple guarded the property, its huge canopy of leaves shading the entire front lawn. I paused for a moment at the base of the tree and gazed upward into those leaves as if searching for something.

For solace?

For wisdom?

I had no idea.

And then without stopping to think, I crouched down and poured David's coffee over the roots of that ancient maple. Little did I know that this would become a ritual in the weeks ahead.

"Here you are, sweetheart. Double-double, just the way you like it." I took a sip from my own cup and sat quietly in the cool grass. Old Maple had a way of sheltering wounded souls and as I eased into her lap, I found myself slipping effortlessly under her spell.

Squeals and shrieks of childish laughter pierced the air, rousing me from my dream-like state. Time to get up and move, I scolded myself. I can't sit here all day. So up I got and made my way around the side of the house and into the sanctuary of Brenda's backyard.

Evan, my son-in-law, must have been watching for me. As soon as I appeared, he broke away from the family to greet me with a quick compassionate hug. His face was solemn as he offered condolences. I took the garden chair he pulled out for me and gratefully sank into it.

As I sat in the yard watching my grandchildren at play, I felt strange; my focus, my awareness was constantly shifting, floating in and out of reality. I was part of this family, and yet I was not. My body was sitting here absorbing the warm summer sunshine, inhaling fresh sweet air. Conversation swirled around me, ebbing and flowing. And yet my mind was back at the hospital reliving the transition of David's passing.

Did he really die?

Was I never going back to Mount Sinai Hospital to visit him? The whole thing felt bizarre, surreal. I tightened my grip around my coffee cup, as if holding on for support.

Incredibly, life continued to flow, even though my whole world had shattered. I could smell a neighbor's BBQ. Was it suppertime? Lunchtime?

I watched as squirrels raced up and down trees, birds pecked at something in the hedges or in the grass, listened as sounds

Wind rustling through the leaves drew my attention upward. The sky had transformed to a deeper more solemn shade of blue. Puffy clouds glowed soft shades of rose and peach, their edges tinged with gold in the dying light.

It was then that a strange and wonderful thing happened. Powerful waves of Love washed over me, through me and around me with a force so intense that I had to hold on to my chair for a minute to steady myself.

Pure, radiant Love, with a strength and clarity I had not known in my earthly life surrounded and embraced my very being.

Face tilted to the heavens, I gratefully opened myself to receive this rich abundance of Love so freely and joyfully given. I basked in the glow, bathed in it, until I was completely saturated, filled to the brim.

I knew at once where it was coming from.

David.

It could only be from David, and in sending this Heavenly Love, it was his way of reassuring me that he was okay. More than okay. He had made it to the Other Side and his Transition had been smooth. Like stepping out into the unknown, taking a leap of faith and at the end of the journey, arriving home safely.

Could I say he was happy? I don't know. Happy is a funny word. It seems more like a word that belongs to this Earth. Not an Otherworldly one.

Content? No, it was a much stronger feeling than contentment.

Radiant? Definitely.

Joyful? Yes, I think so. It was hard to think about joy right now. But one thing I was very sure about was that those waves of love flowing over me brought peace to my confused mind and serenity to my lonely soul.

Sometime later (it could have been minutes or hours, I don't really know) I answered the door.

Peter, my son, my precious son was standing on the front

porch. I was happy to see him, to look into his beloved, familiar face. Peter, 38 years old, tall and strong. When did that happen? A family man now with his own business. I was proud of all he had accomplished as a young man at this stage of life. But more importantly, I was proud of who he was as a person; a trustworthy, honest soul, who wouldn't hesitate to put his own life in the path of danger to protect his family.

He stared at me in surprise.

"Mom. You look fine!"

"Yes, I'm all right. I feel like I'm riding a wave of peace and love. And I'll keep on riding it until I crash."

Under the covers in bed that night, those steady waves continued with a rhythm I found soothing. It felt as if David was wrapping me, swaddling me, cocooning me in his sacred arms with Heavenly Love; to share with me his Otherworldly experience, or perhaps to shelter me from the ravages of panic and fear which would inevitably take over my life, as time swept him further away from me and into the unknown.

I really cannot explain it, nor can I find words to describe these incredible feelings of serenity, of rejoicing, of pure, clear, unmistakable Love swirling around me, holding me tight, keeping me safe in our bed.

The strength of these feelings I've never known before, never knew existed in our earthly realm. I did not expect to feel that way, could not really think beyond the cruel reality that death brings, but on this night, I felt the richness of abundant Love, the protection of a thousand singing angels. I felt treasured beyond anything I could ever imagine.

And slept better than I had in years.

Chapter 2

Early Days

Funeral Home called the next day. I was required to come in and sign some papers. When would it be convenient?

I had no idea.

David had died only the day before and I simply could not grasp what this man on the phone wanted me to do. Handing the receiver to Peter, I put my head down on the kitchen table, closed my eyes and let him take charge. He set up an appointment for later in the day. I was grateful to have his support.

My world had come crashing down this morning, just as I'd feared. Songbirds outside my bedroom window woke me before dawn. I listened to their sweet melodies as I lay in bed, not wanting to face the harsh reality of David's passing, not wanting to feel the aftershock, the acute emptiness, for no matter how "prepared" you think you are – the End is still the End. I could still feel his arms wrapped around me, in a loving embrace, but the feelings were fading, like flower petals scattered over dry earth at summer's end.

No, I did not pat the covers expecting to find him sleeping next to me. I'd stopped doing that a month or so into his hospital stay. Looking back it seems like that hospital admission was a sort of preparation, almost as if God was letting me down gently. We'll keep him here for a while so you can get used to an empty house, to sleeping alone and then we'll take him away forever.

Downstairs in the kitchen, I prepared my coffee. Coffee for one, instead of two.

Where are you, David? I whispered into the stillness of our house. Yes, our house. It is still our house. I was beginning to feel the awful sadness, creeping slowly into my soul.

The separateness.

The aloneness.

Where was that magnificent wave of pure Heavenly love? That ethereal joy that could only be guiding David towards the Light? Why had everything smashed, leaving me with grief, sadness, and pain?

Peter drove me to the Funeral Home. I was so glad now that he had come, and thankful for his strong and guiding presence. The funeral director was very respectful; a professional doing his job. Peter and I sat in his office, filling out the necessary, but tiresome paperwork. How I wish David was here with me!

"Your husband's remains have been transferred from the hospital and are now resting here," Funeral Director informed me in a hushed, comforting tone of voice.

What? Remains? What remains? Oh my god! I can't do this!

Just picturing my dear husband lying in the morgue downstairs was not comforting to me at all! It was horrible!

Yikes! Why can't we just go home? All of us! Come on, David, get up! This is all a bad dream. A nightmare. Let's go home! As my poor brain screamed these thoughts, I focused on the tasks at hand, trying to maintain some sense of balance in a world gone crazy.

My world. And it was in shreds, never to be the same again.

Funeral Director looked down at his documents, preparing to go on to the next section.

Peter looked relaxed as he sat in the chair next to me, but I could tell he was alert, watching me for signs of a breakdown. No, I was not going to cry. Let's just get through this. One step at a time. My mantra for so long while David was sick. I'll just have to continue with it. One step at a time.

"Do you want to know when the cremation will be?"

"NO!" I shouted at poor Funeral Man.

Not perturbed in the least, he merely nodded his head.

Peter gave me a funny look, a question clear in his eyes.

"No," I repeated, shaking my head and sucking in a calming breath. "I just can't go there."

Peter nodded as if he understood.

Driving home I felt myself coming undone. My body was numb, yet quivering. Ripping pain seared through me, as if my heart and soul were being torn apart. How could I merrily go home on this nice sunny summer day, leaving David behind to lie cold and stiff in the dark basement of the crematorium?

How could I open the car window and breathe in fresh air? Feel the warmth of the sun? Talk with my son about ordinary things like what to have for supper? Finally I couldn't take it anymore. I burst into tears. Peter pulled the car over to the side of the road. To his credit, he did not ask me if I was okay.

He just put his hand on my shoulder, while I sobbed and sobbed.

That night I told him to go on home. His wife and young son would be waiting for him in Ottawa, and he had a business to run. I assured him that I would be all right on my own.

The following morning I sat on my back deck alone. Another beautiful day had begun. The sun was up and the air was growing warmer. Summer – my favorite season. A carefree time of long lazy days, flowers and sunshine, swimming and picnics. I adore the heat and relish the freedom of stepping outside in flip-flops or sandals or barefoot as often as not. Shorts, T-shirts, summer dresses, toes in the grass, fingers in the earth, ice cream, friends popping over, outings, bicycle trips, holidays. I love it all and could not fathom, could not imagine dying in the midst of this vibrant time of year. It made no sense. But then nothing was making sense any more.

I felt lost. My focus, my direction, was gone. I had looked after David for so long. His needs became my needs. His care my primary concern. I cooked for him, cleaned for him, saw to all of his basic personal needs. I even learned to cut his hair! I picked up his medications, ran the household: shopping, laundry, bank, library. I was the liaison person. I took all phone calls and made all of his medical appointments.

And now there was nothing.

No loving man in the house to look after. No loving man in the hospital to visit. No worrying about his treatments, care plan, prognosis, medical condition.

Nothing.

I felt empty. Worse, I felt totally off balance like the carpet had been pulled out from under me. I was dizzy, aching. My head spinning. My world turned inside out. Where do I go now? What do I do?

Overwhelmed with feelings of anguish, I put my head in my hands and sobbed. Great wracking sobs. Never had I felt such grief, such excruciating suffocating pain. I was frightened, lost, completely disoriented.

My breath came in short, painful spasms. Tight bands in my chest were squeezing the air out of my lungs. What was happening to me? Blackness lapped at the edges of my vision. Dropping my head to my knees I squished myself into a little ball, hoping to make the world go away. Hoping to dispel the blackness that was threatening to pull me under.

Something whispered to my soul.

Instinctively I looked up. A butterfly was resting quietly on the back of the Other Chair.

The empty one.

The one where David would normally be sitting. It sat quite still as if waiting to be noticed. Calm. Gentle. Serene. It was her peacefulness, her simplicity, her stillness that spoke to me.

A poem sprang into my head: *Do not stand at my grave and weep…*

Was that David's voice I heard in my head? I stopped crying to listen. There was nothing more. I turned my attention back to the butterfly. It was an elegant shade of orange with black markings on its wings, like eyes.

All at once I understood. According to Chinese belief whenever someone sees a butterfly, it is a soul come back from the dead to comfort those left behind. It brings a sacred message, "I am well. I am happy. Do not grieve for me."

I sat up in the chair and rubbed my eyes.

"Did you send me this butterfly?" I asked the air, feeling my spirits lift a bit. Somewhere from the depths of my being, I knew it had to be true. My sadness had shifted, hope was creeping in and I was beginning to feel better. Could this really be a gift or message from David? I'd never seen a butterfly with these markings before. Monarchs, yes, there were plenty of those, but this was not a monarch. Later on I learned it was a buckeye.

Night times are horrible. The house becomes eerie in its absolute quietness; the darkness chilly and frightening. I feel as if I've left this earth too, and I now exist in a whirling vortex, a foreign land, a distorted universe, where nothing makes sense.

Where are the markers? The objects of reassurance to hold on to: his slippers under the bed, pants draped over the chair in the corner, cup of tea resting on the night table next to his eyeglasses. The familiar, comfortable world I used to inhabit is gone; irrevocably and ruthlessly changed forever. I lie awake in our bed, nauseous with worry and fear.

Tears flow down my cheeks, thoroughly soaking my pillow. I miss David's warm body next to mine, as I blindly reach out in the dark to touch his empty pillow. I know his pillow will forever be empty now, but I need to touch it in case he'd left a little bit of his essence behind.

"Please send me a dream," I entreat my newly departed husband, "so I know you are safe. So I know you are not gone to some dark and horrible place."

I awoke in the early pre-dawn hours, vaguely aware of David having come to me in a dream. What was it? If only I could remember! Squeezing my eyes shut I tried to recapture that elusive dream. I willed myself back to that place where I'd sensed my husband. And then I remembered.

I was in a boat. I don't know where it was going. I had a small child by the hand. Try as I would, I could not remember who this child was. I think it was a little boy. A grandchild? Nephew? One of my own boys? My husband as a child? Do you go backwards in time when you die?

Dreams are funny. Time does not run like it does here on earth. My children are grown now, but when they come to me in dreams, often they are still toddlers or teens. So I don't know who this child was.

There was a stethoscope around my neck. David's. He had been a doctor in this life. A gentle and respected physician, who loved and lived for his work. As we sailed along towards an unknown destination, somebody mistakenly addressed me as "doctor". I was too weary to correct him (or her, I forget).

Upon awakening, the message was clear. David was within. We are one.

The house is so quiet. I wander around from room to room shivering. Where is he? Why are his things here and he's not? Is he all right? The kitchen light flickers, but I ignore it. What am I doing in this house? There is nothing to do here. No one to look after.

I've never lived alone before. I was married right from my parents' home when I was 19. Even after I divorced my first husband, I lived with my children. Life was never quiet, never dull. Anyone who has lived with children who grow into noisy teenagers knows the happy sounds of doors slamming, phones ringing, voices calling from every room in the house. A house that always feels alive – even in the middle of the night:

"Mom, did you sign my report card?"

"Mom, there's a spider on my ceiling!"

"Mom, I feel sick! I'm going to throw up!"

It's not just living all alone. It's the nerve-racking conspicuous absence of sound. David's oxygen concentrator was running 24/7, filling our home with a constant humming, droning noise. And yet that noise was reassuring, for it meant that David was alive. He was hooked up to a plug-in-the-wall machine that made oxygen out of room air. He could not survive without it. Absence of this humming noise, meant absence of life. The only time that machine was silent was when we had a power failure. And that was scary.

It was December 2009, somewhere around midnight. David and I were cuddled up in bed, drifting in and out of sleep. Freezing rain slashed at our windows. Strong winds screeched, rattling the glass panes as if trying to find a way in. Suddenly, I heard a loud CRACK, as frozen branches snapped off the trees. One of them hit our roof with a thud.

"Who's walking on our roof?" Hubby asked sleepily.

"Santa's reindeer," I murmured nuzzling the back of his neck.

Delicious waves of sleep enveloped me, yet something was nagging at the back of my mind and wouldn't let go; something swimming through the fog, persistently trying to get my attention.

Go away.

I was tired from all the Christmas busyness. Happy for the celebration with family and happy it was over. Sleep was inviting, beckoning. David was already in dreamland. It doesn't take him long.

The wind continued to howl, blowing and shrieking like a banshee. Did I leave a window open? Not likely in this weather. Something was still tugging at my consciousness; would not leave me alone. I could hear "it" screaming.

Screaming? Piercing shriek? An alarm? Yikes! Suddenly I was up like a shot!

The power was out!

I should have known. That loud crack might have been a tree branch, but could just as easily have been a power line snapping in the storm.

No electricity meant no oxygen for David. In a flash, I switched on the portable oxygen cylinder (which lies like a sleeping dog curled up on the floor beside our bed), popped the nasal cannula up his nose, then ran out of the bedroom and downstairs to shut off that screaming alarm. I pulled the plastic tubing out of the now silent (and useless) oxygen concentrator, picked up a flashlight and ran down another flight of stairs to our dark and dusty basement, where the emergency cylinder lived. It was huge, almost as tall as I, which was why it was hidden away, in the depths of our cellar.

I quickly located the valve on top of that huge cylinder, slapped the wrench-like tool in place and twisted it "open". Then I adjusted the rate of flow, specifically for David's needs. His disease had progressed to the point where he needed a high flow of oxygen. The higher the flow rate, the more oxygen consumed and the faster that life-saving oxygen would run out of the tank.

Fortunately, our supplier had come by the week before and filled the tank, so there was enough oxygen to last the whole night through, if needed. While I was downstairs, I picked up the phone and called Hydro to find out how long this power failure would last. Not more than an hour or two, came the recorded reply. Then I went back to bed. And changed David's nose hoses (took out the cannula attached to the small portable tank, and exchanged it for the one I'd just hooked up to the long-lasting cylinder in the basement).

David was drifting off to sleep again, but by this time I was wired. I could not go back to sleep. What would have happened if I had not heard that alarm? I'd been taking sleeping medication over the past month, which would account for the deeper quality of my sleep; my brain gratefully sinking into oblivion instead of jumping at every little sound. But never in the wilds of my imagination did I think it would be possible to NOT hear that shrieking alarm! If we had both gone to sleep with no electricity in the house, David would not have woken up in the morning. Guaranteed.

The storm continued throughout the night. The power came back on, then went out again. I connected nose hoses and machines and disconnected nose hoses and machines. And then did everything in reverse. Hubby slept on, but I did not get much sleep that night.

That was seven months before he died, and despite the fear and anxiety, I wish with all my heart that we could be back there again, snuggling and cuddling in our warm bed.

My children, bless them, all wanted to do something to help, to ease my pain. I had repeatedly refused their kind offers over the weeks while David was in hospital. What could they possibly do? I couldn't even think. Every waking hour was spent at the hospital. There was nothing of importance to be taken care of at home. I couldn't have cared less if the house flooded and floated away. Housework was not even attempted.

But now I allowed myself to soften, to release, like air slowly hissing out of a balloon. I felt limp, yet open and finally able to receive help. I think it was more of a passive surrender than an actual reaching out for help.

Brenda dove right in (now that I'd stopped resisting), by making requisite phone calls and handling all administrative details with the funeral home. She had been in touch with the Crematorium and was calling to let me know that things were moving on schedule.

"Everything is fine, Mom, the cremation will take place at 11:00 tomorrow."

"Oh Noooooo," I wailed at my poor daughter, "I did NOT want to know that! There is NO WAY I want that picture of

David in my mind. Noooooooo!"

"Mom! I'm so sorry. I thought you'd want to know!" Brenda sounded so upset that I paused to take a deep breath and launched instinctively into mothering mode.

"It's okay," I said feeling my way through this. "It is meant to be. Somehow I need to know this information. It's okay. It's okay."

This last bit was said more to myself than to her. I was attempting to come to terms with this information that I had so adamantly refused to hear. Picturing my dear husband going through the flames was something I Could Not Do.

I hung up the phone, curled up in the chair and wept. I felt sick. I felt weak. How could this have happened? I did NOT want to know. My heart was breaking once again with this new knowledge. How could I handle this?

Agitated now, I jumped up from my chair. I needed to move, to escape. Out of the kitchen and into the hallway.

What to do, what to do?

Nothing. I can't change anything, can't pretend that conversation never took place. I moved on into the living room with its thick, soft, but aging carpet, through the dining room skirting the china cabinet, and found myself back in the kitchen.

Reaching for a tissue, I took a few deep calming breaths and blew my nose. "Now just relax (I told myself firmly), this is all meant to be somehow. I'll just have to go with it. I can handle this. There has to be a reason for it, so just go with it."

During the night I woke up shuddering. I could feel my heart quivering, as David's had in the hours before he died. I could hear breathing and smell the musky smell of death.

I awoke the following morning with a feeling of dread, a wrenching in the pit of my stomach. How will I get through this day? How will my dear husband? Just because he's dead doesn't mean he can't feel anything. What happens if he really can feel the cremation? How do "they" know? How does anyone know what happens after you die. Especially in the first few hours, days, weeks? What if he's really not dead?

I spent the early part of the morning in busy work. Washing dishes, sweeping the floor over and over, cleaning all the mirrors in the house, putting in a load of laundry, walking around in circles. The kitchen lights flickered, dim then bright then back to dim again.

At 10:45 I made myself a cup of coffee and stepped out into the backyard. I crossed over to greet our ancient oak tree, Grandfather Oak. Easily a hundred years old, he doesn't mind that my clothesline is fastened to his bark. He doesn't mind that David nailed a bluebird house to his trunk one fine spring day. He is patient and wise and sits smack in the middle of our backyard.

I had gathered up an assortment of candles from around the house. Most were tealights, but there were some deep blue and white pillar candles too. I placed them all in a circle around the mossy base of Grandfather Oak. Sitting on the ground, I made myself comfortable and lit each candle one by one. I sipped my coffee and poured a little for David under the tree. I sent him Love. I prayed. I sang songs. I told David that I loved him and that I'd never abandon him. It felt like he needed me for this ceremony, this terrible time of "going through the fire", so I put a picture in my mind of David and I holding hands. I wanted him to know that I was with him; that we were going through this together. I encouraged him. I nurtured him with my love, just like I did when he lay dying in that hospital bed only a few days ago.

After a while I blew out the candles and just sat. Quietly. For a few moments more. I needed some time to be still. To breathe gently, to absorb, to assimilate what had just happened. I needed to rest for a moment before leaving this place-under-the-tree, which had now become sacred.

Instinctively, I looked up to the heavens searching for David. Was he somehow flying away? What happens to his Soul now that the body is no more? I thought his Soul had already gone at the moment of death. Was there still a little bit left behind somewhere? Or is it like a process that takes a while to complete, as if the Soul hovers somewhere between heaven and earth for a period of time before finally departing?

Gradually I became aware of sounds around me; ordinary sounds that had been muted as if I'd been swimming underwater. Now I could hear the drone of an airplane overhead, a car door slamming, footsteps, people talking. It was almost as if I were awakening from a strange dream or a long sleep.

The summer sunshine felt warm against my skin; the air soft and gentle on my bare legs. The ground underneath my bottom had become hard and lumpy. Time to get going, I told myself.

I couldn't resist taking another look at the sky. Was David watching from somewhere up in the clouds? Was he nodding and smiling at me sitting in our backyard? I rather felt that he was. Whether that made any sense or not, didn't matter one bit to me.

I stood up and stretched my legs that had become stiff with sitting. I shook off the grass and bits of dirt that had collected in my skirt, and went back into the house. I just had time to put my coffee cup in the sink and fill a drinking glass with water, when the doorbell rang. I was tempted to stay in the kitchen and not answer, but I peeked through the window anyway, just in case. Standing on my doorstep were two official-looking men in dark suits.

Alarmed, I took a quick step back. Had I broken the law by lighting candles under a tree? Had somebody complained? Were those men from the city of Hudson? Did they think I'd been trying to burn down trees in my backyard?

Realizing it was too late to run away, I forced myself to reach for the door handle. Cautiously pulling it open, I was met by eager smiles and in-your-face pamphlets.

Jehovah's Witnesses.

Oh no! I did not want to talk to anybody right now, but it was too late. I had already opened the door.

"Hello," said a pleasant-looking man, "my name is David."

What? screamed my brain. David? And then I lost it.

I doubled over as if punched in the gut and cried and cried and cried. Right there at the door. Those poor men just stood there. They looked at each other, then back at me.

"Ma'am? Ma'am? Are you having a bad day?" asked the man who had identified himself as David.

I could not stop. I could not help myself. I howled.

"Ma'am?" he repeated.

Finally, with a great deal of effort I managed to pull myself together.

"A bad day? A bad day?" I wailed at those men. "My husband passed away three days ago and his name was David!"

They just looked at me.

"I'm so sorry. Would you like to hear a scripture?"

"Excuse me? No!" What on earth would I want to hear a scripture for? I wanted my husband back! Not words or readings, or strange men standing on my front porch.

They tried for a few more minutes to interest me in their literature, but soon gave up. They were not getting through to me. Nor I to them, apparently.

The gentlemen turned to go, but now I wanted them to stay. I wanted to cling to that man whose name was the same as my husband's. Looking deep into his blue eyes, while tightly clasping his hand in both of mine, I asked, "How old are you, David?"

"Forty-five."

"You're still young and I hope healthy, so don't you dare die on your wife!"

"No, Ma'am."

I watched them as they turned and walked away, down my front steps and out onto the driveway. I'll bet they were so relieved to get away from this crazy lady and her house of sorrow. I doubt they'll be stopping by ever again.

Dear God, is this never going to end? My heart was torn in two, did I need the added stress of people coming to the door trying to convert me? Especially someone with my husband's name? Why did this have to happen? What on earth made me open the door to Jehovah's Witnesses?

And then it hit me like a ton of bricks. Here was confirmation. Confirmation that the ritual I had performed under Grandfather Oak was the right thing to do. How else could I possibly know that David (my David) wanted, no not just wanted, needed me to be there with him? He needed my love and prayers. He needed my spiritual presence as he was going through the cremation process. Everything was mysteriously working the way it was meant to. And by David showing up at my door, I knew my David had found a way to say, "Thank you." There is no other explanation. The timing has to be perfect or the message does not get delivered. Coincidences don't happen.

The Gathering

My husband did not want any fuss. He was a humble man, a gentle and kind-hearted healer in this life. And so in death, his instructions were clear: no stone, no funeral, no viewing, no obituary.

However, early one morning, just before dawn, I was walking around the neighborhood in my pajamas and flip-flops. It had been another sleepless night, and not knowing what else to do, I got up to walk. Walk through my grief, move, do something, anything to lessen the pain. Nobody was up at that hour, as evidenced by early morning newspapers plonked at the end of each driveway.

It must have been the rhythm of those papers, as I walked

by. Meaning, I'd walk and look at a newspaper; walk some more and look at another one. But I didn't really see what I was looking at. Instead it was the rhythm that snagged my attention. The persistent repetition of driveway, newspaper, driveway, newspaper eventually poked its way into my consciousness, waking me up. You'd think the hypnotic rhythm would put me to sleep, rather than grabbing my attention. But the pattern forced me to see not one newspaper, but many. Almost every one of my neighbors subscribed to the *Montreal Gazette*.

Well that does it, I decided on the spur of the moment, I'm going to write an obituary, and put it in the paper. I'm sorry, sweetheart, I know you didn't want this. Well, I didn't want you to die either, I rationalized.

My husband was a well-known and respected member of our community. After his diagnosis, however, he chose to hide, to lie low. He did not want people to know he was ill, especially his patients. In his mind, doctors treated patients, they did not become patients.

But (I continued the argument in my head) David's former patients and our small community need to know. Did they have the "right" to know? I don't know. I barely knew what day it was. Somehow, even though everything else in my life was twisted this seemed to make sense. I would write my dear hubby's obituary.

He didn't want one, my mind taunted me. Well then, I compromised, I'll just omit the personal details. Nobody has to know what he died of. In fact, I won't even publish his date of birth, then nobody will know how old he was either.

This is what I wrote:

NELLIGAN, Dr. David John
July 3, 2010
Slipped quietly from this earth with peace and dignity on July 3,

2010, surrounded by his loving family. A gentle healer, a gentle soul, he touched many lives. Gone, but never forgotten, for how could we forget his intelligent mind, wise spirit, and compassionate nature? Raise a toast if you will, say a prayer, make a donation to the charity of your choice, or simply send a caring thought his way, as there will be no funeral at his request.

The obituary was printed in the *Montreal Gazette* on Saturday, the week after David's death, which turned out to be on the very day of the "gathering". I was in no shape to plan and organize anything, however, my dear daughter took on the task. By organizing this gathering, wake or whatever it was called, she was also going against his wishes. But she felt very strongly that David's passing should be marked by a family gathering, not ignored.

I planted myself on the living room sofa and let everybody work around me. Josh, David's youngest son, and his family were staying at our house, as they were from out-of-town. I did not clean up, did not make food or even coffee. For the first time in my adult life, I allowed others to take care of me.

It was an odd feeling, this surrendering, but then, I'd had to surrender David, didn't I? He was gone, cruelly ripped away from me. What more was there to give up? Nothing was more important that David; everything else existed in shadow. I was already hurt beyond repair, nothing could touch me now.

David's brother and his wife arrived, looking tired after their long drive up from Vermont. I stepped forward to welcome them and promptly burst into tears. They had been regular visitors at the hospital, and were present just hours before David died.

"I was not going to do this," I wailed, holding tight to David's brother.

I had wanted to be serene, dignified, and able to cope. I did not want pity or commiseration, for that would send me tumbling over the edge. A good friend of mine who had also lost her husband was able to keep it all together. She was dry-eyed throughout the funeral. At the time, I wondered if she really missed her husband or was just very good at keeping her emotions under control.

Several neighbors rang the front doorbell. They must have read the obituary in the morning paper and kindly stopped by to offer condolences. I could not answer it; did not want to face anybody except family. John, David's eldest son, took me out to the back deck, away from everyone for a while and sat with me while I cried. Somebody brought a cake, somebody else flowers, and somebody else looked after the well-wishers.

I don't remember much about that day. Did I eat? Was the food good? Were the grandchildren well behaved or out-of-control? Who was actually there? The house was full, and I remember looking around the room at all the faces. There were brothers and sisters, spouses and in-laws, children and grandchildren. But where was David? He should have been with us. This was his home. His family were here. Where was he?

Whatever else happened that day is just a haze in my memory now. But I do remember the feelings I had when everybody left and I was alone again. Part of me was relieved. The noise and people were gone. But another part of me was beginning to panic. What do I do now?

Is it time to eat? No, I think we did that. Time to sleep? No, it's still sunny outside. Housework? I looked in the kitchen. Somebody had cleaned up. Should I go for another walk? No, I was tired. So what do I do? How do I go on with life? I can't. Plain and simple.

Where are you, David? Are you all right? Please can't I just see you? Hug you? Talk to you? Why does this have to happen? There were no answers of course. The ceiling lights in the kitchen flickered, but I paid no attention.

Chapter 3

Scattering of the Ashes

It sounds so macabre. This person who I've loved and lived with is now reduced to a pile of ashes. How demoralizing. How strange. Could I even do this?

It had been 10 days since David's passing. Josh and his family arrived a few days earlier, and since they lived clear across the country, it made sense to scatter his Dad's ashes at this time before they all returned home, to British Columbia.

Standing at the bedroom window in my nightgown, I watched as the sun struggled to rise in a rose-tinted sky. Clouds, heavy with moisture, appeared to be suppressing its eager golden glow, as if determined to hold back the day. Eventually they drifted away as if losing interest, and by the time I'd eaten breakfast and showered, only a lingering haze remained. The air was humid with a lazy, mellow feel to it; the kind of day you can relax into as if all was well with the world.

Strange. All was not well with my world, but I wasn't going to argue with Mother Nature. Let's just get on with the day, I thought.

Josh and his family had driven over to Thompson Park, a soccer field that sloped gently down from the road to the shores of Lake of Two Mountains. We had chosen this location to scatter David's ashes as it was close to home. Both John and Josh had played soccer in the park when they were schoolboys, Dad happily coaching from the sidelines.

Josh, Christina and their two children were sitting on a picnic blanket in the grass when John and I arrived. John had offered to pick me up and I was thankful for that. I didn't want to go alone. I didn't really want to do this at all.

The water table was low this year forcing us to wade out a

ways, past rushes and reeds to find a suitable spot. It had to be a place where the water was deep and flowed swiftly enough to carry David's ashes away.

I looked around and saw sailboats in the distance. It was very peaceful to watch the boats as they glided smoothly along the lake. I could hear bullfrogs croaking somewhere in the shallows, and the steady hum of insects. Willows by the shoreline waved their long, slender limbs as if in greeting.

All was serene.

Everything as it should be on this beautiful day, except that my dear husband was about to be scattered to the four winds.

Strangely enough, I did not feel raw or sick or helpless. I felt fine. I felt calm.

David's boys and I opened the small box without ceremony, shaking out the contents until it was empty. I placed flowers in the water, gifts from sympathetic friends. It seemed fitting that they accompany my loving husband on his final journey. As I watched them float away, I wondered where they would end up. I wondered where David would end up.

The Sons were crying, arms around each other's shoulders. They were grown men and yet standing together in the lake up to their knees, I pictured them as little boys, holding tight to each other as Daddy went away; never to return. I walked back to shore, leaving the brothers to grieve, pray and share these private moments together, alone.

Sitting on the grass, a strange feeling of calm, of peaceful release settled over me. It was most unusual and not what I'd expected. Where had this come from? I thought I'd feel torn to shreds at this stage, at this grievous ritual of scattering my husband's remains and watching while they floated away, but I didn't. It was as if everything was all right. David was telling me he was okay with it. Or else my emotions were numb, existing somewhere outside of myself or wrapped up in that soft fog that protects one from shock.

A dragonfly appeared, its translucent wings glistening in the sunlight. Dragonflies are a powerful symbol of transformation, of light, of changes in the wind. I watched it for a bit, before it skimmed away across the water.

Movement out of the corner of my eye turned out to be a butterfly. It was orange and black and pretty, not unlike the buckeye I'd seen on my back deck, except that this one was smaller. It was feeding on a clump of purple weeds that waved serenely in the light breeze. I watched it for a few moments as it delicately sipped nectar or whatever butterflies do and then darted away.

Could that possibly be another messenger from the Other Side? The timing was right. The place was certainly right. Was I imagining things? A moment later it was back. It flew here and there, dipping and fluttering. I wondered what it was doing. And then I saw the other one. Now there were two. Both of them orange and black, flying and swirling about, as if playing a game of tag, or dancing to some inner rhythm. They made a cute couple.

Goosebumps rippled up my arms as a strange thought popped into my head. Was this second butterfly – me? Am I slated to join David soon?

Eeks! I'm not ready to go. Not yet!

But perhaps David was only teasing me or trying to make me smile. They did look happy somehow, and carefree. Or maybe I was making too much out of butterflies and dragonflies, their meanings and behavior.

The boys came back from the lake looking subdued, their faces reflecting the sadness in their hearts. We sat for a while in silence on the shore, our eyes naturally drawn to that spot in the lake as if keeping watch, saying farewell, or resigning ourselves to nature taking its course. Or perhaps we were hoping that by some magic, some last minute miracle, David would materialize in the middle of the lake and come home with us.

Instead I saw sailboats gliding across the water. Were they the same ones as I'd seen earlier? Or were those long gone and these different ones? A heron flew into my line of vision, startling me.

"Oh look!" I pointed excitedly, keeping my eyes on this magnificent bird in case it disappeared.

Just as suddenly a second one appeared. She was a little smaller, but had the same blue/grey coloring as her partner. They looked to be a couple, their movements perfectly in tune with one another as they flew quite low, almost hovering over the water.

I was taken back to a happier time years ago when David and I were at the beach, watching pelicans flying along in tandem, their wings outstretched. Then suddenly one of them would swoop down into the frothy waves to catch a fishy breakfast.

It was wintertime here in Canada, and we had escaped to Florida for a week-long vacation. As we stood together in the sand, I felt like the luckiest girl in the world.

Our days began with lovemaking; it was as natural to us as breathing. Afterwards, David would bring us coffee in bed. I felt like a queen, so spoiled and cared for. We'd sip and snuggle, sip and talk, gradually waking up to a new day.

Life was perfect. I was in heaven.

David appeared at a time when I was going through a particularly rough patch. His warm and gentle presence captivated me. Shy, sweet, and caring, he gently, yet persistently, wormed his way into my heart. Later on I would jokingly call him my persistent little worm.

At that point in time, I was done with men, as in finished, kaput, no more! I'd been through a divorce. I'd been lied to, cheated on and scammed in another relationship, which left me angry and mistrustful of everybody. I also had a full-time job, three teenagers to raise and not much time for anything else.

So when David came into my life, I pushed him away. I

did not return his phone calls. Not that he wasn't friendly or respectful. He was, and intelligent too, but I just didn't want to have anything more to do with men. Wisely, he left me alone.

Then one day I was at Fairview Shopping Centre in Pointe-Claire, browsing in Coles Book Store. That store no longer exists, but on that day in 1995, I looked over to see David reading the flyleaf of a book in the detective and mystery section. We chatted politely for a few minutes. Casually he threw out the suggestion that I join him for coffee and cheesecake at Calories. It was mid-afternoon, and having just finished work, he needed to replenish his energy. Coffee and cake sounded good to me too, but I hesitated.

Sensing my reluctance he quickly added, "My sister will be there."

"All right," I agreed with a smile. That did make things better. It wouldn't feel like a "date" with his sister along. And so our relationship began.

Perhaps it was his eyes, those kind warm brown eyes that sparkled with mischief when he felt safe enough to let his impish side out. Or perhaps it was his aura. He was a humble man, yet sure of himself, giving one the sense that he possessed a deep inner core of strength. Here was someone you could rely on, yet he would never foist himself or his opinions on anyone else. I instinctively felt safe with him. I could trust this man. And he had the most beautiful sensitive hands, full of lines which I could read.

Throughout that spring and into the summer we'd meet at Calories after David's shift at StatCare, the medical clinic which faces Lakeshore General Hospital in Pointe-Claire. Calories was a popular dessert place close by, with a terrace for sitting out on warm summer days. I felt at ease in this public place with this comfortable man, who I thought just wanted to be friends. We exchanged divorce stories. We talked about our children, our love of the ocean, libraries, books and book stores, music, strawberry cheesecake, and anything and everything medical. He was a family physician, and I had been working as a medical secretary for years. We spoke the same language.

And so, in a story as old as time, our friendship blossomed into love.

It was late afternoon when we returned from the lake but I thought I'd go ahead and prepare dinner anyway. Filet of salmon and fresh local vegetables were on the menu as I wanted something easy. It took very little effort to pop fish into the oven and vegetables into the steamer. A loaf of French bread and fresh butter complemented the simple meal. We sat around the dining room table; David's two sons, daughter-in-law, grandchildren and me.

The food must have been good for it disappeared quickly. I barely touched my plate. That peaceful feeling I had down by the lake had evaporated, chilled into the cold, cruel reality that David was not here, would never be here to sit down at the table with us.

Ever, ever again.

I could not eat; even the smell of food was making me feel ill. Listlessly I poked at crisp, green vegetables and pushed pieces of flaky salmon around my plate, pretending to eat. Everyone was talking around me, their voices fading in and out. Was my hearing going, or was this how one experienced shock? Pasting a smile on my face, I nodded in what I hoped were the appropriate places in the conversation. And picked up my fork again, stabbing into an unfortunate piece of broccoli, breaking it open.

I wish this meal were over! My eyes started watering. All I wanted to do was crawl into bed, put the covers over my head and hide. Hide from what? Pain? Nobody can hide from pain. But rational thinking was not happening. I only had my feelings to guide me, and they were raw.

Blinking through my tears, I stared down at the squashed

broccoli on my plate and saw... a tiny worm!

Ewwww!

Quickly I looked up to see if anyone had noticed. Nobody had. I took my plate away and scraped it into the garbage. Why had I been the one to find a worm in my food? A worm of all things! Well, I suppose it was better than if one of the grandchildren had found it – or worse, eaten it!

And then I remembered. David, that dear little imp, who had "wormed" his way into my heart and soul early on in our relationship. He would not give up, yet did not pester me. Instead, he gave me my space, let me be, until I was ready. So this was his way of being with us for the celebratory meal. Had he wormed his way into this too? I wonder.

Recounting the story to Brenda later on, she said, "Mom, caterpillars do turn into butterflies, you know." Ah, the butterfly story again. So was this little worm found on my plate another manifestation of David's energy? Was I really stretching this time?

Chapter 4

Missing Him

I wear his watch on my left wrist.

I sit in his place at the kitchen table, so I don't have to look at his empty chair.

I carry his wallet in my purse.

I sleep in one of his T-shirts.

I drink coffee from his favorite mug in the morning. The one with birds on it: cardinals, blue jays, chickadees, a sparrow and even a tiny hummingbird on the inner rim. This is the very mug I used to bring him each morning when he was in hospital, and take back home in the evenings to wash. I wanted him to feel less isolated in that sterile hospital setting with its Styrofoam cups and plastic cutlery. I wanted him to feel loved and nurtured, as if he were still at home.

Whenever I go to Tim Hortons, I can't help buying two cups of coffee – one for me and one for him. He takes his with two cream and two sugar (double-double). I take mine with a little cream and lots of milk.

Back home, I sit under the oak tree in our backyard where I have a candle burning day and night, in case he needs to find his way home. I carry on a conversation with David while sipping my coffee. Then I pour his under Grandfather Oak.

I just cannot bring myself to buy only one cup. Even my children when coming to visit will bring two cups of coffee.

It's become a ritual; pouring David his coffee under the tree, so he will receive it wherever he is. But as days fade into weeks, I find less of a need to pour his cup under the tree. When I sip my own coffee, I feel we are sipping together, as if we are one.

Am I losing my grip on reality?

Maybe... but I feel him close to me, in my heart.

Our Love is our connection. It's like a bond, gluing us together, even in the face of death. Our Love is our bridge stretching from this world to the next.

David loved pens. There are oodles of pens in his desk drawers. Pens sitting in a cracked mug on a shelf next to the telephone. Pens in every pocket of every jacket. Pens lying on the surface of every table in our home. When David and I would go shopping (that seems light years away now) to a stationery store like Bureau-en-Gros (Staples in the rest of Canada) he would head straight for the pens.

"David, don't you think we have enough pens? We must have a hundred or more. Why are you looking at more pens?"

He'd just smile and head on over to that department anyway, leaving me to wander around or follow him – my choice.

A few days after David's passing I was in the conference room of Notary L, a very business-like woman who was handling David's Estate. Here in Quebec, notaries, rather than lawyers, handle estate management, real estate transactions, etc. We sat around the huge conference table: Josh (who was still staying with me), my Financial Advisor, Notary L and myself. Beverages were offered by a thoughtful secretary. Everybody declined.

I tried to focus on the proceedings, but my head was spacey. Cotton wool, David used to say when his head felt this way. In his case it was the physiological response to a lack of oxygen in his brain.

For me, on this day, it was purely emotional. I could not think. I still could not assimilate or process the finality of death. Whenever we came to this office, David had been with me.

Always.

Now I had to make legal and financial decisions and deal with the required paperwork on my own.

A document was placed on the table in front of me. I looked up at Notary L. She nodded her head as if to answer my unspoken question. I looked back at the paper and noticed there was an "x" waiting for my signature.

Opening my purse, I rummaged around to look for a pen. No pen. Strange, I always carry a pen in my purse. Where could it be? Flustered now, I pushed tissues aside, packets of gum, what felt like cookie crumbs, lip gloss, the odd coin.

Still no pen.

A hot flush of embarrassment spread over me. I shrunk into my chair, feeling like the most incompetent fool. Couldn't I even produce a pen? Did everybody else have to do the thinking for me?

I stole a quick glance around the room, expecting to see frowns of disapproval. Instead, everyone else was looking for their pens too!

The men were patting shirt and jacket pockets. Even Notary L, so composed and business-like, was fishing around in her own purse. Nobody could find one.

Finally, a very red-faced Financial Advisor stepped outside to ask his secretary if we could borrow a pen.

A strange sensation in my gut, a stirring of intuition. Could that have been David?

But how could that be? Do Spirits play tricks?

Well, he did have a playful side to his nature and a little imp that lived inside his spirit (I reminded myself). He knew that hiding pens at that meeting would be one sure way to catch my attention.

But does this make any sense at all? I don't know; and yet, how could I ignore that gut feeling?

Several days later, I felt a strong urge to go to Thompson Park. I needed to be in that place where David's ashes had been scattered. I wanted to see if there was any trace of my husband still lingering.

It was the kind of day to be out and about. Clear skies, warm sun and that wonderful scent of freshly cut grass permeating the air. I think that whole summer of 2010 consisted of perfect summer days. A day for picnics, for swimming and boating, for family gatherings and eating ice cream. Sadly, I wished we were doing these normal things on a normal summer day.

I parked the car in the lot across the street from Thompson Park and sat there for a moment. For some reason, my stomach felt heavy and a little queasy.

I looked over at the lake, for reassurance, for guidance, for something I couldn't really define. It was peaceful and calm, like the day we scattered his ashes.

As I continued watching the lake, it seemed like its Spirit was calling me, drawing me in. Water seems to do that. It's the vast openness, stretching wide and flowing deep that stirs up a longing deep within my soul.

It was time to move, so I climbed out of the car, crossed the road and walked down the grassy slope towards the lake. With each step I could feel the heaviness beginning to shift, to dissipate like storm clouds after the rain.

Sailboats were gliding over the calm waters and I wondered where they were going. More than likely, they were out for a day of relaxation and fun, but in my imagination, they were sailing off to some far away mystical place.

The breeze felt cool as it caressed my face, stirring memories of David's gentle kisses. Cottony white clouds drifted lazily across the sky, their puffiness reminding me of the kind you see illustrated in children's picture books.

The water was higher today than last time I was here. It must have rained over the past two weeks, but I don't remember. It seemed to me that every day was fine.

I sat on a log in the sand and watched some ducks swimming among the rushes close to shore.

I didn't have anything planned; no ritual, no candles, no words. I just sat.

After a while I got up and walked. Bees buzzed, insects

hummed, a dragonfly hovered; all seemed as it should be. Except for the heaviness in my heart and ache in my soul.

Tired all of a sudden, I plunked down on a rock under a willow tree and let the tears flow. Willow trees (according to the ancient Celts) symbolize death and rebirth. Their roots reach deep into the water, their branches sweep the air as if propelling spirits along, or moving the wind instead of the wind moving them.

"I love you, David," I cried into the wind.

After a while, I got up to leave. I looked around as if to imprint this peaceful, yet sorrowful place in my memory; this spot where I had last seen my husband, where the last little bits of him remained on this earth, in a world where I now lived without him.

A quick last look at the lake, and I was on my way back through the soccer field towards the road and my car in the lot just beyond. A wave of sadness came creeping in to my soul as if to steal the calm I'd felt earlier.

A melody floated through my head:

Oh Sisters, let's go dow-ow-own,
Let's go down,
Come on down!
Oh Sisters, let's go dow-ow-own,
Down to the River to Pray...

Oh, did I come here to pray? I really didn't have anything planned, but perhaps I should have.

The morning of David's passing, I kept hearing a voice in my head saying, "Call a priest, call a priest." So I asked the nurse to call him. When the Father arrived, he asked me to join him in saying The Lord's Prayer.

That prayer came back to me now as I walked that grassy field towards the car.

"Our Father, who art in heaven..."

And when I had finished, I looked down on the ground, and saw...

lying in the grass...

a pen!

Our Twelfth Wedding Anniversary fell on day nineteen. Nineteen days since I watched my dear husband draw his last breath. Why couldn't he have waited? At least we could have celebrated together. I would have brought a special cake to the hospital and... I guess that's just it. Who wants to celebrate an anniversary in the hospital?

One afternoon Gillian, one of the social workers, walked into David's room with a piece of scrumptious-looking birthday cake on a plate.

"Oh, whose birthday is it?" I inquired politely, wondering how she would handle this situation.

I had overheard a conversation at the nurses' station, just minutes earlier. Somebody had ordered a birthday cake for a patient. Unfortunately, that poor soul had passed away sometime during the wee hours and it must have been too late to cancel the cake.

Or, more than likely the family had totally forgotten about it in their sorrow. I'm sure this happens from time to time in Palliative Care. And I imagine, offering the cake to the other patients was not only a nice gesture, but practical too.

Gillian flushed a little and told me it was the birthday of one of the other patients. Now she didn't lie, she just left out all the details, which really was a good way to answer my nosy question.

David and I shared a piece of the cake. It was moist and sugary-sweet, but I felt a little weird eating cake that was meant for somebody who was dead. I never told David. He had no reason to doubt Gillian's word and assumed the cake was large enough to go around.

Today is Our Anniversary, dear David. Twelve happy years, even in sickness. I wish I could tell you once again how privileged I felt when you asked me to be your wife. How filled to the brim with joy. How blessed.

And when we were dealt that awful blow, your diagnosis of chronic lung disease, never once did it enter my mind to let you go. I held on tight; probably too tight, but I could not even think about life without you.

You could never, ever become a burden, and I know you worried about that, particularly towards the end of your life. There is no way I'd ever abandon you, my sweetheart. I love you to the very depth of my soul.

Will you send me a sign today? Something to let me know that you know today is Our Anniversary? Something with a special meaning for us? Something that only the two of us would understand?

He'd already sent butterflies, a caterpillar in the broccoli, herons, dragonflies, pens in the grass, what else could he possibly send me? I couldn't imagine anything else that would carry such a strong significance for us. Couldn't imagine a sign or message potent enough to be that link between his world and mine. And it had to be something I would instantly recognize, and know...

But that's just it. You don't know, you can't know ahead of time. And you certainly can't force things to happen. My only advice for people yearning for a message from the Other Side is to be patient and keep an open mind. It's just not possible to control what happens in the Afterworld, or plan a visit or message from those who have crossed over.

Today I would be spending the day babysitting my grandchildren; well half a day really, as the other grandmother and I share the time. She takes the early shift, and I the afternoon. Maybe there will be no sign today, as I won't be home.

Feeling a little low, I issued Spirit a challenge. Ha! I dare you to send me a sign, one that you haven't sent before.

Was I actually teasing and taunting Spirit? Oh the bad karma! Never mind, after the agony of losing David, nothing could hurt me any more. The worst had already happened.

I walked in to my daughter's house to find Irish Grandmother sitting in the rocking chair, by the window, little Nathan cradled in her arms. He must have already finished his bottle and now it was nap time. Was I late? I looked at my watch (or David's rather). No, I was on time.

Older sister Jasmine was putting together a puzzle on the living room floor. I plopped down next to her. She was doing well on her own and evidently didn't need any help. I sat for a bit watching her. I could hear Irish Grandmother singing little Nathan to sleep. It was rather early for his afternoon nap, but maybe he was tired today. I'm usually the one who gives him his bottle and puts him to sleep after Irish Grandmother has gone home.

Things seemed to be flowing along as they should. The rocker rocked, little granddaughter quietly and skillfully fit pieces of her puzzle into place, the dog slept in a corner of the room, and I leaned back against the living room sofa to rest my head for a moment.

Nobody needed me just now, so I closed my eyes. I listened to the rhythm of the wooden rocker, back and forth over the hardwood floor, listened to soft doggie snores, and listened to the lullaby Irish Grandmother was singing,

Toora, loora, loora, Toora, loora, li...

What?
My head snapped up. Could it be?

Toora, loora, loora, Hush now don't you cry.

I couldn't believe my ears! This Irish Grandmother was singing the same lullaby that David's father had sung to him when he was a little boy. David adored this song. His mother had been French, his father Irish. It had been his father who'd sung lullabies to David, rather than his mother and I don't know why.

I just remember David telling me how close he was to his Dad; how much he loved him. It seems his father was the one to look after him throughout the illnesses of childhood. His father had stayed with him at the hospital when he had his tonsils removed. And it was his father who had passed on his love of education and books to David.

Mom was simply Mom, loving and kind. But Dad was extra-extra special.

I was filled with awe. Could this be the sign? Really?

"David – how did you manage that? Irish Grandmother never puts the little ones to sleep. I always do! Thank you, sweetheart! This is one of the best anniversary gifts ever!"

And it came from the Other Side.

Chapter 5

Slipping Away

I could feel movement in the air, a gentle brushing against my cheek, like a summer breeze. My eyes instinctively flew to the window, but it was closed; sealed shut in this hospital room, as I knew it would be.

It was subtle, this movement, this change, yet there was no mistake. My skin prickled at this slight, yet sudden shift in energy, as if a hidden signal had been given that something important was about to take place.

I looked at David. He was sleeping peacefully, his chest rising and falling with each breath, yet something was different. The pattern of his breathing, the rhythm was beginning to change.

We had been drifting in a place of hushed quietness, lulled by a lack of activity in our oasis, our safe little space. There was plenty of action in the hallway, but we were removed from that stream of life, as David lay in a coma.

People came and went outside "our" room with schedules to keep, but we had none. We floated as if on a cloud. Clocks ticked away the minutes, but we didn't notice. In those quiet moments, we had no place to go. There was nowhere we had to be.

For a long time there was only drowsiness, as I sat by his bedside holding on to his hand. It was quiet in the room. The only sounds were the soft hiss of oxygen as it flowed into David's face mask. He slept peacefully, unmoving, while I spaced out beside him, as if in a dream, for none of this seemed real. I kept hoping he would wake up, look around and say, "Where's my lunch?" or something of that nature.

But now there was a definite change, a quickening sort of vibration like angel wings stirring the air. It was a little unnerving, as if warning that we were about to be taken to another level. Our peaceful illusion would soon come to an end, as a bold new energy swept in, pushing us forward.

I could sense a hovering, a whirring of wings which made me think of a dozen hummingbirds all gathered around in this room, poised in mid-air as if waiting for instructions from a higher source.

Did I actually see or hear anything? No, it was just a feeling, a sixth sense, an inner knowing, as if Spirit had suddenly entered the room.

It is time now.

Was this David's Spirit? Hovering over him, quivering, looking down on his earthly body one last time? Or something else?

Earthly time is running out. This is my last link, last bit of precious time both in my body and in the air, as I move away from this Earth and onwards to the Light.

The ripples in the air continued, echoing the breathing of a body growing tired. The rhythm had changed to a shallow, quicker pace, as if wanting to accelerate the process, wanting to get on with this sacred journey.

What could I do? My brain was frozen. It came up with nothing. Besides, nothing made sense anyway. I felt like we were being swept along with this invisible force, like a river flowing to the ocean. The ending was inevitable. He was dying, but I could not accept it.

"Please don't go, sweetheart," I cried softly, tears beginning to flow down my cheeks.

"Please don't leave this world."

I knew in my heart I shouldn't be saying this. I should be letting him go. I should be encouraging him to leave, to go in peace and with love; to have a safe passage. Yet, I could not. I didn't *want* him to go!

"Call A Priest! Call A Priest!"

What?

I swiveled my head around, trying to locate the voice. Where had this come from? There was nothing more, so I turned back to focus once again on my sleeping husband.

"Call A Priest! Call A Priest!" More loudly this time. Where was this coming from? There was nobody about. It must be from inside my head.

"Stop it! Go away!" I commanded, feeling rather annoyed.

I turned my attention back to David. What are you feeling, My Love, I murmured, wishing I could take some of his misery away.

I wanted to put a cold face cloth on his forehead to ease his pain, wanted to change his clothes, shift his position, but I did nothing. Somehow I knew he did not want to be disturbed, did not want to be touched in that way.

He was leaving his body; he needed to let go of it.

His brain, meanwhile, was still active, was transmitting his thoughts into mine.

An orderly walked into the room.

"Does he need a diaper change?"

"Excuse me?" I arched one eyebrow and gave him a scathing look. "He is not wearing a diaper," I informed him in my most haughty tone of voice. The orderly didn't say anything, so I went on, "My husband hasn't had anything to eat or drink in the last 24 hours."

The poor man looked miffed. He was only trying to do his job. And I was being difficult. Well, too bad. So he threw out a warning.

"The nurse will come along shortly to insert a catheter in his bladder." Over my dead body, I muttered to myself; sorry, sweetheart (to David), bad choice of words.

"Sorry," I shook my head curtly, "not a chance in hell!"

He left in a huff. I turned to David and whispered in his ear, "You are NOT going to die in a diaper. They are NOT going to traumatize your body with a catheter. I will look after you, my sweetheart, don't you worry."

David slept on.

"CALL A PRIEST! CALL A PRIEST!"

Where was that coming from? David? Somebody else? It was louder now and very insistent. I figured I'd better do something, or it would *never* go away. The nurses would know how to reach the Father.

I walked over to the nursing station and made my request. There had been a Father Somebody, a pleasant, grey-haired gentleman who had been in to see David on occasion, while making his hospital rounds. Even though Mount Sinai is a Jewish Hospital, other faiths were accepted and welcomed.

Nurse made the phone call. I hoped that I had done the right thing. David was raised Catholic, but had not practiced his religion for some time. We had not discussed calling a priest at the end of his life. In fact, we had not discussed much at all. The cold reality that David was going to die was totally unacceptable to both of us. We could not face it.

David's brother Bill walked into the room. I looked up in surprise. "Who called you?"

It was his turn to look surprised. "Nobody," he answered.

I took Bill outside the room and told him that David had been in a morphine-induced coma since the day before. The shocked look in his eyes didn't even touch me. I felt nothing. It was only after he'd left that I realized somebody should have called to tell him. But who? David's boys? Shoot, I hadn't even called them! My brain, my head, my thoughts were exclusively focused on David. I had nothing left for anyone else. His boys lived far away. By the time they arrived here, it would be too late. How did I know that? I just knew.

Bill didn't stay long, for which I was grateful. I did not want to converse with anybody. Did not want to make small talk while David lay on the bed, hovering between life and death.

I watched as Bill leaned over the bed rails and whispered something into his brother's ear. I assume it was words of love and a final good-by. He left the room in tears.

Something shifted inside me. Instinctively, I knew it was time. I had to begin to let David go. Leaning over the bed as Bill had done, I stroked my husband's face, kissed his lips and whispered words of my own into his ear. "You are the best father, husband, lover, doctor, most wonderful man in the world. I love you so much."

Tears spilled onto the bed, but I didn't care. I clasped his hand and found it stiff.

When had that happened?

I noticed then that his breathing had changed yet again; it was even shorter and quicker than before.

When had that happened?

I jumped up from the chair and ran out of the room to get the nurse.

"He's in pain! He can't breathe! Do something!"

"Okay," agreed Miss Hollywood complacently, "we'll give him some 'break-through' medication." David had dubbed this nurse Miss Hollywood a few weeks earlier when she first appeared on this floor. A gazillion bracelets snaked up and down her arms, wild curly locks flew around her face as she walked, and her eyes glittered with show-girl type makeup. Totally inappropriate for a nurse in my opinion. Brenda called her Lady Gaga behind her back.

She was back a moment later with the syringe. I watched as she drew back the bed covers and plunged it into my husband's emaciated thigh.

Anxiously I waited.

No change.

His breathing remained the same. It was rapid and shallow. No, he was not fighting or struggling. He was not agitated, yet it was obvious he was laboring. His body was undergoing profound changes, which my mind refused to accept. I sensed somewhere in the depths of my soul that he was actively dying; that he was in some kind of transitional phase. There was no turning back. His Soul was preparing to leave, but I still could not accept this.

It simply could not be.

Not yet.

As his breathing became even shallower, I grew more and more distraught. How could I just sit here and watch? I had to move, I had to do something. Frantically I paced the room. What could I do? How do I stop this?

Once more I turned and ran out of the room. Where was everybody?

People were walking about in the hallway. How could they all be going about their business when my dear husband lay dying in his bed? How could the earth turn? How could meals be served, medications given, visitors come to call? It made no sense. Worst of all, it was Saturday. The regular staff were not here. Those familiar faces I had come to count on and to trust were somewhere else.

Where was his regular nurse? Where was his doctor?

I had spoken to Dr. Q the night before. She was reluctant to order round the clock morphine initially. I don't know why. But after watching David's body shiver and shake hours after the initial dose had worn off, I insisted on the orders being changed. My dear hubby was in distress.

I knew that his greatest fear was suffocating. He did not want to die gasping for breath or to feel like he was drowning. The last thing he said to me before the morphine took effect was, "I just want to go to sleep."

I respected his need to ease into this transition in a state of unconsciousness. He did not want to be awake for this frightening part of his journey.

"Help me!" I begged Dr. Q. "I don't know how to do this!"

She lay what was meant to be a comforting hand on my shoulder and said something. I have no idea what she said, as I was not listening. I would not have been able to take in her words of reassurance or guidance in any case.

And then she walked away.

Home.

To her family, as she should.

At that moment, I felt totally and utterly abandoned.

This woman, this physician, who had been our strength, our compassionate guide throughout David's nine week stay in Palliative Care, just up and walked away.

To go home for the weekend.

How could she?

How could she leave her patient, my husband, as he lay trembling in his hospital bed?

Intellectually, I knew there was no way each doctor could stay 24 hours with each patient. That's totally unrealistic and just does not happen. I know the real world doesn't work that way.

But intellect had nothing to do with my need at that moment. I needed comfort and strength. I needed Dr. Q to perform some miracle. My mind was teetering on the edge of sanity, trying to make sense of it all and I needed her to make it better.

I ran back to David's bedside. What do I do? How could I ease this passage, this suffering?

Looking back, I don't think he was suffering. I was.

The lines between us are blurry, flowed into my brain without warning. I stopped in my tracks.

Those were the very words David spoke to me one rainy afternoon, three or four weeks ago, from this same hospital bed. I was surprised to hear him say that out loud, because I had been thinking the very same thing.

As the days melted into each other, and time seemed to drift, I was aware that somehow we were merging. We were closer now than we had ever been before and that puzzled me. I couldn't quite figure it out, since he was leaving this world and I was not.

Yet it felt like we were blending together, face to face, soul to soul, our boundaries becoming fluid, dissolvable, like the ebb and flow of the tides. This merging of boundaries or energies allowed us to tune into each other's needs as effortlessly as we would our own.

"What do you need, sweetheart?" I whispered anxiously to my sleeping husband, trying to squash down my rising panic.

The constant hiss of his oxygen was my only answer.

In my heart the answer was clear, "I need you." Well maybe it wasn't that clear. It was rather fuzzy if you want to know the truth. My thoughts and feelings were becoming tangled. Nothing made sense. I was caught up in a strange whirlpool that was threatening to pull me under, to suck me into a deep black hole of nothingness.

In a panic, I ran back out into the hallway. Ah, here was a nurse who looked familiar. She must have been one of the regulars, called in on a Saturday.

I grabbed her arm and pulled her into the room.

"What's happening?" I beseeched, wishing she could somehow make it all go away. "Why is his breathing so shallow? What can we do?"

This nurse was kind. My husband was not her patient, but it did not matter. She looked at him and made a quick assessment. Then took me gently by the arm and led me back into the corridor.

"It won't be long now," she said softly with compassion.

I just stared at her. Long for what?

My heart knew.

But my brain would not, could not accept that David was about to die.

I flew to David's side once again. Stroked his forehead. Held one of his stiff hands in my own and stared at him, willing him to wake up so we could go home. This was all make-believe, wasn't it? Weren't we in some kind of play or movie?

My cell phone rang.

I ignored it.

Five minutes later a nurse came to the doorway.

"Your daughter is on the phone. Can you come and answer it?"

"At the nursing station?" How odd, I thought. Why would she call there?

"Hello?"

"Hi, Mom, I tried to reach you on your cell, but you didn't answer. Are you okay?"

"No."

"Do you want me to come?"

"No thanks, I just want to be with David."

I hung up and went back to the room.

Five minutes later, I pulled out my cell and called her back.

"Yes, please come. I don't trust any of the nurses here. I want *you* to assess him."

In my confusion, I had forgotten Brenda was a registered nurse. But it went beyond that. Just the sound of her voice dissolved a tiny bit of that protective wall I'd erected around David and me, forcing me to admit, with some relief, that I did not have to do this alone. I needed her comforting presence at this critical time. She and I were close, often on the same wavelength and now I couldn't wait for her to arrive.

Twenty minutes later I looked up to see her striding through the door. She, like Familiar Nurse, took one look at him and knew.

"Mom," she said gently with a sad smile, "it won't be long now."

She walked around to the other side of the bed and sat down. We talked softly over David's sleeping form, mindful of this sacred time, his sacred impending journey.

I don't know how long we sat there. Time meant nothing.

Movement at the door. The Priest had arrived. Having completely forgotten about him, I could do nothing but stare.

Brenda was far more gracious. "Oh hello, Father, please come in." She smiled and rose from her chair to greet him.

"I'm so sorry. I was out of town when you called," he explained, huffing and puffing as he hurried into the room. "I came as soon as I could."

"Thank you," I answered automatically. I do not remember when or who called him.

"*Let us pray. Our Father...*"

I joined in partway through The Lord's Prayer. I had not thought of praying. I had not thought of anything.

"*Hail Mary...*"

I did not know the words of this prayer, so kept silent. I vaguely wondered if the Priest thought I was disrespectful or a bad person. However, not being Catholic, I had never learned this prayer.

"*... pray for us sinners now and at the hour of our death. Amen.*"

Three-quarters of an hour after the Priest left, David died.

Chapter 6

Difficult Days

I feel a constant buzzing in my body, as if there is a motor running inside me but going nowhere. It's grating on my nerves, like a crackling radio tuned to an annoying talk-show. I feel raw, exposed, vulnerable. I've never felt this way before.

I open the medicine cabinet in the bathroom and gasp. There is nothing there. Where are my husband's medications? Who took them? Then I remember that I'd thrown them out; possibly just the day before.

I open his sock drawer. Where are his socks? How can he keep his feet warm if his socks are gone? And then I remember that Josh, David's youngest son, took them home.

Who would take socks?

Well, actually, I did. I have a pair of my mother's warm, purple knee-socks that I wear on cold winter days. Mom must have bought them in a mad moment. In those days, respectable grandmothers did not wear purple! However, during the 60s, colorful fashions were the new norm and I remember my younger sisters wearing rainbow dresses and lavender tights. I preferred long flowery "granny dresses" in shades of fuchsia and tangerine.

And why not? That was the hippie era where radical changes in society took hold. Gone were traditional white shirts or blouses paired with black or navy pants dictated by business or school institutions. A whole world of color exploded along with the Beatles, "make love not war" and Flower-Power.

Mom died in May 1998; my Dad followed her eight weeks later. As my sisters and I sorted through Mom's clothing, I was drawn not only to the warmth and cozy-homey feeling of those socks but also to the freedom they represented. Freedom from the conformist attitude of the 50s.

Besides that, I like the color purple, and her socks were soft from many washings. So I took them home. And now I understand Josh's wanting to warm his feet with his Dad's socks, perhaps longing for the closeness they once shared.

I'm scared. Frozen some days, easily startled most others. I should not be driving the car. I've lost the car keys anyway. It took me hours to find the spare set, on a hook in full view in the kitchen. I should not be cooking on the stove. I walk away and leave pots to boil over. Throw them out, rather than clean up that blackened mess. Wander onto the back deck. Sit on my garden chair and stare at David's empty one. Or sit on his and stare at mine. It doesn't matter. One is always empty.

I walk over to Grandfather Oak and just sit. Somehow from the depths of my tortured soul I'm praying that David will appear from out of that tree, since this is the tree I pour coffee under for us to share. This is the tree I leave a candle under to burn all night long, in a vigil for someone who will never come home.

But there is hope, they say. You can never lose hope. But for what? Can I hope David comes home to me? That this is all a bad dream?

I sleep on his side of the bed now, so I don't reach out in the night to find an empty place, but it doesn't feel right. The bed is huge with all that extra space. I throw the extra pillows on the floor. I'm restless most nights and don't sleep, anyway. That buzzing, droning motor keeps me up, the nervous agitation forcing my mind to go round and round in circles. So I get up, wrap myself in his warm blue bathrobe and go outside. I walk around the street in flip-flops. All is quiet and calm. There is nobody about, of course. Houses are dark. Even though this is a safe community, I don't go far. I just seem to need to keep moving, no matter what time of day or night it happens to be.

Then I come back to sit once again on the deck. I'm glad he

died in the summer. "Who wants to die in summer?" I asked my daughter rhetorically, moments after David passed away. "It's so nice outside." As if that is a determining factor in someone's death.

Now I'm grateful he died in summer. How selfish is that? Had it been winter, I'd be locked in the house. Nowhere to go in the freezing cold; darkness ruthlessly cutting the days short, as if mirroring the anguish of my soul.

At least summer evenings are warm. I can sit outside as the soft night air wraps around me in a protective cloak. Butterflies appear in summer, as do pens lying in the grass and caterpillars in the broccoli. In summer, I can see and experience all the signs David is sending me. What will I see in winter? Will there be any signs once winter comes?

And yet there are times I question these signs, I question my sanity. How can it be possible to send someone signs from the Other Side? Is it just my longing, my imagination creating these messages?

Yet, I have to believe he exists somewhere, in some realm, on that mysterious Other Side. Then why can't we just push back this curtain, tear at this Veil as they call it? And see, touch, and speak to our loved ones? Just for a minute, just for a day, I plead to the heavens, so we know they are really somewhere, not gone into some black void, never to return. That's cruel. Are we being punished for something? Well, I'd like to know what it is, so I can change it. I suppose they call this the "bargaining" stage, as I still cannot accept that he's really and truly gone.

The other morning I was driving to Brenda's home to babysit my grandchildren. The sky was dark with rain clouds and the air felt humid and heavy. Driving, like raking leaves or washing dishes, leaves the mind free to run, and on this day, my mind was in overdrive, churning out thoughts I would have preferred to push away.

Where is David? Why doesn't he come home? How can I

go on without him? Maybe I should just turn this car around and go home. Hide. Hibernate. Until this whole bad dream goes away. Tears rolled down my cheeks and dripped onto the steering wheel. Fortunately the light up ahead was just turning amber, so I coasted slowly to a stop. Too bad if anyone behind me was in a hurry. I needed a minute to compose myself or I'd get into an accident.

My purse was open on the seat beside me and I fumbled around inside for a tissue, but found none. Oh who cares, I thought savagely wiping my nose on the back of my hand.

Still sniffling, I looked out the car window and lifted my eyes to the heavens. Perhaps there were answers there. Perhaps somebody could tell me where my dear husband had gone.

Billowy white clouds floated about unconcerned, as if this was just another day. I briefly wondered what happened to the dark rain clouds I'd seen earlier.

Then right before the light changed, I noticed something wonderful. I blinked back my tears and rolled down the window to get a better look. There in the sky was a heart. A blue sky heart, shaped perfectly by the surrounding clouds. As perfect as a cookie cutter heart!

Just for me!

As if David was smiling from the center of that heart, drying my tears. Joy bubbled up inside me, and for the rest of the drive I felt radiant, basking in the glow of his heavenly love.

Food makes me ill. I have no appetite anyway, so what's the point? Some days I eat only to stay alive. Other days I forget and wonder why I have a headache. I stand at the kitchen counter and eat out of a can. I sit at the kitchen table and stare at the vacant spot that used to be David. I order pizza or make toast, take a few bites, then throw the rest in the garbage. Mealtimes used to be enjoyable, now they make me miserable.

I do a lot of throwing out these days. Cleaning, sorting and trashing. All my Christmas decorations went into the garbage. I just cannot face Christmas without David. It's months away yet, but even thinking about it makes my stomach turn.

Long ago in happier times when December rolled around each year, we'd bundle up, get into the car and go Christmas tree shopping. It had to be a real tree. Real trees smelled fresh, like a pine forest growing in our house.

Pulling into the parking lot of our local IGA, we'd head straight to the far end where fresh evergreens stood, their branches covered in white fluffy snow. The IGA grocery store was close to home, and living in a small town, we would naturally support our local entrepreneurs.

"Hi, Chris," David called out a greeting to the young fellow in charge of the trees. The first year I met Chris, David whispered to me in an offside, "I used to give him his baby shots." I smiled. This was no surprise.

Over the years David must have given half the residents of Hudson their well-baby shots.

"Hello, Dr. Nelligan, what size tree would you like this year?"

"A big one," we'd say in unison.

Way back then, we always bought a huge tree as if proclaiming to the world how happy we were to have found each other. The size of our tree represented the size of our joy.

As we put up our decorations, we'd talk about those Christmases long ago, when we were children.

"I remember the year..." one of us would start. And inevitably the other one would chime in with a fond memory to share as well.

Sharing those memories became part of the ritual. And we both had ornaments saved from our childhood.

I had a moss-green elf from those precious days. One Christmas morning when I was about six or seven, I came downstairs to find this cheeky little elf sticking out of my stocking. It had a tiny red cap, pointy ears and a mischievous face making it look almost real. I snatched it up and named it Tinkerbell.

"It's not a fairy!" teased Ron, my older brother.

"I don't care, I like that name." And Tinkerbell has been with me ever since.

David's treasure was a bright red cardinal, which his father had given him one Christmas when he was about 10 years old. It was sitting on a nest with tiny eggs glued to the inside, but over the years they must have come unstuck and rolled away. Every Christmas David would place his special bird near the very top of the tree, right next to the angel.

In those happy years once the tree was up and glowing, we'd sit by the fire holding hands while sipping a glass of spiced wine or ginger tea. Baking was also an essential part of the holiday and either a plate of shortbread straight-out-of-the-oven or my mother's old-fashioned Christmas cake sat on our coffee table waiting to be eaten. And it was.

David liked to dunk his cookie or piece of cake in his tea. I've never been fond of that custom, but David was. Baking was a joy and it was doubly so to watch my dear hubby dig into whatever I'd created in the kitchen. We were happy in our home and in our life together.

As the years went by, however, our trees became smaller and more manageable. With David weakening over time, our lifestyle changed and the size of our tree wasn't important any more.

Now Christmas looms ahead like an aching void, a black hole where I don't want to be. Our house is lonely now, the fireplace neglected.

Throwing things away seems to be my way of trying to rid myself of grief. As if the action of throwing away would somehow take the hurt with it. If only it was that easy.

Junk from the basement and garage – screwdrivers, nails, hammers, sandpaper and bits of things I couldn't even recognize

– went into the trash.

A week or so later, I was reaching for a towel in the bathroom when I noticed that the rack had become loose. Oh no! Where are the screwdrivers? Dang, I think I threw them all away. Never mind, I'll just rip out the rack and throw the towel over the shower door. It's not important. Nothing is important any more.

The kitchen lights are flickering again. What's up with that? Flickering lights and spirits? Puleese, how silly. Looks like I'll have to change those bulbs. Not something I'm looking forward to as they are fluorescent bulbs, long and awkward to put up in the ceiling fixtures behind some kind of plexiglass that has to be carefully removed first. Yuk.

I bring some new ones up from the basement anyway and leave them on the kitchen floor. Another day I'll worry about that. Mornings and afternoons melt together. All of a sudden I realize the day has gone. What did I do today? I don't remember.

I called Videotron to come and disconnect our TV cable. I don't watch television. So why pay for the cable?

A couple of weeks later, I thought I might turn on the set to catch the Weather Channel. I figured it was a basic news channel and wouldn't require cable. Besides, David always watched the weather.

I'd be in the kitchen more often than not when the weather report came on. David would call out from the TV room, "They're predicting some unstable weather for tomorrow." And I'd smile as I chopped vegetables for supper, or stirred pasta sauce on the stove.

Unstable is a word used by doctors to describe a patient's condition: unstable angina, unstable blood pressure, unstable course of an illness. So whatever the weather forecaster had said, this was David's interpretation and he wanted to share it with me.

I pushed the Power button on the front of the television.

Nothing happened. I checked to see if the plug was in the outlet. It was. Tried the button again. Still nothing. Just because the cable was disconnected, does this mean the television set doesn't work anymore? Strange.

I call Sean, my youngest son. "No way," he said. "Maybe the TV is broken."

"Hardly," I told him, "it's only a few years old."

A day or so later, I entered the room and absently flipped on the wall switch. Voila! On came the TV!

I walk a lot. Every morning, every afternoon, every evening. It helps. It feels like I'm doing something; something to change this pain in my soul. Something to shake off the nausea that creeps up on me without warning, day or night. Something, anything to rid myself of this cruel new reality I've been thrown into. Activity is the only thing that keeps me sane.

I made a firm decision to stop looking all over the house for bits and pieces of David. I have to make myself understand that he's *not* coming back. Perhaps if I see empty clothing drawers (not just his sock one) then I'll stop being shocked whenever I open them.

With a lump in my throat I open his dresser drawers and stare at his lifeless clothing. At one time, there was life here, there was energy in each T-shirt, sweater, pair of underwear. David wore these clothes next to his body. Nostalgically, I lift up a purple T-shirt and press my face into its folds inhaling David's lingering scent. I remember when we bought this T-shirt. We were on holiday in Barbados. Those were happy days, happy times I wish we could have back again.

Quickly, I sweep all the clothing into plastic garbage bags, as if sweeping away those memories, painful now that he's gone. One day I will look back on those memories with love and joy in my heart, but not yet. Why does something so happy conjure up such pain? Why does looking at our old holiday photos bring on tears?

Because those days are gone, you ding-dong, I scold myself. And will never come back. But aren't you supposed to focus on the good memories? On the gifts of love? This is way too much thinking, my head hurts. Just sort through the clothing, not the memories, I instruct myself severely.

I plonk the heavy garbage bags on the floor of our closet. Tomorrow I'll bring them over to the Salvation Army.

But the next day I couldn't. Nor the next. Every time I walked over to that closet, I'd remind myself that I had to give those clothes away. But I just couldn't. So I unpacked the lot, threw them into the washer and dryer and put them all back into his drawers again.

Ahhhh, that's better. He just might need them one day.

Am I going crazy? Sometimes I think so. But according to everything I've read, this denial, paranoia, and all the rest of it are part of the package of grief. These behavior patterns are apparently normal. Well, I certainly don't feel anywhere near normal!

Widow brain they call it. I can't make even the simplest decisions. Do I cancel the daily newspaper? It sits every day in my driveway, unread. Did I pick up the mail today? Did I pay my bills? Or did they not send them this month? I can't find any. Where is my checkbook? David was always so organized. And I'm not. David looked after all our finances. He loved it. I didn't.

Somebody came into my house and took some artwork. Who would do that? I had stacked the pictures up against a wall in the living room; cleaned and ready for the appraiser, who was to come by the following day.

How could anyone come in the house? I was out all day, how did they get in? I was devastated! In a flurry, I ran around collecting all the good silver, china, and jewelry, threw it into the car and drove over to my daughter's home.

"Keep this here for me," I instructed. Brenda looked baffled, but did as I asked.

"What's wrong?" she asked me.

I told her.

"But didn't you give David's son the key specifically to come and pick up whatever pictures he wanted?"

Oh! That's true. I did. I think. A glimmer of memory stirred my tired brain. It must have been a long time ago – probably two weeks or more. And I had totally forgotten. Now it was coming back to me, slowly, bits and pieces as if in a dream. Is this what it feels like to lose your mind?

My thoughts are hazy; like clouds or cotton wool wrapping up my brain. Every day I have to orient myself. Today is Tuesday. All day. Still Tuesday. What month? I look to the calendar.

August. It's still summer. Summer is when David died.

I go to the grocery store and forget what I need to buy. More often than not, I don't even make up a list, or if I do, it sits at home on the kitchen counter. All the way in the car, I repeat to myself, "I'm going to buy groceries, I'm going to buy groceries." If not, I'll end up somewhere else. This repetition of words helps to ground me.

There are times when I look around and wonder when I entered the library, or the drugstore, or post office? And why?

This is when I focus on my feet. Two feet planted firmly on the floor. I am here. There is a purpose to whatever I am doing in the moment.

Right now.

It would be so easy to just let go, to drift through time and space. But I am afraid. I'm afraid I won't find my way back. I'll go insane. As much as I want to be with David, I have my children and grandchildren to keep me firmly attached to this world. They help to ground me in the here and now. And certainly in the future, but at this moment, my mind cannot comprehend any future.

Bedtime again. It seems it's always time to go to bed or time to get up. I lie in the dark shivering with the reality that I am going to long for and miss my dear husband for the rest of my life. My lips quiver, my insides tremble. Why am I shaking? Will it ever stop?

"Oh David," I cry into the night. "Please send me another sign that you are here. I want to feel your loving arms around me once more."

Nothing happened.

Did I really expect to feel strong arms hugging me? Yes, of course I did.

Still nothing.

Well, okay then... how about a little tiny bit of a hug.

Still nothing.

Sighing, I throw the soggy pillow to the floor, grasp a dry one close to my chest and close my eyes and try to go to sleep. And that was when I felt it – a gentle brush of air on my cheek, like a good-night kiss, like a butterfly kiss! Yes! Never mind that it might have come from the air-conditioning vents on the floor – the timing was perfect! It felt good. It felt soothing.

"Good night, David," I whispered to the swirling air. In no time at all, I fell into a sound sleep.

The house badly needs painting. Who do I call? House maintenance and repairs were David's area of expertise. He would look at a problem or task from a logical point of view, carry out the research and then break it down into steps. The job would always get done, usually on time and done well. Sounds easy, but where do I start?

The local paper would be a good place to begin. I perused the ads for house painters and handymen. The good news was that there were plenty of ads; the bad news was I didn't have a clue who to call.

How do I know who will do a good job? What is a decent price for painting? Some men quoted an hourly price and others a price for the whole job. Some had years of experience which seemed like a good bet. Others stated that they could do kitchens, bathrooms, renovations and lots of other things too. How do I choose?

Liam. I called Liam because I liked his name. When he arrived at my home, I immediately took a liking to him. He was full of youthful energy and enthusiasm. I hired him on the spot.

Unfortunately, his work was sloppy. His preparation work was incomplete, and he did not follow instructions well. The trusting soul that I am, I left him to work in the house while I went babysitting for the day. When I got home that evening, I found he'd started painting a wall that I didn't even want done!

I fired him. Called him on the phone and told him not to come back. Now I'm angry with myself. What did I do wrong? He sounded good over the phone. He looked good in person and I was drawn to his youth. And, a little voice in my head reminded me I'd called him because I liked his name. Would David have done that? Certainly not!

Now I'm left with a mess to clean up and sort out. And I still have to hire somebody for this job. I'm not good at this! I don't want to do this! I feel like curling up in a ball and staying there forever. I didn't ask for this. Why me? Why us? We had such a good life, a good marriage.

Where is David?

My daughter has generously offered their home for me to come and stay. Shall I go for it? Do I move in with the family? I hate being alone in this empty house. I hate making decisions about renovations, the heating system, plumbing. What if the roof leaks? Some people would say, just be glad you have a roof. And it's true. I am grateful that I have a home of my own. Others do not.

But if I do make that move, would I be surrendering my freedom? It's only natural that my son-in-law would be making all the "man" decisions in the house. Isn't that what I want? It does sound like an easy solution and one I could certainly go with right now. But on the other hand, would I melt into their family and lose my individuality? Would I begin to feel like a dependent, rather than a free spirit?

I am possessed. There is a woman inside of me who is taking over. It's somebody else.

Not me.

I'd never behave like this.

I walked into the bank, demanding to see the bank manager. I had checked my statement online earlier in the day, to discover that the account was overdrawn. Not by a few dollars or so, but by a rather large amount. How had this happened? Who was responsible? The bank teller was an experienced and kindly lady. She knew me.

"The manager is at a meeting," she said, eyeing me shrewdly.

"Why are they always in meetings when you want them?" the other woman who was invading my body demanded in a loud voice. I heard some shuffling of feet behind me from those standing in line, but I ignored them.

"Let's see if we can solve this ourselves," offered Nice Teller, turning towards her computer screen. With a few clicks she called up my account and identified the problem. In a quiet and professional tone of voice she informed me that I had instructed my investment company to withdraw this exact amount of money.

I was taken aback.

I did? When? My widow's brain was blank. And then something clicked. I remembered. It was at a meeting earlier in the month...

I was back at the notary's office as there were more legalities to be sorted out concerning the Estate. What a horrid word. I hate that word. It means that David is dead and I don't want David to be dead, but I sucked in my breath and entered the conference room.

Earlier in the day, before leaving the house, I made a point of checking my purse. I wanted to be absolutely sure I had a good pen to sign all the documents and forms which would undoubtedly be presented to me over the course of the meeting. This time David wouldn't play tricks on us and hide the pens. This time I'd be prepared.

I checked my purse again. Yes, it was still there. And, just to be on the safe side, I reminded everyone right before the meeting to make sure they had their pens handy.

Notary L stared at me as if I had five heads. She had obviously forgotten our last meeting where nobody could find a pen. I was sure David had hidden them all. Financial Advisor, who was sitting on my right side, must have remembered, for he gave me a quick conspiratorial grin.

The meeting began. A document was produced for me to sign. With a flourish, I whipped out my pen, placed it on the paper and... nothing... but a scratch!

I could not believe it.

Did David do that? Could David do that?

Embarrassed, I tried again. Still no ink. I looked around. Everyone was waiting for me. With a nod of encouragement, Good old Financial Advisor leaned over to offer me the use of his pen. It worked just fine and I signed what was to become the first of quite a few documents that morning.

"You can keep it," he said with a warm smile.

So focused was I on the pen situation (was David really being mischievous?) I did not read the contents of each document properly, and one of them must have been my permission to withdraw funds for The Investment.

I sit and stare out the window for hours. What time is it? Did I eat? When did I wash my clothes? I have no idea. People walk by with dogs. They smile at the neighbors, call to their dogs, pick up poop. Families parade outside my window; mothers and fathers and children, living their normal lives. How can they? What is normal?

I turn the radio on. The announcer is talking about U2 coming to Montreal. U2? What kind of a name is that?

The enthusiastic voice asks people to call in right now! Be the ninth caller and you will qualify for a pair of tickets to the concert.

How can anybody sing at a time like this?

In the next instant there's a commercial for car insurance, mattresses on sale again, cleaning products you can't do without.

What? My mind can't grasp these concepts. Entertainment? Shopping? How can people do that?

A minute later I hear about another contest. Listeners phone in to try and win an all-inclusive trip for two to some sunny destination. How could they? How could their lives be focused on trivial things, when mine is completely shattered? How can everyday life just go on?

"How are you?" people ask me.

Raw. I feel raw. I don't say this to anyone, but this is how I really feel. How can one feel raw? Bleeding and sore, as if scraped all over. You know like when you were a kid and fell off your bicycle or skateboard? Both knees, arms, and other body parts were scraped raw. Blood streamed from your nose, dripped down your skin and soaked into your clothes.

Just like that.

I feel just like that – scraped all over, as if somebody rubbed sheets of sandpaper against my skin and now the blood is oozing slowly down my body like tears. There is no going back. Things will never be the same as they were.

I turn the radio back on again, just to hear human voices. It's the traffic report. People are rushing home to their families; to their husbands or wives. Some of them will be stuck in traffic. It might be hours before they get home.

Wish I had that problem.

They're probably wondering what to make for supper.

Wish I had that problem.

Or what to do this evening. Television? Movie? Reading? Socializing?

Wish I had that problem.

Ordinary people going on with their ordinary lives. How can the world turn, when mine has stopped? Has changed forever?

There are still things in my house that go missing. I really can't find the checkbook. I've searched and searched, but it seems to have disappeared.

Like David.

Summer is winding down. It's late August now and gardens have that untidy, overgrown look as withered blossoms litter the earth. Acorns scatter across our yard and crunch underfoot in our driveway. David used to sweep them up every year. I don't have the energy.

Mornings and evenings are cooler now and I feel a chill in the air as I continue my pattern of walking through my grief.

Days grow shorter and dusk appears earlier as evenings lengthen. I actually miss the cheerful liveliness of long hot summer days with early morning birdsong, scent of freshly-cut grass, laundry on the line, people on hands and knees in their gardens or waving at passersby, dog walkers, children biking, skipping or playing chalk games in the road, and savory smells of grilling hamburgers coming from backyard BBQs.

Evening walks are shorter now as I hurry to get home before dark. The waning year leaves me with a melancholy feeling that settles right into my bones. Tired and discouraged I set out anyway, hoping to shake off the heaviness in my heart.

If I keep moving, I won't feel as much. If I keep moving, and focus on the leaves just beginning to turn, the smell of dampness in the earth, lively grasshoppers popping out at me beside the road, then the sharp rawness inside will ease somewhat.

If I keep moving, I won't think. I'll forget for a few moments that David is dead.

The sun hangs low in the western sky. Time is running out on this day and I can feel the darkness hungrily waiting in the wings, like an owl anticipating its nightly hunt. I shiver as if shadows are already seeping in to claim the land around me.

I've reached the end of my street, the top of the hill, where a panoramic view of the countryside meets my eyes. I can look down now on the trees, which before were obscuring my view of the horizon. Now I have a clear view of the sun's magnificence as it transforms the sky from burnished gold to fiery orange. The air is cool against my skin and I can hear the faint rustle of small animals in the woods close by.

Without conscious thought or understanding, I open myself and surrender to the power of the sun. I spread my arms wide to absorb its strength, its passion, its golden sparks of life. As I breathe in light, my spirits lift as if invisible wings are lifting me up above the clouds where no pain is allowed to exist. Breathing in this divine light, I feel a strong connection to the biggest star in our solar system, and a soothing calm settles over my soul.

"Good night, David," I sigh.

I hadn't intended to say that. It just came out.

I let that thought simmer in my mind while watching the sun slip away behind some clouds. It's not down yet, but a feeling of aloneness creeps over me as I stand on the top of that hill.

Reluctantly I turn to go, but can't resist taking one last look over my shoulder at the fading sky, clouds softening a pathway for the coppery sun, as it inches towards its resting place below the horizon.

"Good night, David," I repeat, liking the images my mind has just created. My heart swells with love as I imagine David as the Sun in all its shining radiance. David as light, warmth, loving kisses, happiness, awakening, growth, glory; my knight in shining armor has just turned into gold.

I have heard people say that if you look up at the night sky, your loved one will be shining down on you, sending love and light through a special star that only you will recognize.

I like that.

It's like an affirmation bringing comfort and strength; a clear strong connection that will never disappear.

I haven't tried that yet. Perhaps once night doesn't feel so terrifying, I will venture out of my safe, comfy cocoon and see how that feels.

But at this moment, I see David in the sun, the brightest star in our universe.

A movement catches my attention. A fluttering, quivering of wings up high. I look up to see a silver shape outlined against the darkening sky.

Silver butterfly wings.

Eek! I rub my eyes. A butterfly? Up so high? I hadn't seen one in days! Or was it weeks already? The silver wings dance and dip, whirl and swirl in sheer delight, as if giving a performance for an audience of one.

The sun is almost completely gone now, with only a glimmer of light against silvery purple-grey clouds, and I see quite plainly, that the butterfly has transformed into a bat.

How strange.

A butterfly one minute, a bat the next?

But the silver color remains. Silvery bat wings. Is this magic? A trick of the light? David reaching out to kiss me good-night?

I don't know, but I notice now that my awareness has sharpened. The air around me feels more alive. My dread of the coming darkness has melted along with the heaviness in my heart. My step lightens to reflect this fresh vitality in my body and I tingle with gratitude as I head back home.

Chapter 7

I'm Not Ready

It was 8:00 a.m. on May 26th. I had just stepped out of the shower and was towel drying my hair, when the telephone rang.

Oh, no, please don't let it be The Call. He's only been in Palliative Care for three weeks. Please not yet, I silently prayed. Shivers ran down my spine as I snatched up the receiver.

"Hello?"

"Mrs. Nelligan? This is Mount Sinai Hospital calling."

My heart sank. The news could not be good.

"Yes?" I managed to croak.

"Your husband is desaturating."

That's medical speak for abnormally low levels of oxygen in the blood. If a nurse was calling it was because something had happened to David and whatever they were doing to correct this problem was not working. His blood oxygen was not rising to proper life-sustaining levels. Definitely bad news.

"Is he conscious?" I managed to ask, trying to stay calm.

"He's sleeping."

"I'll be right there." I slammed down the phone.

My mind went into overdrive. He's in a coma and the nurse did not want to tell me. She did not answer my question directly, but just said he was sleeping. If his oxygen sats were that low, then of course they couldn't wake him up. And we all know there is no resuscitation in the Palliative Ward.

Is he alive right now? Will he still be there when I arrive, or will he have already died? "Please God," I prayed. "Not yet, not yet!"

Trembling with fear, I backed the car out of the driveway, trying to ignore the awful nausea in the pit of my stomach. I drove as fast as I could, my mind sending David signals. "Don't go yet, sweetheart. We still have lots to say, lots to do yet. I haven't given up hope of bringing you home one day. Hang on! I'm coming!"

Deep in my heart I knew he wasn't ever coming home, but I held on to a fragment of hope that one day, maybe, possibly he might be able to come home – just for a weekend. Or maybe for a year, or by some miracle – forever! I was to learn a lot about hope in the coming days and weeks, as its focus changed, evolved, and challenged me to follow.

I don't know how I managed to do it, but I missed the St. Jacques Street exit. Zoomed right by, staying on the highway that would take me to downtown Montreal. How on earth could I do that? This car has been driving to the hospital for three weeks now, doesn't it know the way all by itself? I smacked the steering wheel in frustration.

Anger quickly changed into apprehension and a wave of dizziness swept through me. I took in great gulps of air to steady myself. Honestly, I'm surprised I didn't pass out in the car. My heart was already racing when I answered the telephone, but now it was really hammering.

But then out of nowhere, a sense of calm reached out its arms to comfort me, like a mother's reassuring hug. All at once my body relaxed. My hands loosened their intense grip on the steering wheel and my heart rate slowed to almost normal. I was conscious of my breathing easing up as it softened into a sigh.

If I missed the exit, it was for a reason. And there was nothing whatsoever I could do to stop destiny or change what had just happened. I had to keep going, and no matter what time I arrived at the hospital, whatever was meant to be was meant to be. I had to let go of fear and dread, and allow Faith to lead the way.

But as I continued driving, and those extra minutes ticked

by, that feeling of peace slowly evaporated. It took an extra 25 minutes or so over and above the usual hour to get to the hospital. And by the time I got there, my brain had had plenty of time to conjure up worst-case scenarios, leaving me trembling, my insides twisted and sore.

Finally, finally I pulled into the parking lot. Slammed on the brakes. Jumped out as fast as I could and raced towards the hospital doors. Forget the elevator, I bolted up the stairs to the third floor, my heart pounding away in my chest. I passed the nursing station, but nobody was there. Is that a good or a bad sign? Are they all with my husband, trying to bring him back? But they wouldn't do that, I reminded myself. Was he already dead? Do the nurses guard a dead person or stay with him until family arrives? I had no idea.

I quickly rounded the corner, trying to control my rising panic. Fear was making me shake and my hands felt clammy. Almost there, almost there, my mind chanted, propelling me forward. David's private room was just a bit further. There was still nobody about, and this whole experience was beginning to feel surreal.

My eyes quickly located his door. It was open! That must be a good sign, I told myself. If he was already dead, I hope that someone would have closed the door out of respect or common courtesy.

I lunged through the doorway and in one swift motion tore open the privacy curtain, almost ripping it off its tracks.

"David!" I shrieked in relief.

I was met with the googly-eyed stare of someone who has just awakened from a deep sleep. But that someone was unmistakably, undeniably my living, breathing husband. He was lying in bed, propped up on pillows, eyes glazed and drowsy-looking, but conscious enough to be reading the newspaper!

I ran over to him, threw myself into his arms and gave him the biggest, most gigantic, loving hug you can possibly imagine.

He looked up at me in surprise. "Am I dreaming?" he said over the squashed newspaper. "What are you doing here so early?"

"Oh, sweetheart," was all I could manage. Tears streamed down my face as I sagged against him on the bed. I let myself cry for a few minutes, while David looked at me in confusion. And then I told him about The Call.

"They called you?" he asked, concern sharpening the tone of his voice. "I didn't know that. I'm okay."

Okay? my mind screamed incredulously. How can you be okay? You almost died. You're lying in a palliative care bed, tethered to the wall by an oxygen hose and you're okay? I didn't say any of this of course. I sat as close to him as I could, touching him, absorbing his essence, grateful that he was still alive, while my mind and emotions zigzagged between delirious relief and those horrible what ifs.

David's oxygen mask had fallen off sometime in the wee hours of the morning. Nobody knows the exact time, but when the day nurse came on duty she found him in bed, oxygen mask dangling uselessly over the edge. His face had turned a grey ashen color and his fingertips were purple. She immediately slapped the mask back on his face, turned the oxygen flow up full blast, and yelled for help.

Fortunately, David was still breathing or the story would have stopped here. If somebody stops breathing in Palliative Care, that is the end of their life.

Nurse clamped the oximeter onto David's cold finger, in order to assess his blood oxygen levels. Nothing registered. Someone ran out to summon the doctor. Nurse warmed his fingers between her hands and tried again. This time there was a reading, but it was quite low. I assume that was when one of the nurses left the room to place The Call to his wife. Me.

I could not get a clear picture of how long it took David to revive. I imagine in Palliative Care, charting is not as precise as it would be in an Intensive Care or Emergency Room situation.

Lives are valuable, no question, but you don't expect someone in Palliative Care to get well and walk out the door. There are no treatments or heroic measures to implement. No split second decisions or emergency surgery to consider. Time slows down and stretches in this environment, while comfort rules. And comfort is all we have left to offer the dying patient.

Had this close call, this brush with death not happened to us, I would have questioned the staff's decision to revive a terminally ill patient. Revive is not really the right word, for they simply replaced his mask. His heart was still beating. He was still breathing.

Years ago, I would have thought, "The person is already dying, why not let him go?" Now I know. Once you've watched a loved one weaken and fade away, you want to hold on; you need to hold on to life as much as you possibly can.

For the past eight years, I've stood helplessly by and watched as my beloved husband slowly, progressively surrendered to his illness. We both knew it was a losing battle. We both knew there was no cure.

And yet you go on. You don't give up. The end will come, but you don't want it hastened by a technicality, or an oversight by some fatigued or incompetent member of the hospital team. As humans we hold on to every last shred of precious life we can. He wasn't ready to let go and neither was I.

Dr. Q sat on the bed – the same Dr. Q who would later prescribe David's last dose of morphine and then walk away – home to her family. She was a pleasant woman in her late 40s, rather on the petite side, competent and compassionate. I had a feeling she threw herself into life, living each day to the fullest.

Is this a by-product of working with dying patients? Or just her personality? I don't know, but she rarely left the ward before 8:00 p.m. and often took calls from her teenaged children, excusing herself to answer her cell phone. I never felt those calls were intrusive, rather they showed her human mother-side behind the doctor's white coat.

"That was a close call," she said leaning closer to fully engage with her patient, "but it wasn't so bad, was it? There was no pain, no shortness of breath."

"But, I'm not ready!" came David's sharp retort.

"David," I said to him gently when the doctor had gone, "she's just doing her job. She's preparing you for the end. It doesn't mean your time is up yet. You came back, didn't you?"

My husband has had many close calls over the years. There were times during thunderstorms or high winds when the electricity cut out. Other times it happened seemingly out of the blue. One minute we'd be sitting inside a warm cozy kitchen, blissfully sipping tea or eating a meal, lights on, radio on, oxygen concentrator humming with life, then pop! No sound, no lights, no oxygen. If I were home, that wouldn't be a problem. I'd hook him up to one of the portable tanks we always had on hand and hope the power outage wouldn't last too long.

Being away from the house was frightening. I remember one fine spring day having lunch at the Willows Inn with a few of my friends. The Willows was a landmark here in Hudson, drawing locals and tourists alike, and fortunately for me, only about 10 minutes away by car.

We had finished our meal, paid the bill and were just on our way out when suddenly – Pop! Pow! Everything went black! Instantly the generators kicked in, but I was out the door in a flash!

I sped home not caring if the police caught me or not. I needed to get home and fast!

Heart thudding, I pumped furiously at the garage door opener before I'd even made it up the driveway. Miraculously, the door opened! Thank God!

My legs were shaking with relief as I exited the car and I took a moment to slow my breathing. David would be fine. I imagine that power failure must have been restricted to a small area of the village, but I didn't really care right now. All I wanted to do was make sure David was safe.

It was mid-afternoon and I knew he'd be napping. Quietly, I opened the door and peeked inside.

Yes, he was sleeping peacefully – with two portable cylinders in the bed next to him.

I didn't know whether to laugh or cry. He looked so frail and yet had the foresight to have extra cylinders close at hand in case of a power failure.

I wonder how many wives come home to find their husbands in bed with oxygen cylinders. Better that than another woman!

In the early years David could hook himself up to the tanks in case of a power failure, but as the disease took hold we had to make preparations whenever I left the house. It was crucial to place at least three oxygen cylinders and the portable phone next to David's chair. He rarely ventured out of our TV room towards the end, and spent the time in his favorite easy chair, quietly reading or napping until I got back.

Portable oxygen tanks are for leaving the house. And in the beginning, David would be fine using the portable system, as his oxygen needs were manageable. Over time, of course that changed.

Running out of oxygen away from home was far worse than a power failure, as you can imagine. And this did happen on a few occasions. Luckily, we always carried extra tanks in the car, but even so, those times were scary.

Once it happened at Walmart in the men's washroom. It was winter, a time when breathing in cold air becomes especially difficult, particularly for anyone with lung disease. Even with a scarf over his face to protect from the bitter chill, it was tough for David to walk from our car to the store.

As was our routine, I pulled right up to the doors of Walmart, set my hazard lights flashing, and left David sitting inside the warm car while I located a shopping cart. He needed that cart to lean on, as walking tired him out. I pushed the cart to the passenger side and helped David out, making sure to place his oxygen cylinder in the child seat of the cart. Once safely inside the store, I'd settle him on a chair, run back and park the car properly. The whole performance was taxing for David and he needed some time to sit down and recover, before we could begin our shopping.

An unfortunate side effect of low oxygen levels (which can be caused by any exertion, particularly walking or trying to breathe in cold weather) is an urgency to use the toilet. Elimination is not as important to life as breathing, so the body lets it go. This is why David headed for the washroom almost as soon as we got through those heavy front doors.

The cart could not enter the washroom, so David had to take the oxygen tank out of the child seat and strap it to his back, like a backpack.

It happened while he was standing at the restroom sink washing his hands. Somehow the oxygen tank slipped sideways and smacked against the edge of the sink, loosening the valve. A loud hiss meant that valve was leaking!

Hands wet and shaking, he tried adjusting the regulator, but it did no good. The hissing continued as he fumbled with the mechanism, helpless to stop the escape of precious oxygen into the surrounding air.

Fortunately, he had just enough strength to drag himself out of the washroom and seize the cart, which had been left right outside the doorway. One look at his pale face as he sagged against the cart told me something was seriously wrong. His breathing was coming in short gasps, so I knew there was no time to lose.

Taking him firmly by both arms, I eased him onto a nearby bench and raced back to the car to retrieve a spare tank.

David barely made it through those harrowing moments, but

what would have happened had I not been there? Who would have known what to do? And even if security or an employee had called 911, would they have arrived on time?

And this was just one incident, one close call that happened in the years he could still leave the house. There were others along the way, leading me to wonder if he was living on borrowed time, as the old saying goes.

I was very reluctant to leave the hospital that night. David had spent most of the day either resting or sleeping. Being without oxygen for that length of time (however long it had been) was exhausting to say the least and it took the greater part of a week to recover his strength. I wanted to stay with him, to make sure there would be no more mask "incidents" overnight, but in the end decided to go home. I could sleep better at home in my own bed, rather than on the cot provided by the hospital.

Windows were sealed shut in that ward to control the air quality, but I hated sleeping with closed windows. Even in winter, I crack open the windows to allow fresh, cool air to circulate throughout the room. And being under so much stress at this point in time, I needed my sleep. I needed to keep up my strength to face what I knew was lying in wait for us.

Before I left, I fixed clips in David's hair, tightly securing the elastic strap (that holds his oxygen mask in place) to his head. Now it should stay put. Earlier in the day, I'd walked over to the Dollar Store specifically to purchase hair clips and bobby pins. So what if they were meant for ladies or little girls? There was no way we were taking a chance with his mask slipping off again in the night.

Once back in my own home in my safe familiar surroundings, that near-death experience, that almost-losing-David crisis felt totally unreal. The whole scenario was bizarre, like something out of a movie.

David's life could easily have slipped away in a heartbeat.

I felt the ground under me shift all of a sudden. I had to

sit down. It felt as if the whole world was tilting on its axis. A few minutes later I couldn't sit still. Restlessly, I wandered from room to room searching for something I couldn't even define or put a name to. I felt somehow as if I'd entered another realm, which was drawing me back into ancient times. I sat down at my computer and wrote:

STANDING AT THE BRINK

He is standing at the edge of a Cliff.
Looking down.
Scared. Fearful.
"I do not want to go there."
And he steps back.

"Wife," he says on coming home, "I stood at the Brink today."
"I know," she murmurs, pulling loaves of fresh bread out of the
   oven.

Time passes.
Another Day.
He finds himself standing at the edge of the very same Cliff.
Looking down, he sees fierce-looking animals.
"No, I'm not going there."

Years before, in a dream he saw himself walking to the end of the
   Earth.
To the Brink. Where there was nothing but air below.
"I can't go there. I don't have wings to fly."
Just then an angel floated by. His father.
"Not yet," he sang to him, "not yet."

And so he went back home.
"Wife," he says, "I stood at the Brink today. There was nothing
   below. Just Air."

"I know," she murmurs, ladling out soup for their supper.
Night time. They are sleeping under the Stars.
Wife looks up into the night. And cries softly.
One of those Stars will soon be Husband.
She knows in her heart.
He rarely strays far from Home.

Once again He stands at the top of the Cliff. Afraid to look down.
But he knows he must. He's been here before.
His body is showing him the way.

Looking down, he sees before him a black pit.
"No, I'm not going there."
And he steps back.
To let somebody else go.
Looking around, he sees many Souls taking the Leap.
Some take the plunge with strength and dignity; others hesitantly
    with fear.
Nobody returns.

Now there are people with him as he makes his way to the Cliff.
His footsteps grow heavy.
Second Son says, "It's the natural order of things."
"Have a safe passage," whispers a relative.
"We'll make you comfortable when it's time to go," chants the
    medicine man.
"Are you all right?" concerned friends ask.

"I'm not ready," he tells them all.

And goes home to his wife.
Where he finds her preparing his favorite foods. She knows that
    one day he will not come home for supper.
But every day she cooks.

Every day she waits for him.
Every day she listens for his footsteps.
Every day they sit down to eat.
"How are you?" she asks.
"I'm tired."
"I love you," her eyes go soft as she looks into his.
"I love you too," his eyes speak from his heart.

She knows his time is near; that one day he will not come home to
*   her.*
She knows it will be a time when there is nobody about.
Nobody to watch. No one to interfere.

He will slip away quietly in the early hours.

Turns out I was wrong. He did not slip away quietly in the early hours, but late afternoon, with Brenda and myself by his side.

Chapter 8

The Diagnosis

"You have COPD," said the Doctor to the Doctor. It was January 2002. I don't think this came as a surprise to my husband, the Doctor. Nor to his doctor, the Respirologist. I, on the other hand, had been in denial.

Not that we didn't know something was wrong. We did. We just didn't know what it was. David may have had an inkling, after all it was his body. But from my point of view, he couldn't have anything serious. Our life was going so well and he was *my* husband; bad things wouldn't happen to us, would they?

November 2001. David and I were driving downtown on this chilly day for a routine x-ray. We parked the car and started walking downhill to the medical center. Downhill, not uphill. Suddenly, David slowed his pace, looked at me strangely and said he couldn't go any further.

"What's wrong?"

"I don't know." He looked worried.

"What do you mean you don't know?"

Please don't throw up on the sidewalk or pass out or have a heart attack.

"I just don't feel right," he answered, plopping down right there on edge of the sidewalk.

I sat down beside him, continuing to chat as if having a conversation on a dirty city sidewalk was the most natural thing in the world. People walked around us; some giving us funny looks, most ignoring us.

He did look rather pale, but besides that there was nothing else to indicate what was really happening to him. No cough, no shortness of breath that I could see. After a while we got up and continued on to our appointment.

At the steps of the clinic, he stopped.

"I don't think I can climb those steps." I just looked at him. What was going on? We'd been biking all summer long. There was never a question of not going up or down steps.

Three days later, he came down with pneumonia. And that marked the beginning of this roller coaster ride called COPD.

Chronic Obstructive Pulmonary Disease is a disease of the lungs. There is no cure. Insidious by nature, it sneaks up on a person, silently destroying lung tissue. You can have it for years and years and not know.

Then one day you realize you can't keep up. Your energy levels have diminished. You become short of breath or have trouble walking up the stairs. Activities that used to be routine become difficult – like running to catch a bus, riding a bicycle or even planting flowers or raking leaves.

Colds and flu take weeks to resolve; bronchitis and pneumonia are more common as the lungs weaken.

The primary cause is smoking, but not everyone who smokes develops COPD. Other causes include genetics, long-term exposure to inhaled toxins and lung damage at birth.

Dr. Respirologist sent David across the street to Lakeshore General Hospital for an arterial blood gas test. This is the most accurate way of measuring oxygen and CO_2 in the blood, as it's taken from an artery, rather than a vein.

The results that came back were not good. David was ordered to receive home oxygen therapy, starting immediately.

We were both quiet on the drive back home. In David's mind prescribing oxygen meant you were in serious condition; critically ill and confined to bed in the Intensive Care Ward of a hospital. End of life – almost.

However, we found out over the next eight and a half years that this was not so. There are now thousands of people in North America, requiring home oxygen as a treatment for chronic lung disease. It doesn't cure the illness; it prolongs life and makes living and breathing easier. Some people, we discovered through Internet support groups, live 25 years or longer after diagnosis.

In David's own Family Practice, he had never encountered a patient so severely stricken with lung disease that he or she needed home oxygen. At the first sign of breathing problems, such as asthma, chronic bronchitis or emphysema, he would refer the person to respirology, pneumonology or allergy, whatever specialty best served this particular patient.

It took him weeks to come to terms with receiving home oxygen. Once he finally accepted this course of treatment, a technician was dispatched to our home. Mr. Gary arrived all smiles and politeness as if this was a social call. He didn't realize what a blow this was to David. To us. Or perhaps he did, but professionalism dictated he behave as if this was all routine. Just another day. Mr. Gary set up the oxygen concentrator, attached the hose to one end of it and the other to a cannula which he popped into David's nose. Then he left.

It was very strange to see David walking around the house tethered to a nose hose; this long flexible plastic tubing which snaked all through our house. At first he'd forget and close the bathroom door right on the hose. A couple of times I stepped on the hose and David's cannula was rudely yanked off his face. After that I learned to slide my feet across the floor, as if I were skating on ice. If I didn't know which room David was in, all I had to do was follow the hose.

His nose dripped constantly, irritated by the continuous flow of oxygen.

Sometimes he'd lose the hose in the middle of the night and find it the next morning on the floor beside our bed. Actually, those first few weeks, he only wore the oxygen at night as a way of easing into the therapy. Sleeping with a cannula on his face was hard enough, but to also walk around all day with oxygen hissing up his nose?

No way.

Besides, he was still going to work and just how would that look if the doctor was on oxygen? How would you feel if your treating physician looked sicker than you were?

Portable tanks are available to give the patient freedom to leave the house. David would place a couple of tanks in the car and off he'd go. At work, however, he refused to use his oxygen for obvious reasons, so just left it in the car for when he was driving. Or, he'd conceal the tank, hose and cannula in an empty office where he could pop in and take an "oxygen break" like someone would take a "cigarette break".

With the passage of time, however, it became impossible to leave his oxygen apparatus at home or in the car. As his lungs deteriorated, his oxygen dependency grew to the point where he could not leave the house.

David stopped working six months after being diagnosed. Not because of his oxygen needs, but because of his susceptibility to illness. He had contracted pneumonia once again – from one of his patients. Somebody had coughed in his face; unintentionally of course, but this is a hazard of working with the sick. David had no choice but to give up his beloved career. He could not risk contracting any more respiratory illnesses, particularly one as serious as pneumonia.

Being a doctor was so much a part of David's existence. It was unthinkable that he let go of his practice. To step down from the profession he had chosen in his youth, a profession which was wrapped up in the very fabric of his being, proved to be an excruciatingly difficult decision. One which was not to be taken lightly. One which he seemed to accept with good grace on the outside, yet I could sense within a deep well of sadness, frustration, and the bitterness of unshed tears.

Irrevocably. Regrettably. He had become the patient.

Dr. Respirologist prescribed pulmonary rehabilitation as a

way of managing the disease. David and I both attended the sessions which were held at the Montreal Chest Hospital. He was taught techniques to help breathe more easily and effectively.

Olivia the physiotherapist was competent and empathetic. I was impressed with her teaching skills and the way she seemed to know what each patient needed and how much exercise each person could tolerate, be it the stationary bicycle, treadmill, or simply lifting arms and legs while sitting in a chair.

It is paramount for COPD patients to follow a prescribed exercise program. Consistent physical activity builds strong muscles, which are more efficient at absorbing oxygen from the bloodstream. Cardio or aerobics strengthens the heart, improves endurance and reduces anxiety. And gentle stretching increases range of motion and flexibility.

David did well and settled into a regular exercise program at home. He was religious about his workouts right up until the last months of his life, when he no longer had the strength to do them.

I on the other hand had trouble. Trouble accepting what was the end of our incredible life together. No more travelling to sunny destinations, late night candlelit dinners, strolls along the beach watching for dolphins to surface, or just lying in the sand. No more bike riding in the summer, hikes in the woods.

Visitors coming into our home were screened for colds. Nobody with a sore throat or sniffy nose was allowed in. Feelings were often hurt – there was no getting around that, when someone was denied a visit. It was particularly hard to deny our grandchildren visits, but they were the ones most susceptible to runny noses, sore throats and coughs.

In the first year or two we tried to hold on to our happy, normal lifestyle, as if nothing was wrong. We went out to restaurants, to the movies, ran errands, worked in the garden, and visited family as long as everyone was healthy. But as his disease progressed there was a gradual winding down of activities, and as a result, David's world shrank.

Shopping was done quickly and efficiently, rather than at a leisurely pace. We were hyperaware that he was using a portable tank, which could run out of oxygen at any time, so we always brought extra and left them in the car.

Valves on these tanks sometimes leaked, stuck, or inadvertently slipped (like the time at Walmart) leaving David vulnerable and frightened.

After a while, grocery shopping became too much of an energy drain for David, so he stayed in the car while I ran into the store. It was important that he maintain some sort of normal life, so rather than stay home alone, he chose to accompany me. We could almost pretend that everything was going along as usual – just another day as we went about our routine.

Unfortunately on one of those trips David's tank ran out. The car was parked in a quiet spot under the shade of a tree, where David could read unobtrusively, while waiting for me to return. Things seemed to be under control until he glanced up from his journal to check the gauge and found to his horror that it was almost empty!

Something was wrong!

Immediately, he reached into the back seat to grab onto a full tank.

Right at that moment, his oxygen ran out. He realized at once that the hose was loose at its connection, consequently, all his precious oxygen had escaped into the air. Now he was really in trouble. He had no strength left to haul the heavy tank over the seat and into the front where he could reattach the hoses.

In a panic he twisted around, scanning the immediate area for help. There was a man sitting in a pickup truck a couple of parking spaces over, eating a sandwich. David gestured wildly for him to come. The man gave him a funny look, but stayed put. With no time to lose, David put his hands in prayer position and looked pleadingly at the fellow.

Realizing something must have been dreadfully wrong, the man climbed out of his truck and hurried over. David had no strength to talk, so "explained" his predicament using hand signals. The man understood right away, helped David attach his hose to the full oxygen tank and then went back to his truck to finish his lunch.

He was still sitting there when I wheeled the shopping cart out of Loblaws over to our car and started unloading groceries into the trunk. Good Samaritan stayed to make sure somebody was with David before he left the parking lot to continue on with his day.

That episode so upset David he never went grocery shopping with me again. He remained at home unless it was for short trips to the post office, bank, or drive-through coffee and burger places.

Sick lungs do not regenerate. They worsen as time goes on and breathing becomes more and more difficult. David was housebound for the last three years of his life and could not leave even for medical appointments. His lungs required a higher flow of oxygen than the portable tanks were capable of delivering.

Watching as David's health, his independence and strength gradually slipped away shook me to the very core. Grieving became part of my life, for I knew there was no cure. I grieved for the loss of our sparkling life together; a life that was once filled with joy, passion, and friends. We were active in our work, our play and lived life to the fullest.

Vibrant, happy and in Good Health?

We took that utterly for granted, even at our stage of life (grandparent age). Nothing bad would happen to us. Would it?

I cried a lot. Mostly after David had gone to sleep. I became overly anxious, waking constantly in the night to check on his breathing. Every time I left the house, I was terrified that he'd be dead when I got back home.

Irrational?

Yes. In the beginning of his illness there was no way he'd just stop breathing, but my emotional side fretted and worried.

About two years after The Diagnosis, it became clear that I needed professional help; feelings of anxiety/depression were ruling my life. Medication was prescribed and it worked for a while. I woke up less often in the night and felt calm during the day. So after a year or so I stopped taking the pills. Not a wise decision.

My symptoms returned with a vengeance, and as a result of the constant stress, I developed fibromyalgia. Once again I turned to medication to help calm my skittish nerves. Menopause was in full swing as well adding moodiness and night sweats into the mix – definitely not a fun place to be in.

I must say for what started out as such a beautiful coming together of souls, David and I, we were heading into turbulent waters. Our magical life was slipping away and there was nothing we could do about it, but hold on to each other for dear life.

I joined an online COPD Caregivers group. Here I could voice my feelings, vent and rage. People understood, as they were all living the same nightmare. I searched the clouds for silver linings, asked the inevitable, "Why-of-it all." Why David, why us, why did our world have to come crashing down? And came up empty-handed.

I started my own blog, *Caregiving-Is-Not-For-Wimps*, and slipped into writing as easily as slipping into a cool summer nightgown. Writing helped me to process my thoughts and feelings. It gave me a voice, validation, and morphed into my place of comfort. Blogging became my social life, as I made cyber friends all over the world. One minute I could be in someone's garden in England, the next I could be sitting down to a feast in

India or watching a parade in Japan. How fortunate to be living in a world of such sophisticated technology.

Soul-searching wove its way into my daily existence. Our world as we knew it had crumbled. Our fast-paced social life had been replaced with a quiet, introspective, way of being. I consoled myself with the rationale that we must be growing internally and needed to move away from the bustling social scene. I hated being isolated this way, but it was essential that I find an explanation to ease the frustration building inside me.

David didn't say much. I knew he would rather we had our old life back, but fear and fatigue kept him indoors and away from people and the outer world.

Chapter 9

Turning Point

How does one handle death? Death of a loved one. How can you handle, deal with, come to terms with, go on living in the face of such anguish?

I don't know. No matter how prepared you are the actual death comes as a shock; a shock so deep it shakes you to your very core. And it won't go away.

Even when you know your loved one is going to die, the finality of it is inconceivable. It's impossible to wrap your brain around the horrifying loss that death brings. The cruel reality being you will never see him or her again.

Life is our focus in the day-to-day world. If we're lucky we enjoy our work, our relationships, our leisure time, and don't give our health more than a passing thought. However, when the health of somebody we love is threatened, our everyday world turns upside down and our attention shifts to preserving that life at all costs.

Our days consist of feeding, nurturing, and comforting the sick person. We ensure their medical needs are met: appointments, medications, treatments, etc. We keep them clean and well nourished, not only with food and drink, but with love.

Even though you know they will never get better, only worse as time goes on until they succumb to their illness, you don't give up.

How can you?

We know how to live; we don't know how to die. And when it actually happens the excruciating pain and overwhelming loss inflict a wound so deep that horror is our reaction and numbness our instinctive way to cope with it.

My mind knows David is gone. It's known for a few months now. My heart continues to flow with love, and that will be forever. It's my body that still responds with shock.

Today I woke up feeling terrible. Dizzy, headachy, shaky and shivery, as if I'm coming down with a cold or the flu. I know it's not that, as I've felt this on and off for weeks, since David's passing.

I force myself to get out of bed, drink my coffee, eat something. Baby steps, I remind myself like when he was ill and we were living that roller coaster ride of ups and downs; of waking up one morning feeling fine, but by mid-afternoon he'd be short of breath, shaky and wanting nothing more than his bed.

Another day he might wake up with nausea, headache and weakness, but by evening, those symptoms would have improved to the point where he was actually looking forward to eating supper. His eyes would sparkle once more with renewed zest for life.

Each day was a baby step. Each hour sometimes, as his symptoms waxed and waned.

I can't make long-term plans. I can't make any plans at all. Keep changing my mind. I want to sell the house. It's a big house for one person and I feel isolated here without David. I'd like to move closer to my children.

But can I really do this? Can I tackle the cleaning, sorting and renovations required before a house goes up for sale? Never mind all that – can I leave my beloved home?

I need to renovate the downstairs powder room. Both sink and toilet are a 70s dull brown and yellow. The vanity, although spacious with lots of storage under-the-sink for cleaning supplies and toilet paper, takes up too much space in that tiny room. Perhaps I'll replace it with a white pedestal sink, or a small modern vanity – all shiny and new. I don't know where to start.

Maybe flooring. That shouldn't be too difficult. So off I went to my local Home Depot, hoping to find something quick and easy. Unfortunately once I located "floor coverings" the display alone was overwhelming!

There was so much to choose from. Color (who wants a crimson or icky lime floor?), patterns and textures by the zillions – how on earth was I going to make a decision?

I can't do this! I'm not good at design. Or matching colors, or anything decorative. I wish I was, but I'm not!

A feeling of dizziness swept over me. I desperately needed to sit down for a minute, but there was nowhere to sit.

Calm down, I told myself, taking a deep breath, it's only floor tiles for heaven sake, nothing to panic over.

I chose some plain slate grey ones, some patterned dark-wood colored ones, and boring beige tiles. Not really my taste, but I was "decorating" for potential buyers and maybe they'd like the more blah or neutral tones, to blend in with their decor.

When I got back home, they all looked awful, so I threw them into the garbage. Tomorrow I'll have to start looking all over again. And this is only to re-tile a tiny bathroom.

I still can't find the checkbook.

This shock wears off in little bits. Like the freezing of your gums after a dentist appointment. Some people call it numbness. I call it shock.

I feel fine for a day, an hour, a few minutes. But then it hits and rips me to shreds – the emptiness and profound sadness that is my life now. The empty chair at the table, the empty side of the bed, the empty medicine cabinet, the empty house.

I try to busy myself with projects; can't do people yet for more than a smile and a wave. I don't want to socialize. My mind might be distracted for a bit and maybe even my body as I walk around the streets, but then a little bit of the shock, or the freezing wears off, melts, and the soreness takes over once more. An inflammation of the whole body, sensitive to the lightest touch, the slightest whisper, the frailest of emotions, and tears stream down my face – again.

A deep yearning has taken over my soul. When I step out in the mornings, my eyes sweep over the landscape. Will a butterfly appear today? A special one from the Other Side? Will a pen suddenly appear at my feet as I walk in the grass?

My gaze travels upwards as I earnestly scan the clouds. Will I see a heart, a face, an angel? Something special for us? It's almost gotten to the point of obsession, this searching, wishing and hoping. Hoping for a sign – *any* sign – powerful enough to *be* that connection to David's Spirit.

Where is he? Is he OK? I need to know that.

Sitting on my deck in the cool of the evening (I did a lot of that in the early days), I looked up to see something fluttering amongst the tree leaves. Its wings glowed soft and silvery in the fading light.

A butterfly? No, too big.

A bat?

Bats are not uncommon in this neighborhood. Occasionally one would swoop out of the woods to surprise me as I walked at dusk, like that evening when I strolled to the end of the street and saw what looked like a butterfly turn into a bat, its wings outlined in silver against the darkening sky. But I'd never seen bats in my backyard.

Was this really a bat? I watched it for a bit, entranced with its erratic now-you-see-me, now-you-don't movement. In and out among the leaves. What was this bat doing? Eating insects? Weaving a silvery dance to attract a mate? Absolutely nothing more than fluttering about?

Never in my life have I been so in tune with the Spirit World. Does this sound weird? I would have thought so years ago, but when you lose somebody so dear, so close, you cannot ever imagine severing those ties, that strong connection, no matter what the circumstances.

Our relationship ran so deep that often we'd be thinking the same thing. One of us would make a comment and the other agree before the sentence was finished.

Why should that change in death?

It's common knowledge that communication is not confined to speech alone. We all know about sign language for those who cannot speak, and body language to clarify (or contradict) the speaker. Then there are those gut feelings called instinct or intuition that seem to come out of nowhere, from a different realm or a higher power.

In some deep corner of my being, it makes perfect sense to me that David and I can still communicate – even though he's crossed over into another plane of existence. Yet this concept feels so new to my ordinary way of thinking, that I still find myself wavering between belief and doubt.

Needing to understand why Bat had appeared to me that evening, I pulled Ted Andrews' book *Animal Speak* from my shelves and looked up the meaning.

The keywords for bat are Transition and Initiation...

Interesting, I thought.

... In Babylonia bats represented the souls of the dead. In China they were symbols for happiness and long life. To the ancient Mayans, they are symbols of initiation and rebirth.

Bats also can reflect a need to face our greatest fears.

Well that sounds right. Knowing that David might die was frightening. My greatest fear came to pass when he did die. And living without him is even worse. So yes, I'd say I'm facing my greatest fears right now. And I don't like it!

Ted Andrews also made reference to Bat holding the promise

of rebirth after coming out of the darkness.

Well, that's a little better. Definitely something I can hope for and hold on to. Messages like that are not to be ignored.

Could the appearance of Bat be coincidence? But then again, I had to have been sitting out that night, and I had to have been looking up at just the right moment. Never have I seen a bat in my backyard before, and I never saw one in the yard again.

Over the years, I've found that coincidence doesn't really exist. Sometimes we are not aware of the deeper meaning or the gift "coincidence" presents to us. Often it's much later, in hindsight, that we make that vital connection and truly understand an experience or situation.

It was beginning to dawn on me that the path of communication between our world and the world of Spirit must lie in Nature.

I've always been a nature lover, but with the hustle and bustle of daily life, I rarely paid attention to what was going on around me. It took David coming into my life to change all that and to enhance my relationship with my surroundings.

"What does the sky look like?" asked David one morning as I walked into the kitchen.

I gave him a smile and turned around to plop two cups of coffee and some Timbits down on the counter.

"Oh, a little cloudy, some patches of blue."

I was glad that my back was turned, as in truth I hadn't really noticed. Why did he ask me this question?

Logically it was probably because he hadn't ventured out of the house in the past couple of years. Or maybe he just wanted to know if we would be able to enjoy our morning coffee on the deck, soaking up the early summer sunshine. Some days, even in summer, it might be too cool, especially if the sky was overcast. Or too windy and he'd have trouble catching his breath.

More than likely, he just wanted to have some sense of the outside world. A world he had almost left behind.

Now, I'll never know.

Every day after that, however, I made sure to look up at the sky as I was running errands, so I could tell him what it looked like. And as I became more aware of the sky, I also became more aware of our environment.

Being aware of the ebb and flow of one's natural environment is to feel connected, and David must have needed the strength of that connection.

"There's an east wind blowing," David would inform me as if this was very important to our lives at that moment. In our early days I would look at him as if to say, "Who cares?"

Now I take more notice.

"Let's watch for the hawk," he'd say every time we drove to Ottawa. I never really paid attention to birds on our route. They were always flying about overhead or sitting on the wires by the side of the road. But David had a keen eye and always managed to spot that hawk or a V of migrating geese before I did, even while he was driving the car.

In fact on our wedding day, while en route to Cornwall, Ontario, it was David who caught sight of a curious fawn poking its nose through the long grass by the edge of the road. As our car sped by (we were on the highway and could not slow down), the fawn turned around and bolted into the woods. I hoped its mother was close by.

This past weekend I had been feeling particularly desolate and lonely. It seems I can go for a few days feeling fine or at least on an even keel, when out of nowhere a powerful wave of fresh shock sends me right back down into that well of sorrow. It's like the ebb and flow of the tides, pulling back for a while to allow me to function, but then without warning, pounding me down with such force, all I can do is dissolve in salty tears that sting my soul.

Monday afternoon found me babysitting my two grandchildren. Little Nathan was down for his nap. He had fallen asleep while I was giving him his bottle, so with this little bundle in my arms, I walked slowly and carefully up the stairs; then gently lowered him into his crib. His sister was downstairs in the living room, her attention occupied with a children's program on television. Otherwise, I would be hearing, "Grandma, where are you? Grandma, I have to go potty! Grandma, is Nathan sleeping yet?" So with the TV as distraction, Nathan could be put to sleep undisturbed.

Quietly, I closed the bedroom door. Made sure the baby monitor was turned on. Tiptoed downstairs and peeked into the living room. Jasmine was totally absorbed in her show.

Good.

I withdrew to the kitchen to fix myself a coffee. Just then the dog barked, letting me know she wanted to go out.

Fine.

Coffee in hand, I slid open the patio doors. Whisky raced out into the warmth of an early September afternoon. The sun, bright and strong, shone out of a cerulean sky. It was too nice to be sitting inside, so, I took a couple of minutes to walk barefoot in the yard (no I did not step in dog poop). I just enjoyed the feel of grass on my bare toes, and talked to David as I always do.

"Why are you gone? Why don't you come back? Where are you?"

Silly questions, but I ask anyway.

I heard a chirping sound. Ignored it. The chirping did not go away. In fact it became louder and more persistent. Somewhere in the back of my mind, I must have known it was a bird, but all I could think of at that moment was – where oh where is David?

Then I saw it – a bright red cardinal sitting on a telephone wire, chirping for all he was worth. I watched him curiously for a while. Then looked around for the female. I could not find her.

Just him. Sitting chirping as if trying to tell me something.

I turned around and walked back in the house, leaving the dog outside on the grass, happily chewing on a plastic dog toy.

Peeked into the living room. Jasmine was still engrossed in the program.

"Would you like some juice?"

"Yes, Grandma."

"Yes, *please*," I instructed.

"Yes, *please*," she echoed.

I poured some juice into a sippy cup, then popped my coffee back into the microwave to reheat. Carefully skirting toys, I made my way across the living room to the couch, bent down and handed Jasmine her juice. My hot coffee was put on a side table, out of harm's way. Then I snuggled up to the little girl, enjoying the closeness of her three-year-old body, but at the same time, acutely conscious of the sharp pain of loss, the knowing that David and I will never snuggle up together again.

Enough focusing on pain! (I admonished myself.) Looked up at the TV screen to see what Jasmine was watching. Children's shows are short, usually lasting 10 or 15 minutes, so I thought we'd watch one last one and then turn off the set. As it happened, a new show was just beginning.

A little robin had tears flowing down its cheeks. It was looking longingly out the window of a young boy's room, wanting desperately to fly away. The robin had been injured and unable to fly when the boy found him weeks earlier. The child carefully picked up the bird and carried it home. Over time they had become friends.

Now that the robin was well and strong, it longed to be outside in the open air. The child didn't understand and wanted to keep it caged in his room.

The mother of the boy walked into the room, sized up the situation and gently but firmly instructed her son to let the robin go. Reluctantly the child pushed open the window and the robin flew out like a shot.

But a few minutes later, it was back. It perched on the child's finger, told him, "Thank you for your care. I'm sorry I have to leave, but I must fly free now. Look for me in the spring. I love you."

"I love you too," called the child, wiping away tears as he watched his friend disappear in the trees.

The mother explained to her son that the robin was happy now. It had to feel the wind on its wings. It needed to fly away and join its friends, the other birds. And later on, build a nest and go on to a brand-new life.

Nice little story.

I had just shut off the set and was turning away when it hit me. That story was meant for me! It made perfect sense. And what better timing!

No, no, no, argued my Inner Skeptic. I must be going nuts. Not *everything* is a message.

But how do you explain the timing (my True Self argued back)? I had just sat down at that precise moment to cuddle with Jasmine and looked up at the television to see what she was watching.

Had I not let the dog out, heated my coffee, watched that cardinal, put Nathan down earlier or later, etc., etc., I would have missed that show.

To my way of thinking, it's the precision of the timing that brings home the message.

Is David really flying free now? Free of illness? Free of heaviness, of bodily constraints? I fervently hoped so.

Oh yeah?, insisted Inner Skeptic. Like he's really coming back in the spring.

I soooo wish that were true. Tears filled my eyes, and not wanting to upset Jasmine, I turned quickly away to look out the window.

The cardinal had long gone. Telephone wires hung empty, barren in a yard that moments ago had been so bright and full of life. Dark clouds were gathering now, casting a pall over the hedges, gardens and children's toys. All was quiet, deserted as if birds and animals had taken shelter from something ominous, or simply from an approaching rainstorm.

Little Jasmine took my hand, pulling me away.

"Let's play, Grandma!"

As we sorted through the "dress-up" box for something fun to do, I couldn't help wondering what that determined little cardinal had been trying to tell me.

I kissed his screwdriver the other day. Don't laugh. I saw it sitting on the kitchen counter. I don't know how it got there. I thought I'd thrown it out with the garage things. Maybe it was headed for the garbage bin, but luckily I saved it and planted a kiss on the handle. Well, he did have his hands all over it – many times while fixing things around the house. Did he leave some of his unique energy behind?

Actually no, darn, I felt nothing and it smelled a bit funny like old socks, but I didn't care. Then I went looking for other signs of him. Why oh why did I wash all his clothes? Even the winter jackets, hats and scarves. Now there is no smell of him anywhere – except his hairbrush and comb. I expect that will wear off in time.

I look at his pictures on the nightstand. I kiss those too, but they are so cold and flat. I wish he would just jump out and be alive once again.

Is this denial? Bargaining? Longing?

I still can't wrap my head around the fact that he's really dead. Body gone. Not coming back. Especially when there is evidence of him all over the house: the bird feeder he filled with sunflower seeds now hanging empty outside, favorite rake with the red handle propped up against the shed, his towels on the rack, toothbrush, shaving cream, condiments in the fridge which I don't eat, but won't throw out, bathrobe hanging in the closet, well-loved books on the shelf, notes on the calendar in his handwriting, which suddenly stopped, and on and on.

I lie in bed at night, talking to him in the dark. Am I nuts? I don't really care. Sleep won't come anyway, so I open the bedroom closet and yank one of his sweaters off the hanger. It's a soft grey one; one he particularly liked. Back in bed I cuddle it close to my heart, willing myself to go to sleep. The bed shakes, ever-so-gently.

An earthquake? Not here, although we did have a mild one when he was in hospital. Just a rumbling of the earth. But that was very unusual.

Then I feel a gentle pat on my knees. What the heck? Throwing back the covers, I sit bolt upright in bed, heart racing. I suck in a breath and listen in the darkness.

Nothing.

Cautiously, I lean over and snap on the bedside lamp.

Still nothing. Everything looks normal. Was that a dream? No, I hadn't gone to sleep yet.

As time goes on I welcome these gentle pats in the night. What used to be unsettling is now comforting. His hands pat my legs, like someone would pat a small child. At first it felt as if a cat had jumped up on the bed and was walking across my legs. But I don't have a cat. Or a dog. I'm alone in the house.

Once it felt like he had placed his hand on my shoulder, to ground me as I wept. Another time I swung my feet over to his side of the bed and was shocked to feel a "hot spot" at the exact place where he would have been sitting, sipping his tea before lying down. Those last years of his life, David could not lie down in bed right away. The transition from sitting to lying caused him to gasp for breath, so the process had to be gradual. He would sit for a while at the edge of the bed, sipping tea or water until his breathing became stable enough to lie down.

I tried to make sense of this "hot spot" at first. Had I rolled over to his side? No, but even if I had, this was a round area of heat – just the size of somebody's bottom. I wracked my brain trying to come up with some kind of sensible explanation, but there was none. I kept my feet on it for several minutes, trying to absorb any vibrations or echoes of David's spirit and also because I wanted to see how long it would last. I don't think it lasted for more than a few minutes, but it definitely felt like David had been sitting there.

I now embrace the bed shaking that frightened me at first. It only lasts a minute or so and never happens in any other part of the house. Just in bed at night. At those times, I feel his presence swirling around me, almost tangible, especially when accompanied by a smell that is distinctly David. (Once it was a whiff of chocolate on the pillow, another time it was cigarette smoke and another time it was coffee.)

One afternoon, I was at the gas pump filling up the car. After replacing the nozzle, I reached into my purse to pay for the gas and pulled out something that did not feel like my lumpy wallet. It was smooth and flat and brown. David's wallet! I wondered if David was reminding me that he could still pay for "our" gas – in his own way now.

Yes, I carry his wallet around with me. For comfort. His hospital card, library card, and pictures are still there. His driver's license and Medicare card had to be surrendered to the provincial government, but as long as I carry a purse, his wallet will be safely tucked inside. And thinking David wanted to pay for the gas, put a smile on my face.

Every day I draw an affirmation card. David and I started that years ago over the breakfast table. We'd choose either a Faerie Wisdom card, an Animal Medicine card, or a Well-Being card.

I don't remember exactly when or why we started drawing cards, but as time went on, it became part of our morning routine. It was fun to see what good thoughts, affirmations, or words of wisdom turned up for us to focus on each day.

After David was admitted to hospital, I felt a need to continue that ritual at home before leaving the house. I'd draw a card for me, then one for him. Sharing that little bit of normalcy when I arrived at his bedside, helped to keep some of our fears at bay, if only for a little while.

Something strange happened in that last week of his life. The cards I turned over every morning were identical! First I chose one for me. I'd read it and put it back in the deck. Then I'd give the cards a good shuffle and take another card. It turned out to be the very same card – every time!

I was shocked at first. Not that it hadn't happened before. There had been random occasions in the past when we both drew the same card.

But during this crucial week, it happened every single morning without fail. Clearly something beyond my comprehension was going on. And more often than not the Moose Card would appear. David had a fondness for moose and this was one of his favorite cards from the Animal Medicine deck.

After a few days of this, I was beginning to anticipate, to expect that both cards would be the same. I knew what the message was. It was something profound David said to me, from his hospital bed a few weeks before he died: *"The lines between us are blurry."*

And now David's messages come through strong and clear. The Love Card from the Faerie Wisdom deck appears at times when I need it most. It's a pic of a man and a woman, gazing deeply and lovingly into each other's eyes. It's a beautiful card, rich with feeling and I can't help tearing up for a minute or two.

The Commitment Card as well. Same message – a man and a woman arms around each other in a loving embrace.

The Rabbit card from my Well-Being deck often pops up too. The very first birthday card David ever gave me all those years ago showed a picture of a cute little bunny on the front. Partially hidden behind its back was a present, carefully and sweetly wrapped up with ribbons and bows. "We're lucky rabbits!" he used to say. Lucky to have found each other. Lucky to be sharing our special love.

Yes, sweetheart, we are. Except that you're gone now.

If someone had told me years ago that Spirits communicate through cards, I would not have believed them – not in a million years. In fact, I wasn't even sure that Spirits existed except in the imagination. But now I know differently.

I chose the Waiting Card from the Faerie Wisdom deck this morning. It was time for breakfast, but as I sat there, elbows on the table staring at David's empty chair, I could think of nothing that I wanted to eat. Instead I frowned at that Waiting Card lying on my placemat. The faerie crouched low hiding in the rushes at water's edge looked placid enough; the message was nonthreatening, but it irritated me.

What do I have to Wait for? I want this grief journey to be over. I'm tired of feeling sad and sick. Impatiently I shove it back in the deck. Must have been a fluke. Shuffled and picked another card. It was the Waiting Card again. Darn. Now I have to pay attention, and figure out what it means.

I think the message for this one is to stop running around like a chicken with its head chopped off and let things evolve. Sometimes the hardest thing to do is Wait.

A card that turns up regularly for me (from the Well-Being Cards by Esther and Jerry Hicks) is the "Life Everlasting" card. A serene meadow with what looks like a transparent person, or an outline of someone's body, fills the card. Grass, flowers, blue sky and fluffy clouds can be seen through this transparent person, giving one the impression that she is a spirit. The card reads:

I am Life Everlasting, I am an Eternal Being.

On the back of the card it continues…

You cannot die; you are everlasting life. In grace you may choose to relax and allow your gentle transition back into your Nonphysical state of Pure, Positive Energy. (Your natural state is foreverness.)

This card is so encouraging, so comforting that it brings tears to my eyes. My fears are banished for a while and a feeling of calm envelops me. It's as if David is speaking to me through this card, reassuring me that he really is alive – somewhere in some other form. It's no coincidence that this "Life Everlasting" card pops up when I am feeling totally and utterly miserable.

Late afternoon and I was in the garden with my two young grandchildren. After mucking about for a bit in the dirt, I spotted a fuzzy caterpillar crawling up the low garden wall.

"Oh, look!" I called to Jasmine, not sure if I really should be drawing the attention of a three-year-old to this innocent caterpillar. Little fingers reached out to grab its brown and orange fuzziness. Immediately the caterpillar curled up into a ball and lay still as if dead. I told Jasmine we'd better leave it alone.

"Let's play on the swings for a while until the caterpillar feels safe enough to uncurl."

We went back to check on the caterpillar a couple of times, but it was still curled up tight. Before I left to go home, I noticed it quietly resuming its journey up the garden wall.

That night, while resting on the living room sofa, I thought I'd choose a card from my Animal Medicine deck, just to see what would unfold. Sometimes I will focus on a question, but other times I pick a card at random to see what turns up. Spreading the cards over the coffee table in an untidy mess, I paused to take a sip of lemon soother, while absently turning over a card.

It was Possum. Possum? What did that have to do with anything? Playing possum? Isn't that a game we played as children? I took another sip of tea and started gathering up the cards to stuff back into the box.

Wait a minute. Possum?

Playing possum? No way. How could I have chosen that card? I did not even have to look up the meaning. It was clear as clear could be and my heart knew it. The caterpillar playing dead, the possum playing dead.

That must have been David's way of capturing my attention. His way of sending me a reassuring message. "I'm not really dead, it just looks that way to you now. I've changed – that's all."

Ahhhh, I sighed with relief, sinking deeper into the couch. For the next few minutes I just sat and sipped quietly, allowing my thoughts to wander. Are these really messages from the Other Side? Is David really speaking to me through cards? How does it make me feel?

Good, I answered myself. Comforted. Loved. With a sense of wonder that Spirit could be so wise as to guide my hand over a particular card.

And how else would I explain those strong feelings of Love I felt just after David died? How could I possibly explain that man ringing my doorbell right after David's cremation saying, "Hello, Ma'am, my name is David"?

I don't believe I'm imagining all these signs. There are far too many. And if I slot all these signs into an "imagination folder" isn't that denying the world of Spirit? And by denying the world of Spirit, isn't that saying the only things that are true are the ones we actually see with our eyes? To me that's very narrow-minded. Do we see air?

It was right then and there I made the conscious decision to stop my endless questioning, to cast aside those taunting doubts and embrace my transformation into this new world – a world where spirit communication does not belong to science fiction, but to Nature.

I felt as if some unseen force was taking me by the hand, encouraging me with gentleness and love to step out boldly like the Fool in the Tarot; to take that leap of faith with confidence and trust. Trust that "those who have gone before" are capable of reaching out to us through Nature's gifts. Reassuring, comforting, offering the one left behind a beacon of hope that all ties with our Beloved are not severed forever and ever. Their essence is still close – loving, protecting and guiding us from another level, another realm, as we grieve and struggle to find our way in this frightening landscape, that has become our new home.

It's autumn now and as the days cool down, I turn to fall cooking as naturally as squirrels gather food for the winter. All summer I avoided cooking simply because I could not eat. Grabbing an apple or munching on crackers was about all I could manage since my stomach was twisted in knots much of the time. I lost weight over the weeks and months after David died, but didn't mind so much, as some of those extra pounds I'd blamed on menopause.

But now I needed to feel the comfort of "routine". In autumn we carve pumpkins, spring we plant flowers – that kind of thing.

Pot roast sounded like a good, solid dish to start off with. Pot roast for one. Now how was I going to do that? It looked ridiculously tiny sitting in that big pot, so I added potatoes, onions, carrots, celery, spices and herbs, and threw in some frozen veggies for good measure.

I must admit, the most delicious smells were coming from my oven all afternoon. I hadn't cooked a roast in a year and I found myself actually anticipating sitting down to dinner.

However, as I cut into a tender slice of meat, all I could think of was how David would have enjoyed this meal. True, he liked pasta better, but my melt-in-your-mouth roasts always disappeared completely, without a lick of gravy left on the plate.

I speared a carrot, remembering the carrots we had planted in our garden and harvested over the years. Well, this year there was no garden. The carrot stuck in my throat.

It was no use. I could not enjoy this meal, particularly with that Empty Chair staring at me from across the kitchen table. A tear rolled down my cheek.

Oh, please, I said to myself – you are not going to cry over a pot roast. But it's my first pot roast of the season and David will never eat pot roast again.

Nor will he enjoy my fall baking, which he especially loved. Apple pie was his favorite, then oatmeal raisin cookies, Nanaimo squares, butter tarts and chocolate chip cookies. How can I bake ever again?

That's when the dam burst wide open. I did not hold back anymore, but let the tears come. The dinner went into the garbage and I sat there in the lonely kitchen feeling sorry for myself. I stared out the window at the darkness. When had the sun set? Days were shorter now and I was dreading the coming winter.

Goosebumps shivered up my arms. Abruptly I got to my feet, pushing back my chair. My eyes darted around the room seeking reassurance. Were our familiar things still in their places? Hugging myself protectively, I took stock: the clean white appliances, pine cupboards, big round mirror over the sink, copper stars and key holder in the shape of a wild duck David and I had hung on the wall one rainy afternoon, wooden bowl of overripe bananas on top of the microwave. My eyes swept back to the window where the comforting presence of ordinary knickknacks, an African violet, several tealights and a wooden fisherman all sat placidly on the sill, as if everything was just fine.

The carved fisherman was David's and I don't remember where he got it, but it looked like an old sea captain in his yellow rain slicker, shaggy beard and curvy pipe clenched between his teeth.

Everything in our kitchen looked much the same as it had

this morning, and yesterday, and the day before, but I needed to wrap myself tightly in a cloak of protection against the growing darkness of long winter nights that would soon creep in to steal the light.

It was then that I noticed something strange. The ceiling lights had stopped flickering. When had that happened?

Involuntarily my eyes flew to the spot on the floor where I had left those fluorescent bulbs back in July or August. They were still there. I'd never gotten around to replacing them.

Chapter 10

The Lines Between Us Are Blurry

"The Lines between us are blurry," whispers David from his hospital bed.

Startled, I shift in my chair.

And lean in closer searching his face. Where had this come from? We hadn't been talking about anything in particular. In fact, we hadn't even been talking – just being, resting together.

"I know just what you mean," I reassure him with a smile, for in truth, that's exactly what I had been thinking, but didn't want to say it in case it sounded foolish. But David had no such qualms about voicing his feelings and I'm glad he did.

How strange that at the end of his life we are becoming closer, as if the sharpness of our physical boundaries is dissolving.

How can that be? With each passing year, his body grows weaker. In some deep part of my consciousness, I know I have to let him go.

It is time.

Holding on to someone as tightly as I've been to David simply cannot go on forever. At some point, there needs to be a separation, an uncoupling. It's as if we've come to that proverbial fork in the road. A time when he goes on his way into the Unknown, and I stay behind to finish my life on Earth.

If I think back, however, this "letting go" process actually began in the fall of 2008. I had come to the end of my rope. Exhausted from constant worry and anxiety, I had to withdraw my attention from David in order to focus on my own health.

There was absolutely nothing I could do to change the fact that my husband was suffering from a chronic, incurable disease – a disease that would eventually kill him.

There was no way either of us could control the course of

his illness nor the outcome. All the worry and anxiety would not make things better. In fact, they made it worse, for as a consequence my muscles grew stiff and sore to the point where I needed daily medication.

The tighter I held on to David in fear, the more my body would react with painful muscle spasms. I felt depleted and depressed.

This was definitely a wake-up call.

Apparently, the time had come for me to loosen my grip, to give up any illusion I had of keeping David alive forever. I had to begin the process of letting go or we would both drown.

The day I came home to find David sleeping, totally oblivious to the piercing shriek of his oxygen alarm, marked the beginning of this process for me.

I had been babysitting on this fine June day. There was not a cloud in the sky, no thunderstorms on the radar; absolutely no reason to worry about a power outage. However, as I pulled into our driveway and pushed the remote to open the electric garage door – nothing happened.

Odd. I tried again.

Still nothing.

I was beginning to feel sick. There had to be some explanation for this, other than no power. Maybe the remote was just stuck.

Hands shaking, I squeezed down on the control as hard as I could. "Come on, come on, Open Up!"

The garage door remained firmly closed.

Panicked, I threw the remote on the floor and slammed out of the car.

"Please, God, please, God, don't let there be a power failure!"

David always slept in the afternoons and would not awaken if his oxygen supply was turned off. Whether or not he would hear the alarm, I had no way of knowing.

Running strictly on adrenalin now, I jerked open the other garage door which was manually operated, raced through the garage, shot into the house and jumped full force right onto the bed where David lay sleeping.

"WAKE UP!!"

Poor David. What a shock it must have been to wake up like that, being shouted at and violently shaken by his loving (and usually gentle) wife.

His eyes looked glazed, but instead of offering an explanation, I just kept kissing his sweet face, over and over. I was desperately relieved to find him still alive. Had I arrived any later, the outcome would have been different.

But I did arrive early and he did survive. By "coincidence" my daughter had left work an hour earlier than usual, enabling me to make it home in time to wake up David.

I was beginning to "get it", to understand that this journey we were on is not mine to control. Somehow, I had to find the strength to let go and let God; to allow the natural order of life to flow without the constant battle raging in my mind between reality and denial. No matter how tightly I held on, David would one day slip through my fingers. I could not save his life and this fight was proving to be utterly useless and in fact destructive.

In the spring of 2009, I took a much needed "time out" and went off to Florida for a week. I let go of his care for a little while and allowed his son to take over. That didn't mean I didn't call home.

I did.

Every night, just to hear his voice. And to make sure he was okay.

After a week of nothing to do but lie on the beach, soak up the sun and let the rhythm of ocean waves soothe my soul, I was ready to come home. My energy levels were back once more, my balance was restored and those bodily pains mysteriously gone.

Unfortunately, during this short week, my husband took a

step down. He could no longer follow his daily exercise routine. It was just too much for his tired body. Not only was this a serious sign that his disease was worsening, it was utterly discouraging and weighed heavily on David's spirits. If he could no longer exercise, then what could he possibly do to hold back, to fight the relentless progression of COPD?

Did this happen because I went away? I don't know.

Did I feel guilty?

Of course I did. Terribly. But once again, do I control his illness? I think not.

Now a year later, we've come to the top of the mountain. We both know this journey is coming to a close. We both know the time is approaching where we will take that frightening step into the unknown.

We are fortunate this process has been gradual. Others don't have time; they leave regrets, unfinished business, and final words of love unspoken. And yet, as we stand on this strange threshold, this "holding area" before our final separation, we feel this incredible closeness.

I know what he is thinking and I know what he needs. I can feel his internal struggles and he must be feeling mine – my helplessness at not being able to stop him from dying.

We are not growing further apart as I would have expected. The defining edges of our bodies are disappearing. Our souls, our deep inner beings dissolve into each other, as if this must be a necessary step before a loved one leaves this Earth.

Maybe this always happens at the end of a life.

Maybe not. I don't know.

Chapter 11

Hospital Madness

April 9, 2010. I feel like I'm in the Twilight Zone these days. David was taken to hospital in an ambulance around lunchtime. We'd celebrated his 67th birthday on April 4th, which sadly would prove to be his last.

Three weeks earlier I returned home after a day of babysitting to find David weak and sick.

"Why didn't you call me? I would have come home!"

"Well, if it had gotten any worse, I would have."

Worse? How could it get any worse? I thought. David had been walking to the bathroom when suddenly, he could not breathe. Just like that. A feeling of nausea and dizziness swept over him and he had to hold on to the walls to keep from falling. Sliding down the wall, he ended up on the floor, gasping for breath.

After a few panicky moments he began "purse-lip breathing", a technique used to calm anxiety while expelling excess CO_2 from the body.

Frightened, but unable to call anybody, he remained on the floor and focused all his attention on this method of breathing. It wasn't long afterwards that I arrived home.

What he was experiencing was that dreaded "air hunger" which means his lungs were failing. I've heard it feels like drowning.

Over the next three weeks, David's level of energy was practically nil. He was so depleted that it was all he could do to make it through the day. He could barely walk, so I brought a wash basin, facecloth and toothbrush to his bedside. Some days he was too tired to get dressed, so he stayed all day in warm pajamas and housecoat.

I helped him to the kitchen for meals. He needed to walk a little and a change of scenery was good. Stairs were out of the question, so he never entered our bedroom again. Nor his upstairs den where all his financial papers and computer were kept. For the rest of his time at home, he stayed in our TV room, sleeping on the pull-out couch. I slept with him, as there was no way I could leave him at night to sleep upstairs in our own bed. It was too far away and what if he suddenly got worse in the night?

The only bright spot in all of this was that whole Easter weekend (particularly Sunday, which coincided with his birthday) the weather turned unseasonably warm and we took full advantage of this by sitting out on our back deck. I remember how grateful he was to feel the sun on his face, particularly after such a long winter!

We called his family doctor. She really had no advice. David needed to be seen and examined by his respirologist. But that meant a trip to the hospital, and the only way that could happen was by ambulance. David did not want that. Somewhere in the dark recesses of his mind, he knew that if he left in an ambulance, he'd never come home again. Sadly, he was right.

Family doctor ordered some blood work before she left, and the following morning, a CLSC nurse came and drew David's blood.

We were both hoping that this was just a setback, and he would return to "normal" after a while. Sometimes recovery from these exacerbations was spontaneous; other times a course of antibiotics and prednisone was necessary to get him back on track.

Finally we could not put it off any longer. Three weeks had gone by and David was no better. We needed answers and, God willing, an improvement in his condition.

Perhaps with a few tests, treatments, and some new medication he'd be back in our happy home again.

Unfortunately, this did not happen.

He's been in hospital ever since and we're going on 18 days now.

The ambulance arrived. I had the garage doors wide open and was waiting for them. Three attendants hopped out and I showed them into our TV room, just a couple of steps away through the inner garage door.

They marched into the room and took over. Two young fellows set up a heart monitor and clamped the electrodes onto David's chest.

I had no choice but to stand back and let them work. There's nothing wrong with his heart, I thought. Why are they doing this?

I was beginning to feel dizzy and irrationally wished they'd all go away. Go back where you came from and leave us alone! Leaning against the wall I closed my eyes for a moment to try to regain my composure.

"Ma'am? I have a few questions for you." The older of the trio was holding a clipboard, pen in hand ready to take down some information.

I quickly looked over at David to see how he was doing.

Same.

Hunched over at the edge of the bed, meekly allowing the attendants to take charge. A blood pressure cuff was wrapped tightly around his thin arm.

I wanted to scream. Don't you know this man is a doctor? He's strong and competent and professional and good! He is NOT supposed to be sick. He is NOT supposed to be needing you to take care of him. Heart monitor? Blood pressure cuff? He gives the orders! He calls the shots for medical care – he doesn't bow submissively to receive it!

The man was waiting, concern sharpening his eyes. Taking a deep breath I managed to pull myself together enough to answer his questions.

When I looked back at David, one of the men was switching his nasal cannula to a specialized mask; the other end of which was hooked up to an enormous portable oxygen cylinder.

"Are you sure you have enough oxygen for the duration of the trip?" I asked, nervously shifting from side to side. Gooseflesh crept up my arms and the room suddenly felt chilly.

Did they have any idea how much oxygen David needed? Would they run out en route?

"Yes, we have plenty," one of the younger ones assured me with a smile. I did not smile back. Did they know how serious this was? Did they know what would happen if David ran out of oxygen? What if they were stuck in traffic? I hated to surrender David's care to these strangers, confident and professional as they appeared. He was only their patient, but he was my husband. *My husband.*

"Can you walk?" one of the attendants asked David. He shook his head. I wondered if he could even talk through that contraption on his face. It was a full mask covering both mouth and nose. Quite a change from the simple nasal cannula David usually wore. Oxygen flowed from soft plastic tubing with two prongs that fit into his nostrils. This method of oxygen delivery left the mouth free to eat and talk.

However, since you can't clamp a person's nose shut tight, about 50% of the oxygen escapes into the room.

The snug fitting face mask he now wore was far more efficient, increasing his oxygen uptake to about 70%.

This frightful-looking mask, however, went one step further. There was what looked like a large-sized zip-lock bag attached to the mouth portion, which hung down to about the middle of his chest. The purpose of this was to deliver the highest quality of oxygen possible, by not allowing any room air to be inhaled by the patient.

I didn't know it at the time, but this "non-rebreather" mask was used specifically in crisis situations; later on once the patient was stable it would be replaced by the usual nasal cannula, or a smaller less complex face mask.

What I also didn't know was that David would be wearing this ghastly-looking mask for the rest of his life. He was never to take it off again. It made me think of my Dad's gas-mask, left over from World War II, which hung on our family room wall and scared me as a child.

While the technician left to get the stretcher, I looked over once again at my dear husband. He looked so small and fragile sitting there hunched over on the edge of the pull-out sofa. Lying back was not an option for it made breathing almost impossible.

I felt sorry for him.

He had an air of sadness and resignation about him, as if he knew there was no turning back. But he gave me a weak smile and I smiled back, hoping he wouldn't sense my fear or see the tears welling in my eyes.

Just at that moment, I looked up to see an empty stretcher coming through the door. My heart sped up and I had to bite down on my cheek to keep from crying. This was real. It was not going to go away. These men were putting my David on top of that bed-on-wheels, securing him with straps, covering him with a red blanket and taking him away!

I stood by helplessly, watching in silence as they proceeded to wheel him through our garage and into the waiting ambulance. The older attendant must have sensed my distress for he turned to me.

"And when you come home..." he instructed, looking me right in the eye.

Home! Oh, please God, I prayed, please bring my dear husband home. But some gut instinct told me that David would never come home.

He was admitted to the Emergency Ward at Lakeshore General Hospital, and immediately hooked up to the oxygen outlet at the head of his bed. Pure oxygen of the highest concentration flowed from tubing connected to the wall. With a central supply somewhere in the depths of the hospital, there were no worries of it ever running out.

The portable tank used for transport was sent back with the ambulance crew.

Blood tests, ECG, CT scan and x-rays were ordered to determine the cause of this recent decline. Hopefully, it would turn out to be something treatable. Perhaps a course of antibiotics, I prayed, and he'd be back home in no time.

The Emergency Ward was a nightmare, as anybody who has spent even one night in that environment knows well. It wasn't the crowding; we understand ERs are overflowing with people needing immediate care. It wasn't the noise. Same thing. People are sick. They call out for help. Bells ring, medical staff walk in and out. Visitors too. Nursing care is done around the clock.

It was the apathy and ignorance of some hospital staff. Oh there were good nurses. No question. Compassionate, down-to-earth, competent people. But with some others the quality of care was downright dangerous.

For some reason, one of the night nurses decided to turn down my husband's oxygen. Why? I have no idea. David almost passed out. Had I not been there, he would have gone. Expired. Died in the ER. Sounds too dramatic? Like a TV show? Sorry, it's completely true.

David was shifted over to a tiny cubicle probably due to overcrowding. Unfortunately, this meant his wall oxygen outlet was located in the next patient's cubicle. The hose ran from the oxygen outlet along the floor and into my husband's face mask. We could not see the regulator from David's bed, because of the privacy curtain, so I could not monitor it properly.

The following afternoon, somebody decided to turn it off. Not down. Right off! David's oxygen is set at 13 liters per minute. Yes, that means 13 LPM of 100% oxygen going through his lungs in order to keep him alive. I vaguely heard a voice complain that the hissing sound was too noisy. At that high flow rate (15 being tops), there would be a loud hiss. But so what?

All of a sudden, David was gasping for breath. He gulped for air that wasn't there, while instinctively clutching his throat as if to prevent someone from choking him.

I shrieked! Tore open the privacy curtain and yelled: "WHO TURNED OFF THE OXYGEN!!"

The medical attendant just looked at me. Her patient, a middle-aged man lying in the bed, appeared indifferent. I lunged for the oxygen dial and turned it up as high as it would go. I was shaken to the core. How on earth can any responsible medical attendant just decide to turn off an oxygen regulator without first checking to see if anybody was actually using it? It was outrageous to think negligence of this sort could happen in an acute care hospital. That this was happening to David in the very hospital where he used to practice medicine blew me away.

In a rage I marched up to the head nurse and told her what had happened. Magically, a bed in the "overflow" area appeared. Overflow is a holding unit for patients awaiting admission. It was quieter here with more privacy and space to keep personal items. There was actually a closet for clothing and a nightstand. Luxury! And most important of all, the oxygen regulator was on the wall at the head of the bed – where it should be.

Oh how I wished I could just take David home! End this nightmare and leave! Instead, he spent another few days in this Overflow Unit, waiting to be admitted to the nursing floors.

And once again, one of the nurses took it upon himself to turn down the level of David's oxygen. This particular nurse decided that it was time to "wean" David off his non-rebreather mask and high flow of oxygen.

This was protocol for a critically ill patient, once the crisis had passed. However, these nurses did not bother checking the Doctor's Orders to see if weaning was indicated for David. It emphatically was not!

With a determined and confident air, Nurse #1 whisked off David's face mask. I stared at him. As smooth as silk, he produced nasal prongs and slid them into David's nose, like a magician performing an act.

What the heck?

I watched in horror as he then proceeded to turn the oxygen setting down from 13 liters per minute to 6 – all at once – just like that!

"ARE YOU TRYING TO KILL HIM??!!" I shouted as loud as I could.

I leaned over Crazy Nurse and jacked the oxygen flow back up to 13.

"Ma'am, I know COPD patients. Don't worry."

"LIKE HELL YOU DO!"

"Ma'am, calm down, this is Doctor's Orders."

"WHICH DOCTOR?" I accused, incredulous at this outright lie. I knew nobody had given him any such order.

No answer.

"WHICH DOCTOR TOLD YOU TO DO THIS?"

Still no answer.

"CALL RESPIRATORY THERAPY!" I demanded. It was evening and presumably David's doctor had left the hospital, but I knew Respiratory Therapy would be available and would most certainly back me up.

"I know what I'm doing. This is not my first patient and I haven't lost any yet." I was appalled and thoroughly disgusted with his lame attempt at humor. I looked over at David, for instruction. He was my doctor-husband and I always looked to him for answers, particularly when it came to medical matters. He looked at me with tired eyes and shrugged in defeat.

Helplessly pacing back and forth, I watched as Crazy Nurse #1 turned his attention back to the oxygen flow meter and reduced the setting once more. The saturation level in David's blood descended like a stone. There was no way his diseased lungs could support such a drastic drop in oxygen.

Seconds before I was about to punch Crazy Nurse, something must have sunk in and he realized he'd made a grave error. He was actually doing something wrong. Without fanfare this time, he removed the nasal prongs and placed the mask back on David's haggard face. I had already turned the oxygen back up to the proper level. Without another word, he retreated to the safety of the nursing station.

Respiratory Therapy arrived soon afterward. No, not because Crazy Nurse had called them as I had requested, but because it was time for David's treatment. I told the therapist exactly what had transpired just minutes beforehand. She marched straight over to the nursing station and gave Crazy Nurse #1 shit!

As a consequence of this little episode, the prescribed breathing treatment had to be cancelled, as hubby had absolutely no strength left to do anything more than lie in the bed, close his eyes and rest.

To my horror, the very next day, Nurse #2 decided to pull off the same stunt. (Don't they read the patient's chart or look at Doctor's Orders?)

Being of Caribbean origin, Nurse #2 had a more casual, laid-back attitude. Without a word to either of us, he sauntered over to the wall outlet above David's head as if on a whim, and turned the flow meter down. I couldn't believe my eyes! This absurdity was happening all over again! And he did not even bother to put an oximeter on David's finger!

COPD patients need constant monitoring of their blood oxygen levels, and this is done with an oximeter. If the level is too low, they need to increase their oxygen flow, or sit down and rest. If the levels fall below a certain number, the patient becomes unconscious. Then they die.

"NO WAY!" I bellowed, shoving him aside. I quickly flipped the dial allowing the oxygen to shoot back up. "ARE YOU NUTS?

AND YOU'RE NOT EVEN GOING TO MONITOR HIM??"

"Oh," he responded. Totally unperturbed, he turned and walked away, choosing to go on to another patient rather than fight this Dragon Lady.

By this time I was frantic. I felt I could not leave my husband's side even for an instant. Who else would take it upon themselves to turn David's oxygen down – or off, for that matter!

Fortunately, it wasn't long before Dr. Z (David's respirologist) appeared. I told her in no uncertain terms what had been happening with the nurses. She was angry; I could see it in her eyes, but she kept her feelings under control, as any good professional will do.

"I'm glad you told me," she said through tight lips. "I will put a note in the chart with instructions that NOBODY UNDER ANY CIRCUMSTANCES is to touch the oxygen setting on your husband's regulator." And with that, she squeezed David's hand, turned on her heel and strode briskly over to the nursing station. I watched her slap his chart on the desk and begin to write.

Finally! Somebody who knew what she was doing! Somebody rational and responsible. I was beginning to wonder if the whole world was going crazy! Or was it just us?

Finally, after three long days in this Overflow Unit, a bed became available up on the Medical Floor. David was transferred to 4 North, and immediately put on a special mattress that cushioned his body to prevent bedsores.

Unfortunately, because of his frail body and the hard mattress in ER a pressure sore had already developed on his coccyx – the area of the body most often affected. This was not good news, but I hoped with better nursing care up on the Floor and the softer, gel-filled mattress it would heal quickly.

It never did. But it did not get any worse, nor did he develop pressure sores anywhere else on his body. For that we were grateful.

It was a relief to be up on the Medical Floor, where the pace was slower and less noisy. People came and went outside in the hallways, but there were no monitors beeping, ambulances arriving or patients screaming with hallucinations or dementia.

Nurses were more intent on their nursing routine: taking vital signs, administering medications and checking for worsening symptoms.

No, I wouldn't let them give David his bed bath. I insisted on washing my husband every day. This was my role, my responsibility as Caregiver and I did not want to give it up to strangers. I still wanted to nurture and protect David – whether at home or somewhere else.

Lulu, one of the nice nurses, understood completely, as she had washed and dressed her own husband while he was in a different hospital, before he eventually died of cancer. I did not want to think of that possibility, but thanked her for sharing her story. I just wanted to bring David home to our house in the country, where he could sit out on the deck under the leafy canopy our many trees provided, and breathe in fresh and healing air.

Please, please, I prayed silently while dipping a clean washcloth in the basin of warm, soapy water, let this nightmare end and bring David back home where he belongs.

Even though David was in a less stressful place, that didn't stop the negligent incidents from happening. One evening they forgot to start his IV antibiotic. The nurse came in to take vital signs and left before opening the valve to begin the drip. Not a big deal, but David could not go to sleep until the medication was finished and I only noticed it late into the evening.

Another time, they left his food tray in the kitchen. I had to go downstairs to pick it up, as nobody could take the time away from their duties. A nurse brought in the wrong dressing for his bedsore and a lab technician drew his blood early one morning, when it had not been ordered. Apparently, he had walked into the wrong room and did not even check the patient's hospital bracelet. And on and on.

I understand nothing is perfect, but it puts one on edge, and totally reinforces the necessity of having someone stay with the hospitalized person. A family member preferably, a friend or even a kind neighbor – someone to advocate for the patient.

The worst of the worst, however, was in the cardiac lab. David was to have a cardiac ultrasound – the last of many tests. Routine blood work was normal, as was his ECG. Chest x-ray and CT scan revealed severe chronic lung disease. Not unexpected, but definitely not good, as there is nothing you can do. Lungs don't repair themselves.

Our last hope was that some condition would be found in his heart – something that could be easily corrected. Then he could take the prescribed medicine or treatment and go home. Strange to be hoping for a "positive" result of a medical test; normally you hope everything turns up negative.

The morning of his scheduled cardiac echogram, Good Nurse (there were some of those) entered the room wheeling a huge oxygen cylinder. She was coughing. Worried that she might spread her cold to David, I asked her to please put on a mask. Agreeably she did so, but mentioned that this was not a cold – it was her normal state. I shuddered inwardly. She was young, and most likely had chronic bronchitis from cigarette smoking or allergies. I silently wished her well, and hoped she did not end up like David.

Two orderlies wheeled a stretcher into the room.

"Are you ready to go?" Good Nurse asked David reaching for his wrist to check his pulse. I noticed her eyes sweeping her patient from head to toe, making an assessment of his condition – an essential part of proper nursing care.

David nodded. With efficiency that comes from experience, and a certain pride in her work, Good Nurse smoothly unhooked David from the wall oxygen outlet and plugged his hose into the portable cylinder. Then he was transferred from his bed to the stretcher. The two orderlies left.

Good Nurse accompanied us in the elevator, down to the first floor where the cardiac lab was situated. David's stretcher was parked next to the receptionist's desk while he waited his turn. Good Nurse took one last look at her patient, checked the oxygen flow meter on the cylinder and left to go back to the Nursing Floor.

Looking around, I could see the waiting room was full. People were sitting quietly, reading magazines or chatting. Others were milling around; arriving for their appointment or leaving. Hospital employees wove in and out, some with medical reports in their hands, others accompanying their patients. Telephones rang. It was a busy place.

"Excuse me," I called out to the receptionist, interrupting her conversation with another employee. "My husband needs to be plugged into the wall oxygen outlet."

"Oh, don't worry." With a wave of her hand, I and my annoying concerns were dismissed. She turned her back on us and continued her conversation.

Time passed.

I looked at the flow meter on David's oxygen cylinder. It was getting low.

"Excuse me," I interrupted, edges of panic making my voice tremble. I was met with a frosty stare.

"Excuse me!" I repeated a little more forcefully to get her attention. "He really needs to plug in. The cylinder is running low."

"Oh all right, I'll call the technician." She picked up the phone with a sigh.

Call the technician? Couldn't she do this herself? How long will it take for the technician to get here? I would have done the unhooking and hooking myself, but I didn't see any wall connections in the immediate vicinity. They were probably all inside the actual treatment rooms.

I was starting to get panicky again. Gee, I'm so sorry for the inconvenience, I thought to myself to keep my nervousness at bay, but if you don't attend to my husband's needs you won't have a patient to do this test on.

What was wrong with everybody? I can now see very clearly how a patient can die in front of the nursing station, in an emergency room, in the hallway. People mill about, nobody paying attention, nobody checking, and the patient suffers a heart attack, a stroke or stops breathing.

Sad, very sad in this day and age.

Seconds later the technician appeared. David was wheeled into the procedure room and hooked up properly to the wall outlet. Now I could relax.

We waited another 20 minutes before the cardiologist appeared to perform the echocardiogram. He and David knew each other and for this small blessing I was grateful.

It must have been reassuring for David to have someone familiar administer this test; someone who spoke his language and would answer his medical questions honestly and intelligently.

By the time we got back to David's room, lunch was long past. He was too tired to eat and wanted only to nap. I encouraged him to drink a few sips of water before settling down, made sure the call bell was clipped to the sheet, kissed him on the forehead and quietly left the room. As I rode the elevator down to the cafeteria my thoughts turned to what our "daily life" had become.

The Hospital. From morning till night. I left the house early and only returned late in the evening. It was such a strange way of living, but there was nothing we could do.

Sleeping alone was tough.

One night I awoke feeling jittery – my stomach churning with nausea. What was going on? Was I coming down with stomach flu?

I propped myself up on one elbow and squinted at the clock. One a.m. I had only been asleep for about an hour.

I took a tiny sip of water to see if that would help, turned over and tried to go back to sleep. The nausea kept building. There was no way I could fall back asleep, so I got up and walked to the bathroom, hoping I wasn't going to be sick before I got there. Opening the medicine cabinet, I quickly found the antinausea pills and swallowed one, crossing my fingers that it would not come back up.

The medication worked and I was able to go back to sleep after about half an hour. In the morning I felt fine, so I put that episode out of my mind and focused on my morning routine.

I arrived at the hospital to find David lying in bed looking a little peaked. That in itself was not unusual. It was just that I could sense an air of uneasiness about him and I wondered where it was coming from.

"Hi, sweetheart. How was your night?" I asked giving him a kiss on the forehead before settling myself into a chair beside his bed.

"Just awful. My oxygen mask fell off and I couldn't find it!"

"What?"

"I woke up feeling short of breath. My mask was gone and I didn't know where it was! I grabbed the call bell and pressed hard on it. Fortunately, the nurse came right away. She found the mask in the bedcovers and put it right back on."

"Oh my God. You must have been scared!"

"I was frantic!"

Then something clicked in my mind. "What time was that?"

"Around one o'clock in the morning."

Now I knew where that nausea had come from. I could actually feel David's panic and fear, which translated to nausea in my body.

Another night I woke up thirsty. Reaching for the glass of water beside my bed, I took a sip, which turned into a gulp, spilling down my front. In a flash, I had a picture of David doing the same thing. Reaching out for water and spilling some in the bed.

It was true.

I didn't know it then, but this was to become a pattern. This transmission of thoughts from one to the other. We were becoming closer or perhaps I had been so in tune with his needs over the past few years it had created a heightened sensitivity between us. The physical distance separating us made no difference.

Doctor Z came in to see him. She told us all his test results were negative. This was not good news as we were hoping for a miracle; something in his heart that a medication would cure. But our hopes were dashed. There was nothing to fix. His lungs were very, very sick, and you can't fix lungs.

David would have to remain in hospital. Not this hospital, of course, but one that would provide chronic care until the end of his life.

I felt like somebody had punched me in the stomach. David being David, however, was always one step ahead. At some point in time, he must have prepared for this outcome and had already chosen Mount Sinai Hospital for its specialization in respiratory care. The doctor informed us that she would get started on the paperwork.

I was still reeling. "Why can't you come home?" I wailed. David tried to be reassuring by telling me he'd be better off in hospital with pure wall oxygen. No worries about the power going off and medical staff would be available round the clock, in case he suffered episodes of air hunger. Never having experienced this, it was not my fear. But apparently air hunger is like drowning, and I could only imagine how frightening that would be.

Liaison Nurse met with us at David's bedside a few days later. She brought some brochures to show us and explained meals, visits, nursing care, and other services offered at Mount Sinai Hospital. The good part was that I could stay overnight right in David's room.

Liaison Nurse was very pleasant and I began to feel marginally better with this decision. Until she shook David's hand in farewell.

"Wow, that's a strong grip," she remarked, "for somebody who's going to Palliative Care."

"Excuse me?" my head snapped up.

"Well, Palliative/Rehab," she amended, heading out of the room.

What was going on here? Was David really going to Palliative Care? That meant he was dying! Deep in my heart I knew the truth, but I did not want to think about it, much less vocalize it. I preferred to think that if he had to be in hospital it was because he needed some time for rehab. He'd build up his strength and *then* come home. This "not coming home – ever" did not compute in my brain.

After she left, I turned to David, "What is she talking about?" He just shrugged. Deep down inside he must have known as well.

Chapter 12

The Transfer

The house is so quiet. It's been three weeks now. His heavy-duty oxygen concentrator lies sleeping in the hallway. One gets used to noisy machines, but once they're turned off, the quiet is unsettling. David was admitted to the Palliative Care Floor at Mount Sinai Hospital yesterday. It was snowing. Very strange for the end of April. April 27th to be exact. And we'd had such a warm spring this year.

We waited most of the morning for the ambulance to arrive. In the meantime I packed up David's belongings and took them out to the car. I was surprised at how much he had accumulated in three weeks. Clothing, warm blankets from home, books and pens, personal items and toiletries, all his bedside medications including inhalers and puffers, cards and small gifts from family members. I packed it all in the trunk to bring to Mount Sinai and scooted back upstairs to his room as quickly as possible.

We sat together quietly, holding hands and waiting. There was not much to say. The ambulance attendants arrived just before lunch. As with our experience at home, they were respectful and attentive. David was carefully placed on the stretcher, the oxygen hooking and unhooking professionally carried out and he was all set to go. With what I hoped was a comforting smile, I squeezed his hand, kissed his forehead (his mouth being covered in mask) and told him I'd meet him at Mount Sinai.

As I watched them wheel his stretcher down the hall, I prayed with all my heart and soul that he be kept safe and warm on this unsettling journey. I shuddered to think of all the awful things that "might happen" along the way. There might be an accident, they might get stuck in traffic and run out of oxygen, the equipment might malfunction, he might not survive the trip. On and on and on.

Tears threatened, but I held on tightly to them. No way could I fall apart now! David needed me to be strong and I needed me to be strong. Who really knew what lay ahead of us in the days and weeks to come?

With one sweeping glance around the hospital room, I turned and raced past the bank of elevators towards the stairs. Before I could reach the stairwell, however, Lulu (one of the Good Nurses) reached out to pluck at my sleeve. I remembered that she had been the one to care for her own husband throughout his hospital stay, until the day he lost his battle with cancer.

"Have courage." She spoke with genuine concern, clasping both of my hands in hers. She must have known what I was in for.

"Thank you," I responded automatically. I was touched by her kindness, but quickly disengaged my hands from hers and flew to the stairwell. I was desperate to follow the ambulance as it was important that I arrive at the hospital at the same time as David. I needed to know that he had survived the trip and was all right. And for some urgent reason I wanted to be there as they opened those ambulance doors at Mount Sinai. I wanted to reassure David by my presence. He wouldn't have to search for me, or wait for me to arrive. I was there for him, forever and ever.

Racing through the hospital lobby I nearly collided with Respiratory Therapist. She must have seen the near panic in my eyes, for she grabbed at my arm in a compassionate gesture. Not wanting to be rude, but not wanting to stop either, I hesitated.

She looked straight into my eyes and smiled. "You are an inspiration to us all."

"Pardon?" I stopped in my tracks and searched her face.

"The energy surrounding you and your husband – it's so strong and loving, you've given all of us here the gift of hope."

Hope? What hope? What's she talking about? I had no time to process this information that appeared to have come out of nowhere.

"Thank you," I automatically responded again.

By now I was getting desperate. I dashed to the parking lot, cleaned the snow off my car, paid the exit fee and barrelled down the road, looking everywhere for the ambulance. Snow was falling steadily, forcing me to slow down as it accumulated on the roads faster than the ploughs could clear it away.

Snow ploughs? How odd to be thinking of snow ploughs at the end of April, particularly in light of our warm Easter and spring flowers earlier in the month.

I finally caught sight of it a block up ahead. Hard to miss a big yellow ambulance with red flashing lights.

Visibility was poor due to the swirling snow, but I could easily follow this vehicle and not have to worry about finding my way.

Until it took a wrong turn. Hey! Where are you going? Oh, no, I must have been following the wrong ambulance! I had no choice but to keep on going and hope I would find my way. I'd never been to Mount Sinai Hospital and was unsure of the route. And I hate driving when the weather is bad.

Somehow I made it to the hospital just as the Real Ambulance was arriving. I don't know how that happened for I had missed the sign and consequently the turnoff for Mount Sinai. Looping around and doubling back took up precious time and I could feel anxiety gnawing at the pit of my stomach. Visions of David all alone as they wheeled him into the jaws of that unfeeling institution propelled me to drive over the speed limit and to make an illegal U-turn. I didn't think or even care about the consequences.

Real Ambulance was backing up to the hospital entrance, as I raced across the parking lot. Hoping and praying that David was indeed the passenger inside and not some stranger, I ran right up to the ambulance doors just as the attendants were pulling them open.

Yes! It was my David. Eagerly, I reached out to give him a big hug. He looked funny swaddled in blankets like a newborn, or a little old lady, but he was fine. He had not worsened en route.

Once admitted to a room on the third floor, we could relax a bit. The frantic pace of an active care hospital was gone. This was a place to rest. Yes, a final resting place truth be told, but the calm and peaceful atmosphere erased our anxiety and fear for the moment. Knowing he was receiving good care allowed me some breathing space. I could go home and not wake up in the night in a panic; not worry that somebody was turning down his oxygen or ignoring a call bell. In fact, comfort is the primary goal here, and the willingness of the staff to accommodate David's every wish, took my breath away.

The nurses were professional, yet nobody rushed through their work. After medications were given or some measure of comfort administered, each nurse would spend a few minutes talking with us.

Social workers, psychologists, recreational and physiotherapists all made a point of stopping in to see David. It felt to me that beyond their professional duties, they were making sure no patient was left alone for too long a period of time. It would be so easy to fall into a depression, lying in a hospital bed knowing your life would soon be over.

Even the doctors spent quality time at the bedside. No rush, no hurry. All our questions were answered without hesitation. We felt we were in good hands.

It was lunchtime when we arrived. The staff kept a tray hot while David's physical needs were looked after. I was impressed with the level of care, the swiftness of the whole admission process. And the simple kindness of keeping his lunch hot, while he was transferred to the bed, washed, changed, and made comfortable. I almost cried with relief that, finally, my husband was being "looked after".

That first night I slept on a cot beside his bed. David slept well, but I was not at all comfortable and woke up frequently. I wanted so badly to open a window, but they were sealed shut. Air quality had to be controlled, particularly for patients with lung disease, as any change in temperature or humidity could trigger an acute exacerbation of their illness.

A very noisy air exchanger was mounted on the wall at the end of the hallway. Not only did the noise keep me awake, but so did the overhead lights. I was aware each time one of the nurses tiptoed into the room to check up on David.

Sometime during the night, I had to get up to use the bathroom. I hadn't thought to bring any clothes with me, so ended up sleeping in one of David's T-shirts. It was long enough to cover me – just barely. Of course, I had no slippers either, and did not want to walk on the floor with my bare feet, so I groped around under the cot for my shoes. As I dashed for the bathroom, I hoped nobody would choose this time to walk into the room. Nobody did and that suited me just fine.

Tonight I will sleep in my own bed at home with windows open. I hate being away from hubby, but I just cannot sleep in this environment. I am sooooo tired. The stress is taking its toll; has been for a long time. And I realize that I am gradually letting go, whether I want to or not. And I definitely do not.

However, life as we know it has changed. Our daily routines at home are no more and I feel as if everything is being taken out of my hands. I am being forced to stand on the sidelines and watch as forces beyond my control take over. The man I spent the last few years holding in my arms, shielding and protecting, loving and nurturing, has grown invisible wings and is beginning to fly away from me. My empty arms ache with wanting to capture him again and hold him close. But the natural flow of life carries him away, like a stream of water flowing through the forest. Gentling the journey is the gradual course of events, like steps, giving me time to adjust.

The First Step was giving up his care to the nurses and doctors at Lakeshore General Hospital. Since it was only about a 20-25 minute drive, I could be there early to bring David a taste of home. Every morning I prepared hazelnut coffee for us and lovingly poured it into his old familiar thermos; the one he used back in his working days while driving to his office or the Clinic. It was important for me to do this, to nurture David this way.

"Did you stay the night?" inquired a visitor one morning, as she walked into the room and sat down. Her husband had had a stroke and was occupying the bed next to David's. They were an older couple and she visited for only a few hours each day. Every time she arrived, I'd be sitting by David's bedside. And if she chose an evening visit, I'd still be there when she kissed her husband goodnight after visiting hours were up.

I did not respect "visiting hours". I reasoned they were for visitors – not wife or husband of a patient. Every night I stayed until eleven o'clock or so, chatting (we never ran out of things to talk about) or reading from a library book. Some evenings I'd read to him from my repertoire of guided meditations. As he closed his eyes and imagined himself in a sunny meadow, by a waterfall or walking along the beach, he could relax and let go of the hospital environment. He felt soothed by my voice and I in turn felt better at being able to do something to ease his discomfort.

The nurses didn't mind me staying so late and in fact they often poked their heads in the door and smiled to see David relaxed and comfy with me sitting quietly beside him in the bed.

The security guard, however, was not pleased. One night he stood at the door and asked me to leave. I told him "no" – point-blank. He insisted I leave. I stayed right where I was. He walked off with a warning that I was to be gone, or else.

Or else what?

Well, pooh. I wasn't going to let him come between David and I.

But after that, whenever he made rounds, I'd make sure the curtain was pulled around us so he couldn't see me from the doorway.

The Second Step in this separating of our paths in life was his transfer to Mount Sinai, a hospital much further away from our home. Twice the distance in fact. It made no sense for me to leave early in the morning, as I'd only be caught up in rush hour traffic.

And I simply did not have the energy to stay until ten or eleven at night any more. As much as I love my husband, I could not be there constantly.

Yet it was stressful to leave him. Was he *really* being taken care of properly? Would he die in the night? I hated leaving him in that hospital room, but at the same time, I was wearing out. The fear and worry of his condition, the daily drive back and forth, our laundry to do in the evenings, housework piling up, combined with all the ordinary activities of daily life left me completely and utterly drained.

I had no choice but to crack open my sore arms a little wider and surrender his care to the nursing and medical staff.

At home in my own bed, it's the middle of the night once again. I gradually become aware of the sound of breathing, almost snoring in its depth. Feeling comforted by the rhythm of David's breathing, I begin drifting back to sleep, but suddenly jerk awake.

Harsh reality slaps me in the face. David is not here.

He's miles away lying in a hospital bed, being looked after by strangers.

This releasing, letting go process is both frustrating and frightening. The sense of helplessness is overpowering at times, while I struggle to accept circumstances which I cannot change.

There is nothing else we can do but follow our paths, and our paths are beginning to separate. He is taking a path that is right for him as his life here on earth draws to a close; and I am taking the right one for me, as I watch through a veil of tears.

I force myself to remember that we can still see each other. We can hold hands and kiss. Still share coffee and meals, read together, talk, and even laugh sometimes.

But I know time is running out. Soon it will be time for him to move on. And I shudder at that thought.

Over the weeks that David was in hospital, there were nights when I'd wake up at home to feel the bed shaking. It was frightening. We do not live in an earthquake zone, yet tremors are not unusual here, just very rare. Strange, however, that it always happened in the middle of the night. Just for a minute or two. It didn't happen in the daytime while sitting in a chair, or early morning before getting out of bed. Maybe his Spirit could travel to be with me in the night. I don't know. But later after he'd died, that gentle bed shaking continued on.

Another night, I awoke with a start. My bedroom was dark and quiet with only a faint glimmer of moonlight coming in through the window. Nothing seemed amiss, but I listened for a moment or two just to be sure.

Everything seemed normal, so I turned over to go back to sleep. I was just drifting off when a picture of David, spilling his urinal all over the bed, came into my mind. I can only imagine how wet and uncomfortable he must have felt – not to mention embarrassed, and somehow those feelings of discomfort were transmitted to me.

The next day when he told me that the orderly had to come and change the sheets in the night, I nodded my head and smiled in empathy.

"I know."

Years ago, I would have thought all this was nonsense. At one time I had been very skeptical about the Spirit World and thought any unexplained phenomenon was ridiculous. Knocking on walls, radios turning on spontaneously, eerie sounds in the night, and let's not forget flickering lights (like in my kitchen over the summer). I was convinced that there was some kind of logical explanation. And communicating with the dead? Preposterous! Who were these "mediums" who claimed to contact Spirits from the Other Side? Really!

As one who embraces intuition, the spiritual component of hand reading or palmistry, you would think I'd be open and accepting of Spirit communication, but I wasn't. In my opinion "mediums" were all fakes.

Experience is a great teacher, however, and my thinking has changed. There is so much we don't understand about the Spirit World and I think it's best to keep an open mind.

Something else I've learned is how incredibly strong the human spirit is. David's body is crumbling, yet his spirit shines brightly and strongly through his eyes. Even here in Palliative Care.

In the active care hospital a few weeks earlier, his eyes had become dull, glazed and sick-looking. Every time I scanned his face my heart would crack a little more. I was sure I'd never see that dear sparkle ever again. That soft glow that meant David.

My David.

Alive.

Maybe not well, but definitely living, breathing, eating, sleeping.

Drugs were being pumped into him, oxygen levels fluctuated alarmingly, he was being shifted and shunted around for tests. There was constant fear, uncertainty, and fitful sleep at night – all of which was taking a toll on him. I knew all that, but it was still worrisome; I hated to see that flat defeat in his eyes.

Now that he's in the Palliative Care Ward, the pace, the focus has changed completely. Where once there was harsh intrusion, hustle and bustle, now the feeling is calm, respectful, compassionate. The staff is cooperative, willing to do what is necessary to make end of life care a little easier, more comfortable; instilling hope that when the end does come, it will be peaceful.

I am amazed that he is feeling better – his eyes sparkle with renewed hope, with a new zest for life. It seems incredible, since Palliative Care is the last station; the pause, the Still-point at the end of the runway, just before the final take-off.

David's mind is still sharp. I bring the mail to him every morning, and we open it together. He instructs me on managing the household finances, bill paying, etc. He is preparing me to go on alone, but it also keeps his mind active and busy, and even more important, makes him feel as if he's still a part of Normal Life Out There. He tells me he is looking forward to starting a program of physiotherapy.

Physiotherapy? My mind reels again. Why are they offering him physiotherapy when The End is so near. But then again, who knows when His End will be?

He is eager to gain back the strength he'd lost through those weeks of bedrest at Lakeshore Hospital. Is this possible? Can he regain his strength? To what degree? He wants to be able to get out of bed and sit in a chair. He hopes to stand up and perhaps walk again. I am humbled by his strength and determination, under these circumstances. Especially in these circumstances.

As I drive home, I watch people doing everyday things: shopping, eating, walking, biking. My children call to ask, "What can we do to help, Mom?"

"Just tell me about your day," I answer. "I need to know that there is a Normal Life Out There somewhere."

Chapter 13

Palliative Care

It's been four weeks. And David can walk again. The physiotherapist has been wonderful. Slowly at first, baby steps. Using his walker for support, he can now walk from the bed to the chair. Connectors were attached to his oxygen hoses to lengthen them. Otherwise, he couldn't leave the bed. Now he has a bit of freedom, a bit of mobility. It feels like a miracle.

He walks three times from bed to chair, about seven or so steps each way. It doesn't sound like much to anybody else, but for David it's progress. I can see him getting stronger. He's smiling more often too.

Is he getting better?

Were the doctors at Lakeshore Hospital wrong? I'm going to ask Nurse T (our favorite) to have a respirologist see David for a second opinion. The doctor who sees David here, Dr. Q, is a Palliative Care specialist. She deals with end-of-life care only. Respirology is located on another floor where both in-patients and day patients are seen and treated.

Last week I took a whole day off to go to the dentist and the hairdresser. These appointments were long overdue, but I kept putting them off as I didn't want to be away from David. Not only was I afraid that something terrible would happen to him while I was away, I didn't want to miss a single moment of his life.

The clock was ticking.

Ominously.

In the background.

I was brutally aware that we would never have this time together again. One day that clock would stop. And David would be gone.

But now it was time to attend to my needs, as trivial as they sounded. Driving into the West Island from my home in Hudson took about 25 minutes. The sky was overcast and it looked like rain. Strong winds shook the car forcing me to slow down, and it felt as if a storm was brewing. Just as I was pulling into the parking lot, the heavens opened up and rain came down in a deluge.

I waited a few moments to see if it would stop. It didn't. Bracing myself, I opened the car door and made a mad dash for the Salon.

"Hi!" Janet's face was all smiles as she greeted me, arms raised in mid-snip. She took one look at my dripping hair and quipped, "Nice weather, ay?"

I laughed and sat down at the sink to wait for my shampoo. Looking around, I noticed a smart-looking young lady standing at the counter, purse plopped on the top. Her hair was carefully and perfectly styled and her nails looked freshly manicured. I stole a glance at my own nails, then quickly looked away. Hmmm, maybe another day.

Stylish Lady paid her bill, picked up her umbrella in preparation to leave and turned to wave good-by to the Salon and its occupants.

"Good luck staying dry," I called out to her.

The words were barely out of my mouth when I noticed with surprise and relief that the rain had stopped. Sun was streaming through the windows and I could see steam rising from the sidewalks. Whew! Now I won't have to worry about getting wet when it's my turn to leave.

But the weather was very strange that day, as if weird energies were stirring things around. It started raining again about 10 minutes later; big fat drops, the kind that soak you to the skin.

Janet was snipping away at my hair, both of us chatting as women do, when all of a sudden there was a sharp rapping on the windowpanes. Startled, we both looked up to see hail, as big as marbles pinging off the windows.

"Wow," said Janet, scissors poised, "I haven't seen hail that big in ages! And never in summer, have you?"

"Nope. Freaky weather," I agreed.

She finished my haircut and I made ready to leave. Good thing I hadn't bothered to have my hair blow-dried. Imagine paying to have your hair styled just so, only to have the wind and rain whip it all out of shape? It was summer and my hair would dry quickly in the fresh open air.

And as luck would have it, Ms. Sunshine reappeared, just as enthusiastically as before. It felt hot but soothing on my skin after the coolness in the Salon. As I made my way back to the car I couldn't help wondering if there were more freaky storms around the corner.

It was refreshing to spend the whole day out and about, running errands, doing ordinary things, taking the focus off hospitals and sickness. My last stop was at the Garden Centre. No, I didn't buy anything – I had no time to plant, but needed some soothing, some form of TLC. Flowers lift my spirits and nourish my soul. It's as simple as that.

Once home I popped a chicken into the oven for dinner. It was later than normal, but with nobody home, it didn't matter.

Glancing at the oven clock I saw that it read 4:20. Hey! Something's wrong! I knew it was closer to 6:00. In a flash I realized that the storm must have knocked over a power line while I was away. The electricity had been off for over an hour!

Heart racing, I whirled around and zoomed out of the kitchen towards the TV room. I had to check on David!

Then I stopped in my tracks. And remembered.

I nearly wept with relief.

David is safe. He's in hospital where powerful generators keep the electricity going. No worries. How strange to think that my husband is safe in the Palliative Care Ward. Palliative

Care is associated with death, not life.

There is a wonderful magical Healing Garden in this hospital which we can see from David's window. How lucky we are to have access to this hidden paradise, this center of calm amidst the grim reality of disease. It's taken a while, but finally David has built up enough strength and confidence to leave his room for a short turn in the garden.

But not without preparation, however. One of the volunteers smoothly enters the room with a wheelchair specially designed to hold two oxygen cylinders. Most wheelchairs are equipped with only one holder, for that is the norm. David, however, needs two.

He stands at the side of his bed and I hold his arms while he pivots neatly into the wheelchair. Once settled, I wait until he is comfortable and able to breathe easily. Then, I carefully unhook the hoses attached to the wall oxygen device and reattach them to the portable cylinders nestled securely behind his wheelchair. We stop for a moment and check the oxygen saturation levels in his blood. If he is feeling calm and the readings are good, we leave the room and slowly make our way towards the elevator. If the readings are too low we wait, letting his body recover from the exertion of moving from bed to wheelchair.

In the elevator I find myself holding my breath until we land with a bump and the doors slide open. Even though it's only two floors down, I always worry about a breakdown. It's a tiny space and I have nightmares about being trapped inside, watching while David's oxygen dial goes to 0 and he suffocates. I've never liked elevators in the first place, and head for the stairs whenever I can.

Ahhhhh, walking in sunshine! I push David through the outer sliding doors and into the warm welcome of pure summer sunlight as it pours over us. A feeling of peace settles over us as we absorb the outdoor freshness of the Healing Garden.

Flowers, in shades of soft pink, cream or more vibrant yellows and reds, grow vigorously by the walkways as we meander along. Huge koi fish swim past us, their bodies supple in the clear cool waters of the pond. I watch as they dart out from underneath the wooden bridge that rattles whenever anyone crosses over.

David prefers not to cross the bridge this afternoon. For some reason he finds it unsettling so we choose a different path, one that takes us past the pond where a fountain of sparkling water tinkles and splashes. There are plenty of benches scattered here and there, some under shade trees and some in full sun. We head towards a patch of sunlight where I park David's wheelchair at one end of a worn wooden bench and sit down beside him.

"Are you okay, sweetheart?"

He smiles behind that awkward mask and I smile back. Tilting his face up to the sun, he lets out a sigh of contentment, which almost brings tears to my eyes. I am so thankful that he can relax for a short space of time into the warmth and healing rays of a golden summer sun.

Most days he's too tired to venture out. Some days the weather is either rainy or too windy, but when all is well, we go out. At first 10 minutes was all David allowed himself in the garden. He was worried about depleting his oxygen supply. But after the first few times with everything running smoothly, his confidence grew and so did his strength. Now we've stretched it to 25 minutes, not quite half an hour, but at least we have this time out of doors in the fresh air.

Volunteers are true angels of this earth. They are incredible in their devotion, their selflessness, their smiles. I did not know just how valuable to the hospital these dedicated souls are.

One of them is Mr. Sweet Gentleman. I don't know how old he is, but his hair is all white. This devoted soul assured me he'd be happy to bring my husband his morning coffee and newspaper every day.

Every day.

He's as trustworthy as the rising sun and never takes a day off. No task is beneath him as he fetches towels and soap for somebody's bath, feeds those who cannot feed themselves and wipes food off their faces, pushes anyone in a wheelchair who wants to go out either for a cigarette or a turn around the Healing Garden. He willingly accompanies patients to appointments outside the hospital, often arriving back quite late in the day.

Ms. Tiny Doll is a wee, little old lady reminding me of an old-fashioned doll with her china-blue eyes and soft blue/white hair. This dear sweet soul must be in her 80s and she never fails to come around every afternoon with the snack cart.

"Tea, coffee, cookies, ice cream?" she sings with a smile.

I feel like a kid at somebody's birthday party, being served cookies and ice cream. At first I refused, thinking that snacks were just for the patients, but Ms. Tiny Doll assured me they were for visitors too. David and I smile at each other and accept the cookies just to be polite, but we both tuck into the ice cream.

She stops to chat for a minute infusing us with her energy and I marvel at her fortitude. How can she manage to get here in the afternoons, push that heavy-looking snack cart and smile at everybody? I can't help but feel sorry for us as David will never reach 80. Will never have the opportunity to volunteer, or even just kick back and enjoy his retirement. He had to leave his profession six months after The Diagnosis, at age 59. But then there are others so much worse off than we are, I remind myself.

And out the door, Ms. Tiny Doll goes, taking her lovely smile with her, but not her enthusiasm for life and we both feel a little lighter, cheered by her presence.

And then there's Spa Day. Spa Day happens once a week as a special treat for those in Palliative Care.

Two nursing orderlies enter the room pushing a special bath stretcher. The patient is transferred from the bed directly onto this stretcher, covered up with a flannel sheet then wheeled down the hall to the Spa Room.

The ride is short. From David's room it's right down the hall, around the nursing station and into the bath area. I follow close behind, making sure David is comfortable and has enough oxygen.

The Spa Room is quite dark at first after the bright lights in the hallway, but as my eyes adjust, I notice tiny tealights glowing softly from shelves and little alcoves on the wall. They are made to look like candles, real ones being forbidden, of course. Soothing music is playing in the background and I relax a little as I slide onto a low bench beside the Spa tub.

Someone has painted a delightful ocean scene on the wall facing the tub, to give the illusion of being at the beach. Champagne cooling in a silver bucket beckons invitingly from a shelf just off to the side (no, it's not real – I asked).

I'm impressed at the aura of romance and relaxation that has been thoughtfully created in this humble bath area, and it certainly does the job of spiriting us away from our worries for a little while.

The bath stretcher is lowered directly into the tub and all the patient has to do is lie back and unwind. There is no shifting, wiggling or maneuvering required. Fragrant warm water rushes into the tub, while luxuriant bubbles foam up around the person, as much for modesty as for fun, I think.

There is an oxygen outlet on the wall, so hubby can plug in. No worries. The staff are good. They know what they're doing.

"Are you okay, Sir?" they ask David. In a thumbs up signal, he tells them he's fine. He's relaxed and soothed. It's such a treat that the nurses all joke that they need a Spa too! "Oh no, I'm next!" I joke along with them all. And we laugh. It feels good to laugh.

Back to his room again where we find that the nurses have prepared his bed with bath sheets and towels. He slides from the stretcher back into bed again and I have no qualms about shooing the nurses away. This is *our* time.

I lovingly wrap my wet husband in clean towels, dry him thoroughly from head to toe, then toss the used towels into the linen basket.

Somebody pops their head around the privacy curtain. "Everything all right?"

"Yes, we're fine." I nod my head, dismissing her with a polite smile, then turn my attention back to David. He looks so clean and shiny – like a small child fresh from his bath. I kiss the top of his head then turn around to scoop up two bottles of moisturizing lotion.

"Which one today, tangerine or coco butter?"

"Peach," he teases.

"Coco butter it is," I tease back slathering a generous amount all over his skin and massaging it in. The whole room comes alive with the scent and it really does smell like we've been to the beach!

"Something smells yummy," remarks a passerby in the hallway.

Feeling pleased with myself, I continue David's massage. Then I help him to dress in a shirt and light cotton pants, or jogging pants, whatever feels comfortable. I think it's important to get dressed every day, to shift the focus away from the one-size-fits-all bleached and worn hospital gown of the sick.

I am glad that his hair is washed. Other than Spa Day, he doesn't get into a bath or shower, so the only way of keeping his hair somewhat clean is using dry shampoo. Blow dryers are not allowed in the rooms for some reason, so I just towel dry his hair and comb it nicely. He is tired after all this activity and needs to take a nap. I quietly slip out of the room and outdoors for a walk, or to the coffee shop for a quick snack.

Reflecting on the past two months, I can see that the natural world is full of healing if only we would notice. About a month before David's hospital admission, I looked out the window in our living room to see a pair of mallard ducks waddling across our front lawn. That was quite a surprise, as there is no pond or water source nearby and I'd never seen ducks on our property before. Curious, I looked up the meaning in my *Animal Speak* book. Ducks, I read, bring emotional comfort and protection. Oh boy, I knew right then and there, that we were in for a rough ride.

One evening I happened to look out the hospital window to the Healing Garden below. There on the pond swam a pair of wild ducks, as serenely as you please.

"Ducks," I announced, turning around to smile at David. I was going to ask if he wanted me to move his bed closer to the window so he could see them, but at that moment, Social Worker walked through the door. Eagerly, she made her way to the window to peer out.

"I've never seen ducks on that pond before! And I've been working here for eight years!"

Strange, I thought at that time, maybe she just didn't notice. But I never saw any more after that.

Sitting on my back deck one afternoon about two weeks before David died, I looked up into the sky to see a hawk flying overhead. Now that struck me as unusual. Hawks are known to stick to the wooded areas at the end of the street; never have I seen one in our backyard before.

Curious, I rose from my chair, slid open the patio door and headed for the bookshelves where I knew *Animal Speak* would be waiting for me. Ted Andrews' interpretations of animal sightings are fascinating in my opinion, and I like to consult his book often.

Flipping through the pages I found Hawk: "The hawk is a powerful bird that will awaken visionary power and lead you to your life purpose. It is the messenger bird, and wherever it shows up, pay attention. There is a message coming."

Thursday night, David's last conscious night. He had had

a miserable week. His lungs were failing. Antibiotics were prescribed just in case it was merely an infection, but I think we both knew the truth. David asked me to spend the night. I assured him that I had already decided to stay over.

I sat on the bed and read to him. All week, he had requested I read from my own book *Reading Between The Lines*. It had not been published yet and I had read it to him many times over the course of the writing, to get his feedback. So, it came as a surprise that this night he wanted to hear my story once again. After reading for a while I wanted a change of pace, so asked him if we could do some guided meditations together.

One of the meditations I read to him was *The Shaman's Journey*. I had used this meditation in my healing circles long ago. It's a powerful meditation that weaves its way through each chakra while asking the question: *Which power animal shows itself to you?*

"What animals did you see?" I asked David once we were finished.

"None," he replied.

"None?" How could that be?

"Well, just a hawk."

I believe this hawk was gently leading David into the Afterlife.

Chapter 14

November

I found the checkbook! Finally! Lost my car keys, my house keys, bank statements, important documents and even my underwear (it later turned up behind the clothes dryer). Now I'd like to say that I just asked David to help me and presto – the checkbook appeared. But it didn't happen that way.

There were stories I'd read online in my Widows Support Group, where people asked for help in finding lost items. They spoke out loud to their spouses and mysteriously those items were found, returned to owner, quite often in places that had already been searched.

One woman lost $200.00. This was a portion of her paycheck that she'd stashed away to use for groceries. She was sure she'd placed it in the top drawer of her telephone table, but when she went to check, it was gone. It took her about a week of opening and closing every drawer in the house, before she thought to ask her dearly departed husband.

"Now, Stan, please help me here," she spoke out loud while searching the house. "I can't pay for groceries until I find that money."

Just then the cat, who had been napping on top of the fridge, jumped down onto the kitchen counter, scattering twenty dollar bills as he went. The surprised woman put her hand up on top of the fridge and found the money. It was all there.

I love stories like that.

My problem was not so easily solved, however. I had searched the house from top to bottom, my purse, the car, and even the garage and could not find that checkbook anywhere. I was at a loss. Did I drop it somewhere? Toss it into the recycling or garbage? Where could one skinny little checkbook hide?

It was yesterday afternoon while sitting at my computer that I found it. Needing to use the printer, I first checked to see if there was adequate paper. No there was not, so I reached into an open packet of copy paper and pulled out my checkbook! I could not believe it! In one of my paranoid moments I must have thought that stuffing it into a packet of copy paper would make a really good hiding place, in case somebody broke into my house and stole that checkbook. Turned out to be an exceptionally good hiding place!

I continue to walk.

Constantly.

Every day.

It's gotten chilly, but a few brave moths and bees still hover around. The little bees are sluggish, sleepy as they rest on the last roses of the season, or huddle in clusters of sedum. Butterflies are long gone. How am I going to survive the winter without my beloved butterflies? My beacons of hope?

Autumn leaves in shades of crimson, gold, and flaming orange look so pretty and so lively as they dance in the wind. Like a comet streaking across a night sky, they go out in a blaze of glory before turning brown and falling to the ground.

Dying.

This pattern of nature brings back memories of David's burst of energy about 10 days before he died. It was totally unexpected. He seemed to be almost happy with shiny eyes and an eagerness to get going with his walking routine, rather than hesitating, feeling worried that something would go wrong.

His happiness was catching and I almost burst with joy! Was he getting better? Could I bring him home now? Were the doctors wrong?

Miracles do happen, but sadly not this time. A few hours later after lunch, his eyelids began to droop and I could sense a defeated weariness settling over his body. The rest of the afternoon was spent in a deep sleep.

Christmas is creeping up and I can't stand the thought of walking into stores or shopping malls. I just can't handle all the good cheer, happiness, and bubbly anticipation.

Buy toys! Buy gifts! Buy candy! Buy cards! Ads are in your face everywhere you turn. I can't deal with this overwhelming sensory overload.

Twisting away, I clutch my coat tightly around me and vow not to shop at all this year. It's not going to happen. No way.

Silver Bells, White Christmas and all the other traditional carols are piped into every elevator and every store. Radio stations play nothing but Christmas music, which normally I love. Christmas is a time of joy, but now it brings on a flood of tears as I remember our special times together:

David sitting at the kitchen table, eagerly awaiting a taste of my buttery shortbread or butter tarts straight from the oven. I can still see him swinging his feet like a little kid, eyes glowing with anticipation. How rewarding it was for me to bake for him; he praised everything I made and came back for seconds.

David and I venturing out into a snowy evening or a clear and cold one to pick out our Christmas tree. David and I wrapping gifts together, and placing them lovingly under that tree.

Now I wish the whole thing would go away. Besides, I threw away all our decorations in a frenzy shortly after he died. The house will look bare. Who cares?

November. My birthday month. Where are you, David? Can you just come home? For a minute? For a day? For my birthday? Please?

I was invited to spend my birthday with Peter and his family in Ottawa. Gratefully, I accepted, as I did not want to be at home. Alone.

I can't do alone, as in "no David". How can he just vanish? Gone.

One day he was here and the next, gone. One minute he was

breathing and the next, he'd stopped. Never to draw another breath. Never to be human again.

October 31st, the day before my birthday, I set out for Ottawa around mid-afternoon. There was a chill in the autumn air and a slightly smoky smell from burning leaves. Or perhaps someone had lit a fire in their wood-burning stove. A memory shimmered of David and I cozying up to our fireplace. Impatiently, I brushed it away. I did not want to begin this trip in tears.

Acorns crunched under the car as I backed down the driveway and I was reminded of David patiently sweeping acorns and packing them in small cardboard boxes to be put out for garbage. Raking leaves and keeping our property clean was his way of grounding or de-stressing, particularly after a long shift at the Clinic or in his office. Besides, he liked yard work.

The roads all the way to Ottawa were clear and driving was smooth. I had planned to make a stop at Orleans Shopping Mall, purchase some warm gloves and then head on over to my son's home.

The parking lot was practically empty when I arrived making it easy to find a spot close to the front doors. Shivering in the cold wind, I hurried inside The Bay, wrapping my arms around myself for warmth.

As I entered the store, I saw that the jewelry section was on my right side, hats and scarves on my left. I figured the gloves would be close to the scarves.

I was wrong.

I circled all around the whole store and found myself back at the jewelry counter. Strange. I didn't really want any jewelry, but an elegant silver watch in the display case caught my eye.

Do I need a watch?

Not really. I just check my cell phone when I want to know the time. But this watch was pretty, all shiny and new and I could not stop looking at it.

I was still trying to make up my mind when a memory surfaced; a sweet tingly memory of David's first gift to me – ever – a watch.

A watch! It was just like David – practical, down-to-earth, and so very thoughtful. I remember the joy in his eyes, his wide smile as he watched me carefully unwrap my gift.

That was so long ago, I'd almost forgotten. I don't even remember if there was an occasion to celebrate. Somehow I don't think so. I needed a watch and he bought me one.

Hugging my secret tightly to myself, I smiled at the sales lady and asked her to wrap it up. This watch would be a birthday gift from David. (Doubt go away. Stop bugging me. I am not questioning Spirit signs any more, remember?)

I arrived at Peter's home to see carved pumpkins grinning up at me from the front porch. Darkness was setting in and soon the jack-o-lanterns would be glowing warmly from within. Tea lights, I presume, as nobody used candles any more.

My daughter-in-law answered the door with a huge smile. "Happy Halloween!" A giant bumblebee poked its head around Mama's skirts. "Oh my goodness! There's a bee in the house!" I took a step backwards as if afraid to come any closer, in case I got stung. Giggling with delight, my young grandson dashed away.

"Come in, come in, and don't mind the bee," winked Marcela.

I followed her into the kitchen where Adrian was already pouring candy into a giant wooden bowl. Most of it spilled over the sides and onto the table. "Hey, not so fast!" His mother lunged forward rescuing the spilled candy while at the same time smoothly handing him a snack-size bag of chips. The distraction worked and he sat back in his chair, happily munching.

Peter arrived shortly afterwards. A quick supper of cheese sandwiches and celery sticks was gulped down and off they went into the night, an excited Adrian leading the way. I stood at the front door and watched. Witches and ghosts, dragons and ninjas swirled around in the dark, costumes flowing, parents in tow; little ones running to keep up, older ones running on ahead. As I handed out lollipops and chips I couldn't help remembering those long ago Halloween nights when my own children dressed up and raced through the spooky neighborhood, ringing doorbells and yelling, "Trick 'r Treat!"

Adrian was absolutely delighted with Trick or Treat night and went to bed stuffed full of chocolate. The doorbell continued to ring and when the candy was all given out, we turned off the outdoor lights and settled into the kitchen with a sigh and a steaming cup of chamomile tea. I was beginning to relax in the warmth and caring home of my son and his family, yet nothing could erase completely that empty feeling in the pit of my stomach.

During the night I awoke to feel the bed shaking. And there was that musky death-smell in my nose again. The first time it happened was the night before David's cremation. I thought it was creepy then, yet somehow oddly comforting, as that kind of musky odor could only be coming from David.

A couple of months later (September to be exact) it happened again. I was just falling asleep when that same overpowering smell crept into my nose and throat. It was not very pleasant and I tried drinking water and blowing my nose to make it go away. Nothing worked, but after a while it simply faded away.

And now it was back.

"Ahhh, you've found me, sweetheart, just as I knew you would."

The next morning I awoke early.

November 1st. My birthday. The first without David. It was hard to think of celebrating without my husband. Without his birthday kiss – even before opening my eyes in the morning, the hot, fresh, coffee brewed with love and shared in our bed.

How could David not be here? I still could not get my head around this absence of a warm human body, of "us" as a couple.

Where did "we" go?

It was vital that I receive a sign today. How else could I survive this "first" birthday without my Soulmate? I have to know he is around somewhere, "thinking" of and wanting to be with me as much as I want to be with him.

Do Spirits think?

Would David even know where I was, or more accurately would he be able to reach me in Ottawa? Or did I have to be home to receive these signs? Probably not, since I had received signs at Brenda's home, but I worried and fretted anyway.

Fifty-nine years old today. This year was the first year I'd ever been away on my birthday. It felt strange, but then everything felt strange without David. David was my anchor, my well of strength and support; always there when I needed him the most.

Where is he now? How can he not be here on my birthday?

Coffee mug in hand, I wandered over to the east-facing kitchen window and looked out into the sky. The sun was not up yet, but darkness had faded into the gentle promise of early morning light, a new day was dawning. What would it hold for me?

Are you there, David? Did I really feel you last night in that strange bed?

As I gazed around the garden, my eyes were drawn to a magnificent crabapple tree. It stood out among the rest with its profusion of lush red berries and full branches, reminding me of a mother's loving arms reaching out to gather in and comfort weary creatures. Cold and hungry animals would be fed and sheltered beneath her strong branches over the course of our long, icy Canadian winters.

Strange ropy things protruded from the grass at the base of Mother Crabapple, looking like long, groping witches' fingers in the shadowy light.

Movement between those fingers caught my attention.

I leaned towards the window for a better look. There nestled among the gnarled roots was a round brownish lump with long quivering ears. It was nibbling something in the grass. Enthralled, I watched the little fella for a while, then turned to greet Marcela who had just walked into the kitchen holding her sleepy son by the hand.

"Look, Adrian, a bunny rabbit!" I scooped the little boy up in my arms and brought him over to the window.

The rabbit was gone.

Strange, it was here a minute ago.

Plopping a now wiggly Adrian down on the floor, I picked up my coffee cup and was just taking another sip when Marcela leaned around me to have a look out the window.

"Rabbits? Don't they mean fertility?" she chuckled.

I choked on my coffee, but kept a straight face.

"Hmmm," was all I said, but inwardly wondered if there was something she wasn't telling.

Peter arrived next, hair wet from his shower.

"Hi, Mom," he greeted me with a smile that lit up his whole face.

It was that same enthusiastic happy smile I remembered from way back when he was a little boy. I could picture this dear sweet child stepping out of the bathtub, hair dripping just the way it was now.

Bath time in our home was not only for washing, it was a time for play, for closeness, for hugging and laughing, for wrapping a wet, wiggly little body into soft fluffy towels, while inhaling that sweet-smelling baby fresh scent.

With a pang in my heart I know those precious days will never return, but as Life flows on, Peter is now the parent with a child of his own.

"Good Morning, Peter," I smile back, so proud of my grown-up son.

I can still see that shiny, scrubbed clean little-boy look about him, but I don't say a word. One day he will look back at his own son and cherish those same ordinary, but very precious memories.

The four of us sat down to a scrumptious breakfast of French toast, bacon, bagels, cream cheese and fruit. The sun was full up now illuminating the whole backyard. I could clearly see into all the nooks and crannies that had been darkened by shadows moments before. Garden beds were empty of summer flowers, but hardy shrubs stood out along the borders, offering nourishment and refuge for small animals. A stone bench sat under a huge sugar maple at the west end of the lot, right next to the tool shed. Cedar hedges surrounded the property as if shielding or protecting the home from outsiders.

Brown bunny was back and he'd brought a friend. Now two of them nibbled and munched at something under the tree. This time Adrian squealed with excitement as I lifted him up to the window to watch.

But what was that flash of red? A cardinal had flown in from somewhere and settled in the branches of Mother Crabapple. Its brilliant red hue and lively air told me it must be the male.

"When there's one, there's two," David always said, eyes twinkling. "Cardinals travel in pairs and when you see one, the other will be close by."

"Really?" I asked all those years ago when we were first dating. It was clear that I hadn't observed nature as closely as he did.

Now I do.

I looked around for the female, and moments later, spotted her. She was a gentler version of the male, her feathers toned down to a soft brown, with just a hint of red on her wingtips and tail.

I watched for a while appreciating the couple's instinctive connection. As they hopped from branch to branch weaving between the leaves, each knew where the other was, as if sharing an internal rhythm sensed only by the pair. Yet they were not bound together, but flew freely wherever they chose.

Another couple flew in to join them, then a few more, then all of a sudden the whole tree was ablaze with life. I'd never seen so much red, so many cardinals all in one place! Their noisy chirping filled the air, but it was a sweet melodious sound – the sound of happiness and loving joy. Then just as suddenly, in a flutter of wings they were all gone.

I was impressed. Peter was not. He and his wife were used to seeing cardinals and other birds flock to that particular tree. And at their stage of life, I don't think they realized the full significance of Nature's gifts. Their priorities were earning a living and raising an active child.

I know.

Years ago I was the same way.

As the day wore on, I wondered if that huge flock of cardinals could possibly be a sign from David? He did send a cardinal to me at Brenda's home back in the summer; a message to tell me he was happy and flying free. I just didn't "get it" until a short while later, when I stepped back in the house and happened upon that children's television program about the baby robin needing to fly free.

But rabbits? Was there a message here too?

My birthday dinner was delicious. We sat in the dining room and ate mango shrimp on a bed of coconut rice. A rich-looking chocolate cake decorated with swirls and sprinkles was presented to me with a flourish. I felt blessed to be wrapped in the loving embrace of my family, cared for and protected in this most difficult First.

First birthday without David.

It wasn't until I was driving home that everything became clear. From a place deep in my heart I could hear David's voice, "We're lucky rabbits!"

"We're lucky rabbits," he was fond of saying with love in his cuddly brown eyes, and a smile that made my insides turn to jelly.

"We're lucky rabbits to have each other."

"Oh yes we are," I'd heartily agree, while planting a smoochy kiss on his nose.

Memories now. Of another life.

Chapter 15

Where Are You?

Somebody has lured my husband away, stolen him. He's disappeared without a trace; his body is gone, vanished totally and completely. I can't wrap my head around it yet. And it's been almost five months now. It's as if he's been washed away by a wave or transported to some distant land where I can't follow.

Was it by wings? An angel? A mythical beast? Did he go by boat over a body of water to be carried far, far away? Did somebody just gather his sleeping form up in their arms and take him?

But I was with him! His body was there, lying on the hospital bed.

Where can he be? How can someone be alive one minute and dead the next? How can he just not be in my life anymore? The vastness of death overwhelms me. It's unbelievable. It's cruel.

Why can I not just catch a glimpse of him? Through the Curtain, in the clouds, a reflection in a pool of water?

And life is just supposed to go on? As if nothing happened? What kind of a world is this?

I feel like he's at the bottom of a pit. Or we're standing at the edge of a chasm. He on one side and me on the other. Five months ago we could clasp our hands together tightly. Then that grip loosened just a bit, then a little more, then only our fingers touched.

"No, no!" I scream, but the relentless surge of time, of separation moves on. Contact is lost. I frantically reach out into the air hoping for a whisper of his aliveness.

Nothing.

I stretch and stretch my fingers until they burn.

Still nothing.

I watch silently, suffering inside while my Beloved moves further and further away from me. His Earth Life is over. Every minute, every day, is like the widening of that chasm; he on one side and I on the other. I wish, I pray, I yearn to jump across; if only I could find a way!

But that's impossible.

Spiritual people call this division a Curtain, a Veil. I too have made reference to a Curtain or Veil separating the spiritual from the earthly. It's easy to reassure someone else, easy to tell somebody else their loved one is just on the other side of a Curtain, but when it happens to you, that's not comforting at all.

The whole concept sounds like fantasy, an illusion with the good intention of bringing solace to those left behind.

But for me, right now in this moment, it does absolutely nothing to lift the heaviness in my heart, to banish the terror or calm the shakes.

When feelings become too hard to handle, we instinctively allow our logical mind to take over.

Okay we have a problem here, now how do we solve it? We must first define the problem. What is it?

The problem is that David is on the "other side" of a Curtain.

Okay, then, how do I rip open that Curtain? How do I get through to the Other Side?

There will never be an answer to that question, of course, but the simple act of turning away from emotional anguish to focus on something objective is enough to provide a distraction, a space, a pause which lifts one out of that dark hole for a short space of time. Enough to regain a bit of equilibrium.

Autumn leaves are almost gone leaving the trees naked; their skeletal limbs reaching up to scratch at the sky. The sun sets much earlier now. And I continue my frenzied outdoor walks, as if my brisk pace would somehow outrun grief, would somehow shake off those ominous feelings of gloom and doom.

Even in the house, I can't sit still for long. I walk around from room to room looking at things that were bits of his life; his books, his favorite chair, his desk, his reading light, his calendar. Objects that must still carry some vibration of him. I gather up some nail clippings and strands of hair left in his night-table drawer. What kind of behavior is this?

I did not keep any of his ashes. I felt that I'd been holding on to him so tightly in his illness that I had to let him go. Let him move on to wherever he needs to be.

But I backslide. I am reaching for, grasping at pieces of him. I don't care what I thought was right just after he'd died. I've changed my mind and want every little bit of him back NOW!

I wish I'd never scattered his ashes! I wish I'd kept some of them to wear in a locket over my heart. I had heard others doing that. Why didn't I think of it?

Needles of pain stab me relentlessly. Day after day I'm pounded in the head, slapped in the face, kicked in the stomach, reminding me that he's gone, as if I'm likely to forget. There is no respite, except in sleep. Every thought I think, every idea, every feeling and reaction is suffused with pain and the stark reality of a void left by David's absence. It echoes in my dizzy brain leaving me with a sick feeling in the pit of my stomach.

And it just won't go away.

I've stopped looking for him in every room, as if he'd be sitting at his desk, washing in the bathroom, making coffee in the kitchen. I've blocked that quickening of my heart, that eager, foolish rush of anticipation whenever the phone rings (yes, I used to wish, hope fervently, that somehow he had been misplaced or lost, and by some strange turn of fate that person who died in the hospital bed was not really my David. And now he was calling to tell me he was coming home). Strange fantasy.

I wonder if anyone else thinks such convoluted thoughts or confabulates such impossible stories. Or (my foolish mind would go on), that somehow, he was able to make one phone call from Heaven. If I didn't answer that phone, he'd be lost forever.

I lunge for the phone now.

Am I nuts?

Crazy?

In those early weeks and months I truly thought I was. And most of the time, really didn't care. It was all I could do to get out of bed in the morning, to navigate through the mind-numbing haze of disbelief and heart-wrenching pain that had become my life.

Sadly, I know when the front door opens, it won't be him either. I get that now, but it's still this "goneness", this emptiness where a warm body used to exist, this abrupt departure from our world, my world, that erodes my being, that shakes my confidence, that flings me into a make-believe world of longing and fantasy.

A noise in the night.

Is he back home?

Was this all a dream?

My poor brain cannot absorb this nothingness, this vacuum where a once happy, loving, earthly man used to be; one with sparkly eyes, a sharp brain and gentle kisses; one who would curl up snuggly with me at night and chase away my fears. Even though I was the Caregiver, having David warm and alive in bed beside me was reassuring.

Realistically, if anyone broke into our home in the night, David could do nothing about it, but it didn't matter. His sleeping form and cuddly body kept me safe, warm, and happy. Now there was nobody.

No body.

A sad and hollow emptiness, a void, a cruel and lonely space.

He had to be somewhere. I could not grasp this "nonexistent" David. I wrote a poem:

Where Are You?

I'm in the wind, I'm in the breeze
I'm in the flowers and in the trees
I'm all around, though you cannot see
Please don't weep. I'm still me.

I'm energy now, a beam of light
I watch over you day and night
I'm in your heart, can you not feel?
The depth of our love, does it not heal?

I scattered you tenderly in water deep
Good-by My Love, my heart did weep
The lake was calm, the sky deep blue
I saw a butterfly; then there were two
Please tell me that was you

A pair of dragonflies, glistening wings
Dipping, dancing, shining things
Blue-grey heron swooped into view
I saw another, making two
Please tell me, Sweetheart — was that you?

Just close your eyes, my love, and feel
I'm not gone, I'm real as real
I've only changed, transformed as they say
I'll never leave you, I won't go away

I am the light that flickers in the hall
I am the shadow you see on the wall
I'm all around, though you cannot see
I'm not gone
I'm still me.

Chapter 16

Christmas

Christmas arrived.

When did that happen? I made no preparations this year at all. No baking, no shopping, no decorating. I did not want to celebrate Christmas without David.

Christmas came anyway.

Christmas Eve was spent at my daughter's home with family gathered all around. Happy faces, smiling children, opening gifts and eating turkey. I tasted nothing. The children alternately melted my heart and irritated me.

Where was David?

He should be here celebrating with us. We would be sitting side by side in the living room, sipping our tea or glass of wine, happy to settle back and watch the younger generation; each of us remembering those days when we were young parents. Oh, life was good back then.

Brenda entreated me to spend the night. She did not want me to wake up alone on Christmas morning. "The children would love you to be here when they open their gifts from Santa Claus."

I knew it really wasn't my grandchildren's decision; they were far too young, it was my daughter's kind heart and compassionate nature.

Christmas morning turned out to be a blessing after all. I actually woke up first – before the little ones. Needing my morning cup of java and a little bit of quiet, I tiptoed downstairs and set the pot to brewing. Even though I had been warmly welcomed in Brenda's home, I felt out of place here. This was not my home. Conflicting emotions ran through me. I wanted some alone time here to process my feelings, but I didn't feel like being away from everybody, standing in the empty kitchen, bare feet on the cold floor.

I didn't have long to wait though, for I'd barely taken a sip or two when the excited pitter-patter of little feet brought me out of the doldrums and into a warm glow of anticipation.

The children must have flown down the stairs for the next thing I heard were squeals of glee. Ah, they'd spied Santa's treasures heaped under the tree. Smiling now I picked up my mug and followed the sounds into the living room.

It was a pleasure to watch my grandchildren playing out the story of Christmas; no not the religious one, the story of Christmas morning, of waking early to find Santa's magic had transformed the house.

Stockings that had been empty the night before, were now bulging with clementines and chocolate. Elves must have placed all those bright packages under the tree, for where else did they come from? And this was the only day in the year when *everyone* sat around in pajamas until lunch time.

I remember quite well being a child, peeking downstairs at all the gifts sitting expectantly under the tree, excited and impatient for my brothers and sisters to wake up.

Years down the road it was my turn to be Santa. Love filled me to the brim, as I watched my own children rip open glittery presents in wide-eyed and enthusiastic delight.

Candy canes and chocolate melted in tiny hands, smeared over small faces or ended up being crunched underfoot. Trains, planes, dolls, books and crayons had been mysteriously left under our tree during the night. Christmas was a magical time and the little ones eyes shone with the wonder of it all.

And now I'm the Grandma. Humbling to feel this passage of time, the turning of the Wheel as decades go by.

I was glad I had decided to stay. This was so much better than waking up alone and sad in my big empty house, longing for David, while memories of happier times tore at my heart.

About mid-morning I decided to go out for a walk. I wanted, no, needed to be alone for a bit, so left the family warm and cozy in front of the fireplace, toys strewn all over the floor.

It was cold, but I could see the sun briefly peeping out between patches of foggy cloud. Not having any idea where I wanted to go, I just put one foot in front of the other and set out walking down the street, instinctively turning my face towards the sun. One foot in front of the other, seemed to be my mantra these days, but in actuality it must have been the sun that was beckoning me onward.

After about 10 minutes or so, I realized I was on the street where my husband had lived many years ago, as a young boy. Somehow my feet had carried me in that direction. As it happened, Brenda and her husband chose a home in the very same neighborhood where David grew up. They had no idea.

As I stood on the sidewalk gawking at his childhood home, I took some deep breaths of crisp cold air, as if I could absorb precious energy waves of Christmases long past, of happy voices echoing down the years. I imagined David as a little boy, opening his presents, playing street hockey with friends, eating turkey with his family. David with a smile on his face looking out at the world with those mischievous brown eyes – the ones I'd fallen in love with.

There was nobody about, so I took my time. I wasn't quite sure what people would think of a middle-aged lady rooted to the sidewalk gazing in reverence at an ordinary house. Was she going to walk up to the front door and knock? Was she waiting for somebody to come out? Or was she just going to stand there all day in the freezing cold?

Eventually I turned away, tucked those imaginary visions of Christmas past into a secret place in my heart to savor later on and continued down the sidewalk.

I probably should get back, I thought to myself. The sun had gone. I was getting cold and the kids must be wondering where

I am.

Ahhhh, but in the distance I could see the Lake, the silvery, shimmering Lake, luring me with its charm. What is it about water? Whether it is winter or summer, I feel the irresistible pull of a lake, river, or ocean. Just a little farther, it seems to be calling me.

The sidewalk ended in a footpath which led across a clearing and on to the Lake. Leaving the protection of houses and street behind, I followed the path into the clearing and braced myself to be hit in the face with a cold gust of wind coming off the water.

The air was still.

All was quiet and peaceful.

Spread out before me was a winter wonderland, beautiful in its serenity; quiet, almost surreal in the muted light. Huge evergreens guarded the shoreline, their branches frosted with new-fallen snow. Silvery ice crystals formed around the edges of the Lake, their delicate lacy pattern making me think of sugar cookies.

The Lake itself was eerily calm.

No one was about. No birds sang or flew overhead. Clouds, heavy with moisture, softened the sky.

I stood there for a moment or two, wondering if the greyness of the scene before me was a reflection of my sorrow, even if it was beautiful to behold. And then, as if on cue, the Sun burst through the gloomy clouds instantly transforming the grey misty landscape into glimmering, shining gold.

It was as if David had popped out of those clouds to greet me with a cheery, "Hi sweetheart, Merry Christmas! I was waiting for you to get here!" I stood there absorbing the glorious golden sunlight, feeling David's love and warmth enveloping me.

What a precious Christmas gift! And well worth the long walk and cold toes.

Just then a playful young dog approached, startling me by

rudely sticking its nose right between my legs! The owners were horrified, and called out an apology, but I just laughed and petted the dog. It held my eyes for a long time, as if trying to tell me something.

"Please understand," those soft brown eyes seemed to say. I had an uncanny feeling that David was trying to communicate with me, through the dog.

The Sun had gone back into the clouds now, but I turned to address the sky anyway. "Ha! Still trying to get between my legs, are ya?" Smiling to myself I started back towards my daughter's home.

Christmas turned out to be a happy occasion after all. How grateful I was to have taken that walk, to have received that special gift of David's presence. I utterly and absolutely missed his warm earthly body, but the strength of this connection, this reaching out from the Other Side with Love on Christmas Day, only served to strengthen my belief in the Afterlife.

Love does not die.

David is an eternal being.

His body is gone but his Spirit is still here, along with his sense of humor.

Chapter 17

The New Car

I bought a new car. A spanking, brand-new Toyota Camry. In aloe green. And immediately felt guilty. How could I spend this much money on myself? I'd never bought a new car before; not on my own.

David and I chose our last car together. It was a brand-new Camry as well, but since we needed it right away, there was no choice of color. It happened to be a smooth-as-silk silver and looked splendid.

I liked it. David liked it. So happy with our purchase, we drove off the lot and on to one of our favorite restaurants to celebrate. It was fun. That was 9 years ago and 5 minutes ago.

Now silver Camry was getting old. Parts were wearing out and breaking down. I'd already made several trips to the Garage over the past year. Each time the repairs were costly. And aggravating.

The brakes were shot, shocks leaking and some other weird technical stuff I don't remember needed replacing.

I couldn't put it off any longer, so early one Friday morning, about four weeks into David's hospital stay, I dropped the car off at the Garage. Luckily, I was given a rental car for the day and off I drove to the hospital, totally oblivious to the fact that I'd left my garage door opener back at the Garage – in my car's visor.

Evening came, no word on my car, so I assumed they would keep it overnight. Good thing I had a rental. I'd drive home after the hospital visit and pick up my car sometime the next morning once the repairs were completed.

David and I were snuggled up in his bed, reading library books. I could see him growing tired as the evening wore on.

Time to get going. I hated that long drive back home. It took just over an hour, and by the time I got home, I was exhausted, stressed and worried. Will he be there in the morning when I return? Will this be the night that I get The Call? I just hated leaving David behind.

As I was mulling things over in my mind, I suddenly remembered. How on earth was I going to get into my house? My garage door opener was securely locked up for the night. In the mechanic's Garage.

Darn!

There was no other way I could get into the house. I could not go in the front door because I bolt it from inside when I leave the house via the garage. The back door was securely locked from the inside too and the key had been missing for ages.

What was I going to do?

I could spend the night with my sister and her family. No. I'm too tired for conversation and really don't want to answer their questions about the seriousness of David's condition. Oh I know how concerned they are, but I just don't have the energy. Besides, I wouldn't want to put them out.

I could go and spend the night in my daughter's home. I know I'm always welcome there, but honestly, I'm just too weary. It makes far more sense for me to stay here.

With David.

I'd much rather spend the night with David anyway, for who knows how much time he has left?

All that being said, however, and if I'm going to be completely honest, I also need some time away. Not from David but from the heavy atmosphere of a Palliative Care Ward.

It's important for my equilibrium that I shift back into the normal world for a while, in order to catch my breath.

Even though I don't want to socialize with people, to be a part of the hustle and bustle of everyday life, I need to know that there is a normal world out there; an ordinary world that runs smoothly – almost like a parallel universe.

It's a little hard to explain – this place where I am right now. I seem to be existing somewhere in-between-the-ordinary-world and the unknown. Sometimes it feels like I'm living in the middle of a strange and shifting bridge, the sort of long suspension bridge that sways over a rocky canyon. You don't particularly want to cross that bridge with its treacherous rocks or swift and dangerous currents below, but you do.

Every day.

Every day, I travel back and forth across that bridge between the "normal world" and the harsh temporary world where David rests in his hospital bed, waiting for his life to end. I never know what will happen on that bridge. The only thing I'm certain about is that one day it will vanish.

It's a bizarre feeling, this not fitting into either world. Like (I would imagine) a snake might feel while in the process of shedding its skin.

Ordinary events of the "normal world" don't have much meaning and seem unreal, unnecessary. The Palliative world, as the last stop before leaving this earth, is not a place anyone wants to be part of. But I cannot let David stay there alone.

No way.

I'm afraid for him. I'm afraid for what is happening to his body, to his quick, sharp and intelligent mind. I'm afraid of what might happen when I'm not there. And even more than that, I want to soak up all the precious moments we have left together.

So every day I cross over from side to side, from one world to the next. If I stay too long in one world, I will lose something of the Other.

It's disorienting to live this way.

The next day was Saturday, and fortunately that particular Garage was open for business. I was happy to return the rental car and slide into the driver's seat of my silver Camry. Yes, the garage door opener was still there, under the visor where it was always kept. Relieved, I pulled out of the parking lot and made my way home.

But enough is enough and now it was definitely time to get rid of the old car and buy a new one. I like cars when they work well. Can't stand them when they need to spend time in the Garage.

I walked into the Toyota dealership knowing exactly what I wanted. I ordered a Camry in aloe green. I adore green. After signing all the forms, I accepted a cup of coffee from the salesman, sat back in my chair and felt like a successful, independent woman.

But a few days later I changed my mind. How could I do this? How could I spend so much money? I felt so guilty that I did not answer my phone when the salesman called to tell me the car was ready.

A week went by, with several more calls and frantic messages from Mr. Car Salesman. Finally, I realized I could not keep doing this. It was childish and irresponsible.

When I finally picked up the car the sales manager presented me with a bottle of good Italian wine because, he said, I was such a good client. Good client? Ha, that's a stretch. It was probably because I had paid in cash.

From David's life insurance policy.

What a horrible trade-off.

I pushed these intrusive thoughts away and took myself out to supper that evening. I was determined to enjoy this experience and not allow those sharp shadows of grief to get in the way.

Fifty-nine years old and I'd just bought my first new car. I should be feeling proud, elated! But I was not. I was feeling heavy, heavy with sadness. All that long way home, memories of our last car purchase flowed into my consciousness: David and I at the dealership. David and I test driving what was to be our new car, signing the papers, shaking hands, driving off the lot and into the cold December night feeling pleased with our purchase and ourselves. David and I sitting down to dinner at the Florentine Restaurant and ordering wine. Oh, those happy memories of sharing wine. Something we hadn't done in years. David's body just couldn't handle it, after The Diagnosis.

How carefree and easy life was back then. Those were the days before COPD. Days when we could come and go as we pleased. David was happy and full of energy. He loved his work and was often stopped on the street for an impromptu medical consultation.

"Hey, Doc, did you get my test results back yet?"

We lived in a small town. People expected you to know their business. It didn't matter who was listening and I noticed several people stopping to say hello, ears wide open, before continuing on their way.

"Oh, you'll have to call the office, ask Linda if she's received them yet. Then we can schedule an appointment if we need to. By the way, how is your knee? Is the pain better?"

At first I was shocked at the health issues people openly discussed in public, and would discretely walk away, but as time went on I learned to just go with the flow. If they wanted to talk about personal body parts that was their choice of topic and I didn't have to make myself scarce, inadvertently encouraging a medical consultation in the grocery store.

One afternoon David and I were standing in line at the bank. We noticed Mr. Investment Counsellor standing in line ahead of us. A second later he turned around and said in a loud voice, "Well, Doc, I had my hemorrhoid operation two weeks ago Friday. Everything is running smoothing now."

David smiled and nodded, but I was quite taken aback, as this particular man was very well known in the community, not some hard-of-hearing elderly person who had been there, done that so many times it didn't faze him at all to discuss something so intimate in public.

As for myself, I was happy to stay at home in the traditional role of housewife. Cooking, gardening, and running our home gave me pleasure and not having to work at a full-time job (as I'd done in my younger years) made time for more creative pursuits. I wrote articles for two alternative health magazines, read palms at psychic fairs, at parties and at home, took singing lessons, tai chi, aqua fit, woodworking, and horseback riding. I tried my hand at tole painting without much success, participated in a fast-paced aerobics class because one of my friends was the teacher, went on hikes and lunches with old friends and new.

And the best part of all was at the end of the day, when David and I sat down to dinner, we had so much to tell each other! So much to share of our outer selves, the parts of us we showed to the outside world. Our inner selves we knew intimately, often without a spoken word. Life was so good! How unfair of it all to come crashing down.

How senseless.

Why can't we go back there?

By the time I arrived back at my lonely, empty house, my bubble had burst. With heart breaking yet again and tears coursing down my face, I stumbled through the door in the darkness, crawled into the bathroom and threw up.

Please come back, David! I don't want this car. I'll give it right back, I promise. Please come home!

Seems like I take one step forward and two steps back.

Chapter 18

January

It's been six months. Six months since I've held and comforted my sweetheart. Six long and lonely months. I stare at the cinnamon orange candle burning at the base of Grandfather Oak and wonder how I am ever going to survive all the months that will make up the rest of my life.

It's snowing outside.

When did winter arrive?

How could I have gotten here, to this point without David? I feel like I've just taken a look at the bottom of a dark, black pit. Quickly I clap a lid over that hole. I can't go there. I can't do this. Isn't it supposed to get easier as time goes on?

Well, in some ways it has. There are some nights when I feel his warmth, enveloping me like a soft, warm, wool blanket. I feel his closeness, I hear his voice in my head. I ask a question and he answers me, as if we truly are one.

Is this progress?

I peek out my bedroom window at the solitary candle, hoping its flame is still alive; that it hasn't been snuffed out by the falling snow, but of course it has. Just like our life together, I think to myself, sadly.

But in the next moment, I come to a decision.

Peter and Marcela invited me to join them for a holiday. I told them I'd think about it. Could I leave this house? Would that be leaving David behind somehow?

Of course not – I need to get past that "clinging-to-the-house-in-case-David-returns". He won't. There is no reason for me to stay behind.

I won't be snuffed out like that candle, left alone in the cold snow. I will accept their kind offer and go.

A week in sunny Florida sounded wonderful. Peter had booked a Resort, Hilton Grand Vacation Suites at SeaWorld, which they'd been to the previous January. Geared for young families it was safe and fun, the accommodations condo-style with a full kitchen, plenty of windows overlooking the pool area, small balcony and indoor Jacuzzi. An adjoining room with private bath and kitchenette was provided for me.

As our plane touched down in Orlando, I was filled with a sense of relief, of peace and contentment. Florida felt like a place to come home to with its breezy palm trees, profusion of hibiscus and bougainvillea flowers, and carpets of rich green grass.

Not that I'd ever lived there. It was just this sense of familiarity, of homecoming probably due to the fact that David and I spent a week or two in Florida every winter. Clearwater on the Gulf side was our favorite, but Fort Lauderdale and The Keys were special too. Each spot had its own charm.

Our plan, once David retired, was to spend our winters in Florida. A dream that never came true.

Sadly, this would be a different holiday without my beloved and as I stretched out on the pool chair, soaking my weary body in sunlight, I tried to imagine soaking up David's Soul wherever he may be. I imagined his familiar and loving arms wrapping around me, his warm breath on my cheek, his closeness, his unique smell of strawberry jam and hazy autumn days.

I awoke every morning to the sound of water singing as it tumbled over rocks and into a misty pool just below my bedroom window. What a refreshing change from blowing snow and rattling windowpanes only a few short days ago. Songbirds filled the air with trilling music and warm, fragrant breezes woke up my senses. It seemed as if the whole world had suddenly sprung to life, in direct contrast to that cold starkness of winter back home.

Early mornings, before anyone else was awake, I'd brew

a pot of coffee and take some with me down to the Resort's luxurious pool area. Since we were miles away from the ocean, I pretended the clear water of the swimming pools and gentle waves of the lake beyond were my ocean.

Nobody was about; it was too early, except for the ever-present staff who were busy hosing down the flagstones, emptying trash baskets, retrieving used towels and generally cleaning up in preparation for a new day.

"Good morning, Ma'am," a young fellow greeted me pleasantly while rolling up a stack of clean pool towels. I watched for a brief moment as he squashed them into a tiny bamboo hut, where guests could help themselves to as many as they liked.

Nodding politely, I continued on my way wanting to avoid conversation. I needed to be alone in the quietness of the early part of the day, alone with my thoughts, my just-below-the-surface tears. I was balancing on the edge of grief and did not want an innocent comment from someone or a flash of memory to tip me over the edge.

Leaving the pool area, I crossed over a rustic little bridge and headed towards the lake at the very end of the complex, just beyond the hot tubs and kiddie water park. Flowering bushes lined the path leading up to the water, while natural wood benches invited rest and relaxation. There was a fountain in the middle of this lake and I was surprised to see birds (most of which I couldn't identify) flying gracefully through the spray, as if taking their morning shower. Tall trees separated the lake from the road beyond. I could hear cars motoring along, but could not see them.

I chose a clean wooden bench facing the lake and this became my customary morning spot. It was quiet and peaceful here. I was alone in the coolness of a fresh day, with only the birds and an occasional bee for company.

Moments slipped by, but I was in no hurry. It was healing

to have this solitary time to sip my cup of java and wait for the rising sun to clear the trees, before launching into the day's activities.

Those trees were rather annoying, however, as they obstructed my view of the sun. I looked forward to its gradual appearance over the horizon, changing from deep crimson to orange to gold. Watching the sun rise every morning gave me some kind of hope that all was well. I can't really explain why, except that I always see David in the sun. If the sun comes up, then he must be okay.

Irrational?

No doubt. But who cares?

One morning as I headed over to "my bench", I was dismayed to find someone walking around, cell phone glued to his ear. As he was dressed in a three-piece suit, I wondered if he had just arrived from the airport, or was preparing for a very early business appointment. But what was he doing in the pool area at this hour?

Miffed, I walked a little further away and settled onto another bench. Soon the man left. Perhaps he had wanted privacy and was as annoyed to see me as I was him.

Good. I yawned and turned my face to the sky, waiting for the sun to clear the trees. It was then that I made a discovery. There was a hole in those trees. Well, not the trees themselves, but in the leaves, an opening really between the branches.

Excitedly I watched, hoping that the sun would appear inside the framework of those leaves. A moment or two later I was rewarded. A fiery red glow had begun to fill the hole, turning the soft shadows of night into a golden pink.

Ahhhh, David. David in the glow of a new day. David's butterfly kiss on my cheek in the guise of a gentle breeze wafting in from the lake. I sipped my now lukewarm coffee and talked to the sun. Talked to my dear husband this way every morning for the duration of the trip.

We did the usual things families do on vacation: swam in the crystal clear water of the Resort's pools, weaving in and out of the waterfall, splashed in the water park, shopped at the mall, ate out and ordered in.

Downtown Disney was a new experience for me. As the name suggests, it was like a downtown core with its shops and restaurants, ice cream stands and bakeries. In the daytime there were activities for children, crafts, face-painting, and Lego building.

In the evenings everything was lit up with twinkling faerie lights, making me think of Tinkerbell and pixie dust. There was music, clowns and entertainment galore. It was a fun place to be and I tried to ignore the ache deep in my gut and the empty space beside me where David should have been.

I was impressed with The Disney Store; its sheer size and quantity of gifts. Every single Disney character ever created was there, smiling from shelves, urging the public to "take me home".

At one end of the store, I came upon what I thought was a beauty salon. Strange place for this I mused, until I took a closer look. And saw that all the clients were little girls sitting in front of mirrors while a lady-in-waiting transformed them all into princesses! How exciting for the young princesses-to-be!

It wasn't hard to spend money here and I ended up with a mountain of gifts for the grands back home, which I hoped would all fit into my suitcase.

The days flowed at a relaxing pace as we geared ourselves to the rhythm of a three-year-old. Time means nothing to a child when he's engrossed in licking ice cream or watching water as it suddenly squirts up from a hole in the cement.

But even so, I had to keep moving. I walked around the Resort morning and evening, and swam away my grief as much as possible. The waterfall in the main pool was magnificent, where people could swim beneath the cascading waters. There was also a twisty water slide, but I wasn't brave enough to try that.

The last day before we were to head home, I took my usual morning walk around the Resort. The grounds were always well kept, common areas clean and gardens fresh.

Palm trees shaded my path as I strolled around the complex. Water from the fountains glistened in the sun and popular music played over the sound system. Music I was only half listening to as I preferred the gentle sounds of nature; birds calling, breezes whispering, and water trickling.

Vibrant red flowers growing by the side of the path drew my eye so I stopped to take a closer look. Bending down, I recognized the lantern-shape flowers and rich tones of a bougainvillea bush. A memory of David and I standing under a magnificent bougainvillea tree, while a kindly stranger took our picture, flashed through my mind.

We were vacationing in Barbados, back in the early years and I remember having an absolutely glorious, passionate, and delightful holiday. The ocean was warm, the food scrumptious. We spent our days lounging in the sun or walking the beach; our evenings gazing into each other's eyes over romantic candle glow, and our nights making love.

Sadness swept over me, but I was determined not to cry, especially out here in public. And it was just at that instant the volume of the music escalated, or perhaps my awareness sharpened as I tuned into and listened to the words of this song.

I Will Remember You...

It felt as if David was singing to me through Sarah McLachlan's voice.

I will remember you. Will you remember me? Don't let your life pass you by. Weep not for the memories...

Shivers ran up my spine.

Weep not? How could I possibly not weep for those bittersweet memories? Memories of an enchanted life we never thought would end.

Don't let your life pass you by... Goosebumps rippled down my arms. No, I can't go there. Can't deal with that now.

I hadn't heard that song in years. No, it wasn't "our song", but the timing was uncanny. It had been released the year we met, in 1995. Cherished memories from those tender days came flooding back, blending the past with the present. David in my arms, David and I laughing, dancing, playing, David wrapping me in a warm blanket of love, caressing, whispering, singing.

His presence was palpable on that garden path, as if he was trying to reach me, to reassure me that my senses were not wrong; he'd been right here all along, sharing this holiday, as we had in the past.

I looked for a butterfly, but there was none.

Chapter 19

February

Do Spirits Cry?

One sunny morning a day or so ago, I was sitting at my kitchen table, looking out the window into our snowy backyard. That window was new; a lovely Bay window with a cozy nook just big enough to fit our round pine table and four matching chairs. David and I had had it installed the summer before he died. All that previous winter, he could feel drafts coming from cracks around the window frames whenever he sat down to eat. Chilled and uncomfortable, he would leave the minute the meal was over.

The only solution was to splurge and have the whole Bay window replaced.

It turned out to be a big job, but well worth the time and money, since not only could we feel increased warmth throughout the kitchen, but David now had plenty of time to linger after a meal.

Gazing out at the expansive view (that only a Bay window could offer) filled him with contentment and gave him a sense of being in tune with nature; as if all he had to do was open the door and walk outside – like an ordinary person, unencumbered by oxygen hoses.

Looking through that window now always brings on a rush of tears. Sweet memories, just dreams of our life the way it used to be. An old life now, gone, evaporated, totally ripped to shreds by this bitter new reality I'm being forced to live.

The kitchen table holds no coziness, as it did when we sat together sharing meals, the day's happenings, tidbits of gossip, a silly joke, our triumphs, our failures, our intimate secrets. Whatever needed discussing was done around our kitchen table, in the heart of our home.

The telephone rang but I paid no attention. I was feeling sad, heavy in the chest as I stared at snow-laden hedges, our neighbors' garden shed, a network of squirrel tracks which looked as though they were connecting one tree to another.

A few icicles hung down from the edge of the roof above the kitchen window, too high for me to reach from the ground, even with a long broom handle or an old wooden hockey stick.

Bright purple crocuses and mini daffodils were nestled in pots on my windowsill looking strangely out of place against the backdrop of stark trees and mounds of snow.

Moby, my long-haired grey cat, lay curled up on a kitchen chair, napping in the warm February sunshine. It was unseasonably mild for this time of year and I could hear the soft tinkle of ice crystals melting as the temperature rose.

With a sigh, I hugged myself protectively, tilted my face to catch the golden rays streaming through the window and began a conversation with David as I always do.

"I miss you, sweetheart."

Movement drew my eye to a spot a little further down the windowpane, towards the bottom right corner.

One lone drop of water, like a shiny bead sat glistening in the sunlight. It paused for a second or two as if wanting to make sure it had my attention, then slowly trickled down the window glass, like a teardrop running down somebody's cheek.

At that moment I felt David's presence. It was as if he were standing right beside me in our sunny kitchen, tears of grief rolling down his face, a mirror image of my own.

Where Are The Birds?

Our backyard is empty. David's beloved birds are gone. Where are they? All winter he would watch through the window, safe and warm and cozy in his favorite chair, as winter birds flocked to our feeders. Chickadees and sparrows played hide-and-seek in the hedges. Finches, cardinals and blue jays flew from the feeders to the trees and back again. Juncos usually arrived later in the season, their dark heads bobbing up and down as they pecked at birdseed on the deck. Woodpeckers spiraled up our trees, hugging the trunks and hammering their beaks into the bark in search of grubs.

"You'd think they'd have horrific headaches," David always remarked after watching those little heads snap back and forth without pause.

"Or their heads would fall off," I joked. I never thought about woodpeckers' heads being sore. I guess it was a doctor thing, always observing the body, whether human or animal.

One year I hung a suet feeder on Grandfather Oak but the squirrels totally destroyed it. They were persistent and territorial, and I don't think many woodpeckers or nuthatches got any suet that year, so I never bothered again.

This year there are no birds at all. None.

Every morning I watch for them, but they're gone, vanished, flown away. I've taken down the feeders, washed them, refilled them, but it changes nothing. They remain full. Swinging in the cold winter air. Not a bird in sight.

How strange.

Did David take the birds? Are they escorting him somewhere?

I was at my doctor's office (yes, it feels strange to be seeking the services of a physician when all I had to do before was nudge my husband, no matter what hour – day or night). Dr. A is a very kind, patient, and compassionate person. I booked an appointment for a minor problem, yet she took time away, quite a lot of time away, from her busy office to ask how I was coping. To listen to my fears, to hear my sorrow, and offer comfort and support. She did not push or hurry, but sat back in her chair reading me with her eyes, as I unburdened myself in the safety of her office. Tears flowed, I could not hold back, but let them come.

As I was making ready to leave, I casually mentioned the puzzle of my missing birds. Not quite sure if I should say something so obviously un-scientific to a doctor, I plunged ahead anyway; after all David was a doctor and he was very open to the spiritual world. Dr. A looked up from her charting, a flicker of surprise showing in her eyes.

"Yes, that certainly sounds strange, and yet another female patient of mine had the very same experience. The winter after her husband died, there were no birds at the feeders, nor in their yard. The next year they returned, but that first one, they were gone."

I left her office feeling pleased that not only had she taken my un-scientific question seriously, but somebody else had experienced this strange occurrence. So I wasn't the only one! I was not going crazy or imagining things.

Encouraged with this bit of rapport, this bond I'd established with a patient, who I didn't even know, nor she me (how pathetic is that?), I was determined to find an answer. I would get to the bottom of this.

Our TV room faces south. This is where David used to sit in his comfy leather chair, watching birds out the window, which really is a large glass patio door leading to the back deck. A cedar hedge surrounds the deck offering privacy and a haven for ever-cheerful chickadees. Everything looked the same as it did this morning. Snow glistened on the hedges and covered the wooden planks of our deck. Not a bird was in sight, but I really didn't expect to see any. I slipped quietly into David's chair as if afraid to disturb the Nature spirits, bird spirits, or whatever was inhabiting the space in my backyard.

Feeling supported by the simple fact that David's body once occupied this chair, traces of him must still be here somewhere in the cracks or crevices. He had to have left something behind for me. Every morning when he awoke, this is the place he'd come to, a cup of fresh coffee in one hand and the daily newspaper in the other.

Those "good old days" before COPD seemed so long ago. David would rise early, bounce down the stairs each morning and fling open our front door to retrieve the newspaper from the porch (no matter how cold the weather – he could breathe normally back then). Stepping into our kitchen, he'd set the coffeemaker to "brew" while glancing at the headlines.

By that time, I'd be downstairs too and we'd take our mugs into the TV room where we eased into a new day. There were no concerns about regulating oxygen flow, no hose to trip over, no worries about shortness of breath, weakness, or fatigue.

Did we take good health for granted? Of course, we did. How were we to know those carefree days were numbered? Over the years, as COPD took hold and gradually erased David's professional life, social life, and sphere of existence, he became a recluse, withdrawing to the safety and comfort of his reclining leather chair, the very one where I was sitting now.

I closed my eyes and let all bittersweet thoughts of what was – go – and brought my awareness back to the present dilemma. What had become of our winter birds? I allowed myself to immerse in the energy surrounding my bird feeders; feeders that were overflowing with food, yet empty of birds. It sounds like a strange thing to do, but I thought if I could make a connection, melt into or open myself up to whatever forces were invading my backyard, then I could understand or figure out what kind of energy would repel all the birds.

What happens when someone dies? What kind of energy is released when they leave the earth plane? Why would that particular energy keep birds away from our home?

Nothing came to me. All I felt was emptiness. Discouraged, I gave up and left the room. The next morning while sitting at my computer I thought I'd take a chance and google "birds when somebody dies". I really didn't expect to find anything of value, but figured I had nothing to lose.

Surprisingly, I uncovered a wealth of information. This is what I read from one source: mythencyclopedia.com.

Rising above the earth and soaring through the skies, birds have been symbols of power and freedom throughout the ages. In many myths and legends, birds link the human world to the divine or **supernatural** *realms that lie beyond ordinary experience.*

The Flight of the Soul Numerous myths have linked birds to the journeys undertaken by human souls after death. Sometimes a bird acts as a guide in the afterlife. In Syria, figures of eagles on tombs represent the guides that lead souls to Heaven. The soul guide in Jewish tradition is a dove. In some cultures, it was thought that the soul, once freed from the body, took the form of a bird. The ancient Egyptians believed that the soul, the ba, could leave the dead body in the form of a bird, often a hawk. They built their graves and tombs with narrow shafts leading to the open air so that these birds could fly in and out, keeping watch on the body. The feather cloaks that Central American and Mexican priests and kings wore may have been connected to the idea of a soul journey.

So, I wasn't imagining things. Could these myths be true? Myths by definition are not based on fact, but to my way of thinking, ancient beliefs are rooted in some form of truth or observation. Did this mean that *all* the birds in my backyard were assigned to escort David? And if that's so, then just how long does it take to get to the Other Side?

Something else struck me, as I sat there thinking, absorbing and feeling things out. People say, "A part of me died with him." And it's true. I feel it.

Intensely.

It leaves a hollow emptiness inside that nothing can fill. But what if we shift the focus? Instead of looking at this as something being stolen from us, suppose we change that to something we've given up.

Voluntarily.

We've gifted our loved one with a part of us to carry with them.

Let me explain. David's clothes are here. His comb, brush, razor and toothbrush too. There are fingernail clippings in his toiletry case along with some hair in his hairbrush. His pictures are all around my room. I have learned from others to say, "he has passed within", rather than "passed away". He sends me signs. He is not completely gone.

So if some of David remains with me, it stands to reason that some of me must be integrated with him too, or I wouldn't be receptive to his energy, his signs, the smell he has left behind. This must be our pathway, our link, our connection, like a beam of sunlight stretching from heaven to earth.

Rather than focusing on the black hole of emptiness I feel when saying, "a part of me died with him," I am leaning towards amending that to: "he kept a fragment of me with him," or "I gave him a piece of me." This simple adjustment in thinking has given me the power to temporarily change my emotion from depression to hope. I say temporarily because for every step forward, there is inevitably a step (or two) backward.

Now logically, if David is in Spirit form, then a "part" or a "piece" of me would be too tangible for him to incorporate into his essence. Like a chunk. How can he keep a chunk of me? I think a wisp of energy or a shiver of spiritual essence sounds better. Yet how can I give away my spirit? Even if it is only a wisp?

Maybe that's where the birds come into this. Perhaps it is the birds who have the ability to glide with energy on their wings carrying not only souls to the Afterlife, but also the gifts of spiritual essence from those left behind. With the "swish" of a wing, a wisp of my energy is sent on its Heavenly way. And David is on the receiving end of it, keeping it close to his Spirit heart.

Our connection. Our bridge. Our Love.

It always goes back to the loving heart.

I woke up with a snort in the night and instinctively reached out to touch David. Was David snoring? Strange, he rarely snored. My hand touched empty space. Of course he wasn't there. Miserable, I turned over to punch the pillow and realized it must have been me. Since when do I snore?

A gentle shaking of our bed, my bed now, almost like being rocked in a child's cradle calmed my aching soul; and once again, I felt wrapped in a cloak of love. David's love.

Cuddling his bathrobe close to my heart, I fell fast asleep.

Needing to reach out to others and hoping for some guidance and comfort, I finally crawled out of my cocoon and joined a Bereavement Support Group. The meetings had already commenced the previous month, but I had wavered so long between going and staying home that I was afraid I would not be welcome.

It turned out to be just the opposite. The nurses running this program were completely understanding and encouraged me to join them. The sessions were held once a week on Wednesday evenings in a church basement.

My first meeting went well. There were about eight of us varying in age from 20s to 80s. It was a women's group, men in the community holding their meeting elsewhere. Some of the younger members mourned the loss of a parent or sibling, the older ones a spouse.

A course outline had been distributed at the beginning of this 10-week session with assignments and journaling to be completed at home; no pressure – the "exercises" were to aid in the processing of feelings and emotions.

Guidance and structure were offered at these gatherings setting this group apart from ones where a more casual approach is taken.

Those less structured, often drop-in groups are fine and serve the purpose of letting people share their stories in a compassionate, understanding atmosphere. But this group went beyond that.

Through journaling, artwork, and music, we were to learn coping strategies and skills, tools to integrate into our daily life.

"Healing Through Grief" was the theme we were working with, and I was willing to learn all I could to get through this tortuous, lonely journey-that-nobody-wants-to-be-on.

Our facilitator was a nurse from the local Palliative Care Center, who had lost her husband, three years previously. I'll call her Belle. She knew firsthand what this whole grief business felt like. I respected and trusted her. I noticed that she didn't try to "fix" anybody. As people shared their stories, it was evident that some were further along on their path than others. I expected Belle to jump in and give suggestions or to help people move on.

She didn't.

She just listened.

Unfortunately, after two sessions, I dropped out.

Wednesday evening came and I started feeling sick in my stomach. I could not eat supper. Nerves, I told myself – just push through and go anyway. I looked out the window. It was dark, very dark and cold. I shivered. No, there was no way I could go. No way I could drive in the blackness on a cold winter night. What if my car (my brand-new car) broke down on the highway? I'd be alone, vulnerable to the elements and any stranger who happened to find me, frightened and shaking in my car.

No, I could not do it. Feeling sorry for myself, I curled up in a ball on the living room sofa and wept. Couldn't I do anything right? Must I always fall back into this bottomless pit of grief? This cave where I just want to shut out the world and retreat like a wounded animal?

The evening wore on and I wondered what the other ladies in the group were discussing. I was feeling lonely, and needing reassurance and some form of human contact, I sat down at my computer and logged on to my Widows Support Group. Here I would find compassion. Here I would access the discussion boards and find somebody sitting on the couch crying, just as I was, because she was afraid to leave the house. Here I would learn how others manage to wade through that swamp of fear without being sucked under and lost forever.

Most encouraging with this online group, is that people are willing to reach out and help one another, no matter how much of their own pain they are enduring. I feel validated when I read their stories and hopeful that I just might find light at the end of the tunnel one day.

One woman had recently passed the first anniversary of her husband's death. He had died suddenly in a car accident. She was younger than I with a child still at home. These are her feelings as expressed in a journal entry:

> I am now at a point where I feel as if my husband "has passed the baton to me". Over the past year, I've asked, why, why, why, and not gotten any answers. I think I've finally "gotten it". My husband taught me well over the course of our relationship. He loved, guided and supported me throughout our marriage and now has left the business of "life" in my hands. I have a daughter to bring up, whom I've been neglecting in my sorrow. But now it is time to "take the baton of life" and run with it.

I was impressed. Not only has she found reason to go on living, but she's made a conscious decision to let go of her wounded past. I like the baton analogy she's used to move forward with life and sincerely hope to feel like she does when I reach the one year mark.

Her words have given me pause to think, to see things from a different perspective, as if just noticing that the wind has shifted or the blackness of a night sky is suddenly alight with stars.

I admire her for her inner strength, and wish I could have met her in person.

A few nights later, as I was trying to fall asleep, I begged David to send me a dream. I had not dreamed of him in a long, long time. One of the widows in my support group gave me this suggestion.

"Simply ask. Ask your husband to appear in your dreams and he will."

That's easy, I thought. So, I asked. Usually I talk to David about my feelings, my thoughts, whatever has happened during the day, as I prepare for bed. I don't ask for things. But this night I asked specifically for a dream – once, twice, a half dozen times. Then I turned my thoughts to our early days, days of sweetness and delight, of silliness and sex. Bliss swept over me as I relived those memories that belonged to another lifetime.

Then out of nowhere, images of horror filled my mind. I saw David in his hospital bed his chest jerking with the rapid, shallow breathing of someone about to die. I sat up and screamed! My heart thudded in my chest and I could not shut off my mind as it continued to play out the nightmare. A feeling of dread threatened to choke me as I sat uselessly by and watched David draw his last breath. Then he was gone. Forever.

Chills ran up and down my spine. "Calm. Breathe," I told myself. "It's all over. You can't go back there." Pushing back the covers, I got out of bed and padded to the bathroom. I turned on the faucet and let the cold water run; then filled a glass and drank deeply. "Breathe," I ordered my reflection in the mirror. A pale and very tired me looked back. Definitely time to get back into bed.

Plumping up the pillows, I tried to fill my head with happy

thoughts. David's smiling face. David and I planting our garden, sitting in the sun, riding our bikes, standing in line at the airport – anything to bring back those good feelings. Pouncing on a memory of David's smiling face I fervently asked him to please, please, please send me a dream. I knew I was obsessing with this request, but did it anyway, pleading and hoping as I tossed and turned the night away.

When I awoke in the morning there was no memory of a sweet, loving David dream. Not even one. More than likely, in my anxiety, I pushed them all away.

Feeling sad and out of sorts, I consoled myself by pouring out two mugs of coffee and bringing them both into the TV room. I pretended David was sitting close by as I sat curled up in his easy chair wearing his bathrobe and sipping coffee from his special mug. The other one I placed on a side table next to my chair (where I pretended David was sitting) so he could drink it.

Glancing through the windows, I saw a winter sky, heavy with clouds and gloom. Snow lay in soggy grey mounds here and there, and our bird feeders were still empty. No surprise there.

I lit a yellow candle and set it on the coffee table to dispel some of the dreariness of the morning, while I tried to make sense of the events of the night before.

Mulling things over I realized in that moment just how much of David's life I was trying to live. Sitting in his chair, drinking from his special cup, wearing his clothes, I was holding on so tightly as to almost become David.

By worshiping all his earthly things, reconstructing our days in my mind, and continuing our routines of the past, I was trying to bring him back to life somehow.

"Let go," my mind urged.

"I'll never do that. I'm David's wife forever." My straight-from-the-heart answer.

But a little voice in my head argued back:

"David is here with me at all times; in my heart and in my soul. He is my guiding light, never far from my thoughts. We still share a life, changed though it is. I will still talk to him, out loud in the privacy of my own home; in my mind when out in public. But I cannot continue to obsess about the pain, the loss, while fervently wishing and hoping and praying that he'll come back.

He won't."

It was then that I remembered my grandmother's words about a month after my grandfather died.

"Wendy, your Grandpa and I had a good life together (she was 85), but now he's gone and I just have to accept it."

What a strong and courageous soul she was. And if she could come to a place of acceptance at her age, then I would find a way to follow in her footsteps. I took a deep breath and felt the first small piece of the Acceptance puzzle click into place.

Over the years, I've found that some of my greatest learning, my growth and wisdom comes at times when I am hurting. Last night, I was frustrated at not being able to conjure up a dream of David. I know that visitations and dreams of loved ones who have passed on can be a very powerful experience and I wanted that.

Demanded that.

But it didn't work.

Yet out of that frustration and despair, a tiny root of strength began to take hold, like the first stirrings of new life once the earth begins to thaw after a long, cold winter. I knew I couldn't continue on the way I was. Sadness and longing would not bring my husband back and I did not want to be in a place of suffering forever. It was time to make changes in my life.

The next step might be to wear my own bathrobe and sit in my own chair by the window sipping coffee from my own special mug. I knew I had to stop living "his" life and go on with mine.

And just at that moment, a chickadee appeared at the feeder!

Just one. The first bird I'd seen in our backyard since the summer, and as it turned out, the only one for the rest of the winter.

Chapter 20

Valentine's Day

Valentine's Day was coming up. Would I be able to handle it? I was proud of myself for having gone through some of the most significant "firsts" on this horrendous journey; first wedding anniversary, Thanksgiving, my birthday, Christmas. Somehow I had managed to survive; I'd temporarily pushed away my heavy shroud of grief. Oh, I knew it was still there waiting to snare me in its darkness once again, but for those moments, those festive days of the year I chose to focus on family, on the spiritual strength of Love.

I thought if I prepared myself for battle like a warrior, I could do this. I would smile in the face of romantic roses as they beckoned from flower shop windows. I'd keep my sighs of envy to myself as I listened to *another* radio ad enticing lovers to hurry up and reserve their special table for a special meal with their special someone. I told myself those huge red boxes of heart chocolates would just make me fat.

Who needs that?

I was trying to erase the longing in my heart as I watched others make their plans for this most romantic day of the year.

I have a blog called *Changes With Seasons*. Using this blog as a platform, I'd show the world that I was just fine. I'd write an upbeat post on my blog. Then everybody would know I'm not one of those people who feels sorry for herself. I'm not wallowing in self-pity. After all, I'm not the only one who has lost a lover, a husband, a wife, a partner. Others have and they've survived.

I will survive too.

Most blogs by nature are really just journals. The author chooses a theme, such as knitting, pet care, cooking, child rearing, photography, newsworthy items or whatever they feel like. Some authors just chronicle daily life in their part of the world.

I started a different blog *Caregiving Is Not For Wimps* in the fall of 2007; a time when David was visibly slowing down. That was the year when his lung function deteriorated to the point where we had to exchange his regular 5 liter concentrator (that most people use) for a heavy-duty 10 liter one. That was the year he was forced to give up his driver's license.

The Renewal came in the mail a few weeks before his 64th birthday. Whether because of his age or some other reason, I don't know, but now it was mandatory that he undergo a physical exam before the SAAQ would renew his license.

He looked up from that letter with sad eyes and said to me, "I won't pass this physical – not in a million years."

He waited a moment before going on. "Looks like I'll never drive again."

I could see his eyes glistening, but I held his gaze.

"Why don't you pretend I'm your chauffeur?" I tried to be lighthearted, without sacrificing compassion.

"That's what I told my Mom years ago. But she was in her 80s and a menace on the roads."

"I know. I remember."

"But really and truly, I don't feel stable enough to drive. Especially if I have to worry about my oxygen sats. I know it's time to give up my license – but it's just so hard! It feels like my world is shrinking every time I turn around."

"I hear you," I said placing a loving hand on his shoulder. "But you know that I'll always be with you when we go out anyway, so what's the difference if I do the driving?"

As time went on, he was forced to give up visits to the doctor's office, and eventually got to the point where he could no longer leave the house at all. Even ordinary activities like putting on clothes was becoming a chore.

One chilly winter morning towards the end of his life, David was sitting on the edge of our bed, resting before getting dressed.

"Sometimes," he said quietly, "in those hazy moments before waking up, I totally forget I have COPD. Just for one quick moment, I think I can jump out of bed – the way I used to. Then I remember (he tugs at the oxygen cannula in his nose) and my heart sinks to the bottom of my feet."

Quickly I bend down and focus on helping him pull up his socks. I don't want him to see how easily my eyes fill up with tears.

Blogging became my outlet as we sat together in the evenings. I with my laptop and David, tired from his normal daily activities, curling up contentedly with a good book. Reading is something we both enjoy. It's a relaxing way to end the day, but at this point in time, reading passively was anything but restful for me.

I needed some form of activity that would allow me to channel my anxiety, my worry over David's declining health; a forum to vent and rage, to process my feelings.

I needed to reach out to others who were going through the same Caregiving issues I was. There is a kind of bonding or reassurance in knowing other people share your struggles, your challenges, your heartache. We "get it", we understand. We support one another by offering suggestions or simply an empathetic ear.

Two years later (about a year before David died), I decided to end that Caregiving blog and start fresh. I no longer wished to be defined by my husband's illness.

Changes With Seasons was born with a focus on gardening, grandchildren and happy events. I needed to put away my heartache, struggles, and tears, emotions which made up the very fabric of that Caregiving blog.

This is the post I chose to create for Valentine's Day, 2011, hoping that my readers would think I was perfectly fine:

A Dinner To Remember

Valentine's Day will soon be here. Memory takes me back to another Valentine's Day about a year or so after David and I were married.

Always the romantic, David decided to take me to an elegant restaurant for the occasion. Dressed in our best, we hopped into our car and drove up the mountain to Auberge des Gallant, a well-known, but rather secluded Inn. It was perched at the top of Rigaud mountain, a popular spot for easy-level skiing and hiking.

I was impressed by the massive fieldstone fireplace in the lobby. Our table was not quite ready, so we decided to make ourselves comfortable in front of the crackling fire. A waiter brought us each a glass of Merlot to sip.

It wasn't long before a hostess appeared to take us to our table. We had requested a table by the window, since at this time of year deer come out of the woods to feed. They come right up to the windows as food is put out especially for them, adding a uniqueness and charm to this fine restaurant.

Our waiter was very French, of course.

He set out tasty tidbits and a basket of bread. Water was poured deftly into crystal glasses. He bowed slightly and left.

Resisting an urge to pick up a tasty tidbit with my fingers, I politely stuck my fork and knife into what looked like a toast triangle.

Oops! That hard bit of toast flew over David's shoulder to land on the floor! My face flamed with embarrassment and I quickly looked around. Nobody saw a thing. Phew!

Surprised by the flying toast tidbit, David knocked over his wine glass. Fortunately it was almost empty, so he quickly put it right again.

By this time I thought I'd better be safe than sorry, so I chose an innocent-looking roll from the bread basket. It was crusty on the outside, but nice and soft and buttery on the inside. I'd just finished eating it when Monsieur Waiter appeared at our table with a whisk.

"Vous permittez, Madam?"

I was taken aback. Permit you do to what? I hesitated and then nodded my head, wondering if he was really going to sweep up the breadcrumbs I had carelessly spilled on the crisp white tablecloth.

He did.

David choked on his water.

Monsieur Waiter then asked for our orders.

"I'll have the duck," I decided, wanting to try something different.

"How would you like it cooked?" asked M. Waiter.

Again I hesitated. I didn't know there were different methods of cooking duck. Doesn't one just roast it?

"Sanguine?" suggested Waiter pencil poised and waiting.

I nodded again.

David gave me a funny look but then went on to give his order.

Le canard (the duck) was presented to me on a bed of rice surrounded by tender-crisp vegetables.

It was rare.

Eewwww. I could not eat it.

"Didn't you realize that when you ordered?" David asked, concern softening his eyes. He leaned forward and reached for my hand across the table.

"No." I shook my head.

"We'll send it back then." Letting go of my hand, he turned quickly in his chair. The waiter was gone.

"No, no, it's okay." I'd lost my appetite for duck anyway, especially one that was half-raw. I would be fine with the rice and vegetables. With a smile on my face, I lifted my fork and tucked into my meal. It was actually quite tasty, in spite of having to skirt around the sanguine duck.

A young couple sat down at the table behind me. I could hear M. Waiter asking what they'd like to eat. It was obvious they spoke no French, so the waiter was obliged to speak English.

"Perhaps a salade, Madam?" he asked the lady. "A lettoose salade?"

I had to bite the inside of my cheek to keep from laughing. David, ever the doctor, kept a straight face, but, I detected a glint of amusement in his sparkly eyes.

Lettoooose? Lettoooose? What else would a salad be made of than lettuce?

Okay, it could have been cabbage, but that would be coleslaw. Or potato salad, or Greek salad. But really it was the poor man's pronunciation that had us chuckling in our napkins.

Coffee arrived in delicate china cups. I picked up the silver cream pitcher and poured some into my cup. It didn't look like cream; it looked like milk. One sip of my coffee confirmed my suspicion.

I called M. Waiter over to our table and asked him for table cream. He looked horrified.

"Non, Madam, we do not have cream."

Well, excuse me, I thought. Isn't this a French restaurant? Don't they put cream in all of their sauces? Well never mind. We stopped at Tim Hortons on the way home and picked up coffee to go – double-double for David and just cream for me.

We had had a delightful evening and laughed about it for years.

As this V-Day approached, however, my emotions decided to opt out of this game I was playing. The confident, I'm-just-fine-thank-you-very-much front I had put up was crumbling and even after writing this lighthearted post, I could no longer hold back the wave of sorrow that filled my soul.

For three days I cried. I cried for the lover I missed, the

intimate dinners, red roses and chocolate hearts (yes even if they make you fat). I cried for the man I loved, the man I still love and refuse to let go of. I cried for the loss of bits and pieces of "us" that made up everyday life; our conversations, our playfulness, our shared meals, laundry, library books, bills – everything and anything that defined our life together as a happy couple.

I missed being so close to someone, the depth of our relationship was such that we could read each other's hearts, knew what the other was thinking and feeling. I've never felt that close to another person, almost as if we share a soul. And never did I think I could still feel this closeness, this connection to someone who has died. It's not something you think about unless you are living it.

Grief continued to pour over me as if I was standing in a shower. Every breath was tinged with anguish. Every thought a sad reminder of the incredible loss I'd endured.

This continual flow of grief was becoming my new normal, almost like a habit and I did not like it. I tried to push these feelings away. But they persisted, opening up that deep and jagged wound within, the one that refuses to close.

A week after Valentine's Day while driving to the library, my thoughts turned to David's Palliative Care stay. I remembered listening to David as he voiced his anger to Dr. Q one afternoon, over an incident which had happened the day before. I was surprised at the time, because anger was an emotion David rarely expressed. But this occurred in the last two weeks of his life when he was not feeling well at all, so it was understandable that his irritability would surface.

One of the nurses had made a medication error. David was livid. Not because she had made a mistake, but because she tried to cover it up.

"Why don't you just take it anyway?" was her irresponsible, totally insensitive retort when David pointed out her error.

Thinking about the nature of David's anger, I wondered if a part of it had been because his buffer was missing. I had been his go-between, his liaison almost from the beginning of his illness and more so once he was admitted to hospital. Because his non-rebreather mask covered most of his face, it was virtually impossible for him to talk with hospital staff. He could write out his wishes and thoughts, but that took time and energy. David needed all his energy to breathe, to wrap his mind around the dying process and to just be, for whatever time he had left on this earth. It was much quicker and easier for me to jump in and do the talking for him.

However, I had not been there that day, so David had had to deal with this issue on his own, which must have been overwhelming for him in his fragile state. We didn't know it of course, but he would be dead in a fortnight. His lungs were steadily failing and I'm sure he could feel his life force slipping away. This feeling of powerlessness must have precipitated the angry reaction. Or perhaps this anger was an expression of his own grief; grief for the inevitable end of his life.

Why my mind chose to revisit that time in our journey, I don't know. I had slept well the night before, feeling David's presence enveloping me, helping to heal my cold, which had started just after Valentine's Day. So why this morning was I preoccupied with his stay in Palliative Care and this incident in particular? Perhaps I had some of my own inner anger to process, so naturally focused on an "anger" issue from the past.

Or quite possibly I was in need of a respite from Grief, which continued to swirl around me, pulling me into a swamp and filling my heart with sadness. I don't know why it comes and goes like it does. Time does not heal, it only brings more hurt. It intensifies my missing David; it confirms his absence, making it abundantly clear that time is passing by without my life partner, my soulmate, my reason-for-being. I feel like half a person.

And I'm stuck at the bottom of a well. The Well of Grief. I

don't really know how I ended up right at the very bottom of this black pit. I guess we never do figure it out. It's like being tossed to and fro on an ocean wave, or blown carelessly away on a gust of wind, at the whim of Mother Nature.

Valentine's Day has come and gone. I should be over these endless spasms of grief by now, but I'm not. How can I make it go away? Does anybody have a Handbook on How to Grieve Properly? If we block it, it makes it worse and only comes back stronger. If we make ourselves busy, again, it only prolongs the grieving process (or so I'm told). But to stay in pain and suffering night after night, day after day doesn't seem right either. It feels horrible; feels like I'm backsliding, slithering further into that deep black hole, with no way out.

Night time again. I had the most horrible dream. I dreamed that I had wished David back into existence. Sounds nice, doesn't it? Every night I go to bed and wish and hope and pray that somehow he would find a way to come back home to me. True Love always finds a way, doesn't it?

In this dream, he did come back. Not the loving, smiling face as I picture him in my thoughts, but as an ethereal, frightening blackness. He wasn't even a person; it was as if he had transmuted into something sinister, some dark entity that invaded our home and threatened to choke out any bit of life within. As I struggled to comprehend the significance of this weird smothering presence, who was David and was not David, something snapped in my mind. No oxygen! There is no oxygen in the house! A few weeks after David's passing, I called the oxygen company to come and pick up all the cylinders that were left in the house. There were some empty ones and still quite a few full ones. I donated his oxygen concentrators to the CLSC, the home nursing services we have here in Quebec. Somebody else might as well benefit and I sent a prayer along with the machines. Our journey was over, but somebody else's just beginning. "How could I do that? When one day he'd be back?" my brain screeched at me.

"No oxygen? Now he'd be drowning, gasping for breath. He would die all over again, but this time instead of a peaceful, loving death, it would be a horrible suffocating painful death!" I woke up screaming, but heard nothing. I tried again to scream. I wanted to scream and scream and scream out that gruesome vision. But my throat was paralyzed. Not a sound came out. Shaking with fright, I pulled David's bathrobe close (yes, I still did this even though I'd resolved to wear my own clothes and drink out of my own cup, but who cuddles their own bathrobe?) as if I was cuddling his warm body, and eventually drifted off to sleep. This time I dreamed of the Answers, the Keys to this "how do you grieve properly?" question. Unfortunately, I forget most of them. But I do remember a few. One is to take things in baby steps. That's not a new concept, but one I'm obviously not doing these days, or it wouldn't have surfaced in this dream. I need to focus on the little things that pop up. Deal with them first, rather than with the whole package of overwhelming sorrow and grief. Another Answer or Key or whatever that came to me is actually something I learned when David was first diagnosed with COPD. It's an attitude change, a way of accepting and living with chronic illness:

"Pull up a chair. I see you, I acknowledge you, I won't deny you. But I'm not letting you take over my life. We will coexist."

At least that's a start. And I awoke this time with sun streaming in my bedroom window, feeling much better to face the new day.

Chapter 21

March

Early March. It's been eight months. Eight months since my dear husband passed away and I can't seem to shake this bitter loneliness, this overwhelming anguish of grief. My life has been torn to shreds and it just does not make much sense any more.

Somebody suggested I take a vacation. Really? As if I could "get away" from myself. Did I have enough money to pay for something as frivolous as a vacation? Did I have the strength to pick up and go? Could Brenda do without my babysitting for a week? Was I just running away?

Somehow I found the strength to call a travel agent. I let her pick the location and do the booking. She suggested Sint Maarten, an island in the Caribbean. Intrigued, I agreed and off I went, to a resort on the Dutch side of the island. I'd never been there before and would have chosen Florida, a familiar and comfy spot. Maybe, it was good to get out of my comfort zone... then again, maybe not.

The flight was scheduled to leave at seven a.m., which meant I had to be at the airport at four. In the morning.

Oh joy.

Why had I booked such an early flight? As usual, I was not thinking. Well, never mind, it was a charter flight and I had booked at the last minute. Okay, I can do this.

The night before the flight, I was restless with excitement. I packed my suitcase, then unpacked, then repacked. Unable to sit still, I picked up the phone and called everyone in my family to say good-by.

Even though it would have made sense to go to bed early, I didn't even try. I knew I'd just lie awake, my mind buzzing with anticipation. As well, I never sleep properly before a flight or early morning appointment. Every hour or so, I wake up and check the clock, which actually turned out to be a good thing this time, since I discovered that not one of my alarm clocks (David's actually) was working. I hadn't set an alarm in years, so it should not have come as a surprise. Never mind, I was up and raring to go at two o'clock, after about three hours sleep.

The first evening in Sint Maarten, I sat out on my private balcony alone. Cruise ships were settled into port for the night, their bobbing lights illuminating the surrounding darkness. Shops and restaurants on the shore were lit up too, creating a stunning picture against the velvety black backdrop of the mountains.

Enjoying the extraordinary view but feeling a little melancholy the first night in this strange place, I surrendered to sadness and let the tears flow. I had been holding back for obvious reasons. I did not want people to see me openly crying on vacation. But in the privacy of my room, alone on the deck, I let my heart weep into the darkness.

Who were those people enjoying a cruise? Lovers? Couples? Families?

There were couples at the airport, couples on the plane, couples checking in at the resort, couples lying on the beach. Chairs were placed under umbrellas in twos. How was I ever going to get through this week?

It was then that I looked up, to the slab of concrete which formed the ceiling, but served as the floor for the balcony above. A silvery white moth was clinging to the rough stucco-like undersurface. It was resting quietly in an unobtrusive spot, blending in so well that I almost missed it. I watched it for a while wondering if it would fly away, but it didn't move. It was so still I thought it might be dead. And yet, I could sense a peacefulness emanating from this little moth, a serene energy that had a calming effect on me.

"David, is that you?" No answer of course, but the next day

it was gone, reminding me of the buckeye I'd seen two days after David's passing. I had been sitting outside on the deck, weeping uncontrollably that summer morning when something caused me to look up. It was nothing more than a feeling, a subtle change in the energy surrounding me; a shifting of focus away from my distress towards something significant, noteworthy, important enough to make me sit up and take notice. It was the calm and gentle stillness of the butterfly that had captured my attention back in July and I could sense the same qualities in this silvery winged moth. Strangely, or maybe not, I never saw either of them again.

To say I'd made the right decision in taking this trip was an understatement. It did me the world of good.

Each day I would awaken before dawn, anticipating the glow of a golden Caribbean sun as it woke up the earth. I would listen to the timeless rhythm of ocean waves and relax into the softness of sweet ocean air as it caressed my skin, its tenderness a balm for my raw nerves.

And as the sun rose in the sky and the softness of first light transformed into more intense heat, I would relax into that heat, the warmth spreading throughout my body and awakening a faint stirring of joy – a feeling I thought had been buried in the depths of my unrelenting sorrow.

Stretching out on a beach chair early one morning, I closed my eyes to rest a little before breakfast. Gentle sounds of lapping waves reached out to soothe my soul.

"Braid your hair, Miss?"

I blinked and sat up in my chair. Where had this woman come from? Wasn't it rather early to be working the beach? I looked around. There were people everywhere. Had I fallen asleep? I looked at my watch. But my watch had stopped working at the beginning of my vacation, and had stayed that way throughout.

The brightly-clad, plumpish Island woman looked at me curiously. She was waiting for my answer.

"No thanks," I started to say, sinking back into my beach chair. But then I changed my mind and sat back up.

"Yes," I said. "I'd like my hair braided. Let's do it!"

"Welcome to Sint Maarten!" she sang with a friendly smile and a swish of her skirts. She plunked herself down on the empty chair beside me, reached into her bag and brought out a handful of vividly colored beads for me to choose.

I chose pink and white and blue. And in choosing these colors, I made a decision based solely on instinct. I was reaching for something lighter, something to lessen the heavy darkness I'd brought with me on this trip.

I chose to open up and breathe – to let go of constant fear and worry about circumstances beyond my control. My husband was gone. I could not bring him back.

I chose to go with the flow.

I chose Life.

And looking back I could see that the act of choosing to climb out of my deep well of depression, to take a risk, to embrace life by going on this trip alone proved to be a turning point in my life.

My last day in Sint Maarten. I wished I could magically stretch out this day, to make it last the whole winter long. I would miss the warm, tropical climate, the friendly people, and the pampering one inevitably soaks up while on vacation. One thing I love about vacationing in tropical climes is wearing summer dresses, especially the long flowing ones that swirl around my ankles. This morning I'd chosen a soft peach dress; one that David had particularly liked.

Meals at this resort were buffet style, so I picked up a plate and selected some fresh fruit for breakfast. A table by the open window looked inviting and I settled into my chair, grateful for the small blessing of a cool breeze brushing against my face. I would miss this sweet air, this lazy breakfast time, this wonderful sea of turquoise as it ebbed and flowed right outside my window. Cruise boats were leaving the harbor and I wondered where they were headed next.

"Coffee, Miss?" I nodded my head and watched as the server filled my cup.

People walked by my table, some with full plates, some empty. Conversations flowed around me, but I was used to this now. It didn't bother me so much to be dining alone, particularly at breakfast or lunch. There were others alone as well. Not many, but a few.

Dinnertime was different, however, and I felt awkward the first few nights, but I was lucky, for about halfway through the trip, an older couple took me under their wing.

They were celebrating their 50th wedding anniversary and had booked a two-week stay. Laughingly they told me that they were bored with each other, and welcomed my company. I was touched by their kindness.

Music was playing in the background and strains of the 70s song by Lionel Richie, *Lady*, met my ears. *"Lady, I'm your knight in shining armor and I love you..."*

Oh, puleese, I thought to myself, sappy love songs at (I checked the wall clock, since my watch had stopped working) 7:34 in the morning? In a gesture of annoyance, I stabbed my fork into a cube of juicy watermelon. It was halfway to my mouth when I remembered.

Knight in shining armor? Wait a minute. David was my knight in shining armor. Was he sending this song to me? No. Impossible. How silly can I get?

But as memories of our early days opened my heart, I softened. And changed my mind. Awww, how sweet. Thank you, David.

I finished my breakfast serenely without stabbing any more food and left the dining room as if floating on air. Down to the beach I went to say a last good-by to the ocean. It had been an amazing week, and as I stood watching the waves and breathing in fresh, clean air, I hoped I could bring some of that ocean goodness back home with me.

"Mornin', Ma'am."

"Oh, good morning." I tore my gaze away from the powerful waves to look into laughing, crinkly brown eyes. An elderly man was sweeping the steps that led from the pool area down to the beach. His energetic movements were that of a much younger person, yet he had an air of contentment more fitting to an older soul.

"I'm going home today and will miss this beautiful ocean."

"Oh?" He cocked his head to one side and momentarily stopped his work. "Don't you have an ocean?"

I had to suppress a smile. Wouldn't that be nice, if I had an ocean on my doorstep. I imagine this friendly fellow had lived his whole life in the Caribbean, surrounded by water. It was as natural to him as snow is to us northerners in winter. Though judged to be poor by our standards, he was inordinately rich in his lush environment.

I came home to find my basement flooded. Oh joy, back to reality. But the remnants of golden tropical sunshine continued to warm my skin and lift my spirits, and surprisingly this homecoming turned out to be not as painful as the one back in January. I knew I would be coming home to that dreaded emptiness, no David with his warm smile and twinkly eyes, but each time it was becoming a little easier to bear. All that being said, after a while I could no longer hold off my sadness. Tears flowed as once again David's absence filled our home and melancholy crept into my soul.

After a while I pulled myself together and noticed that the intense heaviness which comes with deep grieving was beginning to subside. I will always miss David, beyond a shadow of a doubt. Yet I'm beginning to get the sense that the pining, the torture in my soul, the fear and panic that sometimes haunts my dreams is starting to dissipate, to loosen its suffocating grip around my chest, as it softens into a mellow veil of sadness.

Now I had to turn my attention to this water-in-the-basement problem. Where was it coming from and how do I stop it? The logical place to start would be to check the sump pump. It was broken. No wonder my basement was flooded. And being March, banks of snow were beginning to melt. Not only that – there had been a heavy rainfall the previous day.

Do I need this? Do I want to deal with this upsetting and potentially expensive problem?

No, of course not. Who does? I decided I would not spoil my vacation glow with worry, so did what the Island people do. "No problem," I said to myself and went out to buy groceries.

One thing I love about life in the Caribbean is their relaxed attitude towards everything. Everything is "no problem". Everybody has time to talk. Everybody has time to play. Life is good. I was trying to hold on to that energy for as long as I could.

Back from grocery shopping, I took my time putting the food away. I was hoping by some magic that the cold disgusting water would have evaporated while I was out. Of course, I knew this would never happen and I still had the sump pump to fix, but I delayed dealing with this wretched task for as long as I could.

In the end I had to call a plumber. Yes, it was expensive, but he got the job done. "No problem," I told myself once again, while watching my money fly out the window. I really did not want to spend any more money on this house, since it was time to put it up for sale.

This was not a new decision. After The Diagnosis, I tried to convince David that we should sell our family-sized home and move into something smaller. He was not comfortable with this decision and so it never happened. At the time I was frustrated at not being able to put into action what I thought was a good plan. However, as the years went by, I realized that a move for David would be like having the carpet pulled out from under him. His familiar surroundings would be gone and the adjustment would have been too much for him to handle.

In order to get the house ready for showing, I'd hired workmen, last fall, to paint and renovate. Not wanting a repeat of the Liam disaster (the fellow I'd hired simply because of his pleasant-sounding name), I asked my neighbors for advice. Don had a reputation for working quickly and efficiently. The drawback was that because of his "regular job" he was only available on weekends.

His painting was good and I was pleased, but wished it would hurry up and be over. The going was slow and I felt a sense of displacement in having a stranger in my kitchen, bathrooms and bedroom.

The master bedroom, the bedroom that David and I so lovingly decorated ourselves sixteen years earlier, was the last to be painted.

I cried as I dismantled our most intimate space in preparation for the painter. Curtains were unhooked from windows, pictures came off the walls and everything else that was special to David and I had to be packed away.

I wept as I stripped off our custom-made wallpaper, a wide border really that we had placed all around the room, just below the ceiling. We'd spent months trying to find something unusual, something lively, yet soothing enough to promote sleep, and ended up placing a special order that took forever to arrive.

The pattern was called "Arizona" and it looked like a beautiful desert with its sunset hills gently rolling across our walls and splats of pink flowers scattered here and there. A border of muted teal could either be grassland or the rim of a magical sea, depending on your imagination.

I couldn't stand this tearing down of what we'd created with such anticipation, such love for the beginning of our married life together.

Finally, I just walked away and let Don do his job.

The renovators were local people and I paid them in cash. It seemed like every other day I was running to the bank to withdraw more money. It's an investment, I kept reminding myself. A house that shows well will sell for a better price.

Whether it was the energy expended in cleaning, decluttering, and preparing the house for sale, or the uplifting of spirits one feels on vacation, or both, I don't know, but grief actually took a short vacation too. Life seemed worth living once again.

I had missed my grandchildren while in Sint Maarten, and was glad to get back into the routine of twice weekly babysitting. They were happy with the trinkets I had brought for them from the Islands. As well, there was mango rum for my son-in-law and a shell necklace for Brenda, T-shirts and summer clothes for my other grandchildren. It felt good to be back in the arms of my family once again.

Chapter 22

April

April. David's birth month. I remember a day about sixteen years ago. David and I were standing in a patch of sunlight outside Chapters Bookstore one afternoon. We had met only a few weeks earlier and were exchanging trivialities, likes and dislikes as people do.

"When is your birthday?" I asked, wanting to know what astrological sign he was.

"Next week – April 4th and I'm going to Florida with my sister, do you want to come?"

"Um, no, thanks."

I hardly know you, I thought to myself. Why are you asking me to come to Florida with you? Where would I sleep?

He instantly picked up on the reasons behind my refusal for he quickly added, "We'd just be going as friends. You'd have your own hotel room."

"That's nice, but really, I can't." Actually that was true. I'd just started a new job and couldn't possibly take time off so soon. His invitation was genuine, and my intuition was telling me I could trust him, but I still felt uncomfortable. Having gone through a divorce two years previously, I was extra cautious about dating men. And we weren't even at that stage yet. We really were just friends. And that was enough for me.

April third fell on a Sunday this year. Nine months since I last held my sweetie. Nine months since his death. It was time to go back to the lake where his ashes had been scattered, to feel some sort of connection that could only be felt where David's remains had last touched the earth. Because winters here in Canada are so long and cold, I had not been back to this spot in months. The river would have been frozen in any case. No point sitting under a tree on a frozen body of water, looking for birds that had migrated south, or butterflies who would be hibernating (if that's what they do), wishing with all my heart David was not dead.

Nine months seemed to be a symbolic time to perform a ritual, so I gathered together a candle, some matches and a plant that someone had given me the day of David's gathering. It was a pretty African violet, deep purple in color, but hadn't flowered since early fall. I did not have the patience to care for it any longer; besides it reminded me acutely of that day in July, and I didn't need any more reminders. Time to let it go.

I drove the familiar route to Tim Hortons and picked up a fresh coffee for us. Next stop was at a fast food restaurant David had particularly liked. I ordered a hot dog and some French fries to go and got back in the car. The sun was warm on my face, but the air was chilly and I was glad for my winter coat. Last April it was like summer. This year it had turned shivery cold.

I parked the car in the lot across from Thompson Park, looked around to make sure I was alone and then crossed the street and on to the soccer field. I wanted privacy and knew I would find it here. Nobody comes to a soccer field or to picnic by the water at this time of year, and I felt conspicuous carrying take-out cups, bags of food, a candle and a plant, and hoped no one passing by in a car would notice and think it odd.

The field was mushy with melted snow and I sloshed through puddles of water and oozie, gooey mud as I made my way towards the water.

Feeling a little nervous (why, I have no idea), I took some deep breaths to calm down. Ahhhh, the tantalizing smell of fresh earth and rain, wet leaves and slimy worms. Now some would think that was gross, but to me, this pungent smell is a clear sign that our long cold winter is finally over. Change is in the air along with awakening energy, renewal and rebirth.

I could hear glee in the songs of birds all around me, their sweet melodies lifting my spirits. Warm sunshine kissed my face and I began to relax into my surroundings, while continuing on through muddy fields, one squishy footstep at a time. Young squirrels ran zigzag patterns around tree trunks, up and down, over and under, chattering constantly as squirrels are known to do.

It was obvious that the world was going on without my beloved. Wistfully, I watched as the hustle and bustle of a new season unfolded before my eyes. Bird couples were engaged in nest building, while pairs of small animals dug burrows in the ground. It seemed the whole world was busy creating – new homes, new life, new growth – as naturally and normally as day follows night.

Was I growing too?

Was David? Do Spirits grow? What do they do in the Afterlife?

Tears rolled down my cheeks, as I continued to walk, so I distracted myself by looking at the ground for a pen or anything else David might have put in my path to find.

Movement in the grass caught my eye. A pair of robins looked up at me briefly, their beaks full. Robins! The first ones of the season! I had heard their distinctive "cheer up-cheer up" singing while on my morning walks at home, but they were always hiding in the trees and I had yet to spot one.

But here they were! Two of them, a male and a female pulling up worms.

Was this a sign from David? A message that he too was rejoicing in these first signs of early spring? My mind went back to the children's program I had watched last summer, the one about the story of a little boy who had found a robin with a broken wing. The wing had healed over the summer and it was time to set the bird free. Reluctantly the child opened his bedroom window and watched the robin fly away.

"I'll be back in the spring," promised the bird.

And now it was spring. Feeling a soft loving glow that I knew was coming from David's Spirit, I lightened my step and continued down to the lake.

The water was frozen as I knew it would be, and slushy in places. It was strange to see low tree branches imprisoned in the ice. I always feel sorry for trees or hedges whose branches are so laden with snow that they are forced to bend down to the ground, and remain stuck until spring.

I found the perfect spot under one of those trees at the shoreline. Its frozen branches curved down and into the ice, forming a loose but cozy shelter. There was even a log to sit on, which turned out to be rather cold on my bottom, but at least I could sit for a bit.

This is so hard, I thought to myself. Why did David have to die? We should be home looking forward to his birthday, instead of me sitting here alone, sipping coffee and eating French fries, while searching the frozen lake for the exact spot where the last remnants of his earthly body were scattered.

Not wanting the tears to start up again, I busied myself with unpacking my bag. I placed the candle in the center of some slushy snow. The plant (yes I knew it would freeze, but it belonged with David, wherever he was), the rest of the food (which I knew the animals would eat later on) and a gull's feather I had found nearby were placed around the candle in a circle. I poured the last of my coffee around the candle, thinking vaguely that I'd stopped doing this a long time ago. Well never mind. Perhaps I'd only stopped when winter began. I really don't remember.

The wind blew the candle flame out several times, so I pushed it deeper into the slush, for protection. I did not have any special words ready, so just said a few prayers, talked to David as I always do and looked over the frozen scene in front of me.

It was so different at this time of year. I longed for summer with its warm blue skis, sailboats on the water, those dancing butterflies I'd seen in July, and a return of the pair of herons I'd also seen that day we'd scattered his ashes.

Not that I wanted to be back to those early days so full of anguish and shock, but somehow this passage of time felt like a betrayal. Time is supposed to heal, but it felt more like a reinforcement of his absence. Things were not getting better. I was not getting over it or through it or whatever I was "supposed" to be doing as time went on. In fact time was proving to be the enemy, as with each passing day, I felt David slipping further and further away from me.

Like the scattering of his ashes to the wind, never to be seen again.

The following day was David's birthday – April 4th. Oh how I longed to hold him in my arms again – just once (I was bargaining again), just on his birthday. Was this too much to ask? Surely on the dead person's birthday, the heavens should open up and allow Spirits to mingle with their earthly loved ones.

"Please," I pleaded silently to a grey cloudy sky.

As I got ready to leave the house, I remembered how sad David's last birthday was. I told myself he was happier now, the heaviness of his sick body long gone. No more COPD, no more fear. Now he was living in the Light. I should be celebrating his joyful release to freedom, rather than dwelling on my own sorrow and heartache.

Today I was scheduled to babysit and I wonder if this was a blessing. I would have no time to brood, no time to get stuck in that well of grief. My focus today would be on the next generation, on the care of my grandchildren. Sippy cups, Play-Doh, endless games and the happy stream of chattering voices never fail to keep me on my toes and in the flow of everyday life.

On my way home I stopped at the bakery and bought carrot

cake – David's favorite. Silly or not, I would put some under Grandfather Oak for David. How could I not share his birthday cake with him? And how could I not pour us some coffee as well? Looks like that ritual was still with me. I was not ready to give it up yet.

Homemade spaghetti was on the menu for supper tonight, another of his favorite dishes. Sitting alone in the quiet kitchen, I picked at my food and let my mind wander back to David's last birthday.

It had fallen on Easter Sunday. The weather was unseasonably warm throughout the holiday weekend and we were lucky to be able to sit on the deck and enjoy some early spring sunshine. After a long cold winter of being cooped up in the house, it was a welcome relief to be out in the open air. Chickadees chirped in the hedges surrounding our deck and rays of nourishing sunlight warmed our souls.

It felt like a gift, a last reprieve somehow before the inevitable happened. And David had been so ill those last few weeks at home. To watch him sink to the level where he could hardly brush his teeth filled me with despair. It was depressing to watch him, yet at the same time I wanted to lash out, to punch something.

I wanted to breathe for him. I wanted to wave a magic wand and bring him back to good health, or at least where he had been before this "step-down".

But David being David, put on a cheerful face and tried to look as if he was enjoying his birthday gifts, cake, and special dinner I'd cooked for him.

Now I wish we were back there – at least he was alive. At least I could cuddle him and hold him close to me. At least we could look into each other's eyes, David's so endearing, so soft with love and tenderness.

We both knew in some deep inner place that this was to be his last birthday. I could feel the horrid knot of dread twisting in my gut and I sensed the weary defeat in David's body as he lay beside me in bed his last birthday night.

Five days later he was taken to hospital.

On April 9th, exactly a year and a day after David was admitted to hospital, our home went up on the market. How symbolic, a year and a day. Isn't that some kind of initiation time? Last April seems like such a long time ago, and only just yesterday. It was last April that David was taken away in the ambulance, never to return home.

I felt a queasiness, a shivering in my bones as I watched the Real Estate Agent slam a For Sale sign into my front lawn.

Am I really moving? Can I leave all of our cherished memories behind? What about Grandfather Oak? How can I leave my secret conduit to the Spirit World? How can I continue my ritual of sharing coffee and cake with David if I don't have Grandfather Oak? I had become so attached to that tree as if it was a telephone to Heaven or ladder I could climb up any time I wished.

Can I really leave all that behind?

What will the new owners do? Will they love Grandfather Oak as I do, or cut him down? I shuddered at the thought, but reminded myself I had to make an effort to detach or I'd never sell this house.

Is David still in our home? His presence? His energy? Oh yes he is, but not as strong a presence as a year and a day ago. Back then, he had only just left for the hospital. His medications and oxygen equipment were still here at home. There was a sliver of hope he'd return one day; that this was just another exacerbation of COPD, a setback only, from which he'd eventually recover. Now, his energy in this house is more subtle. Our bedroom has changed; walls a soft cream and lilac instead of the livelier more vibrant shades we both loved. His clothes still hang in the closets, T-shirts and underwear still hide in his drawers. After my initial frantic activity of giving away his clothes and other things, I've totally stopped. His remaining clothes will stay with me forever.

Even when I move.

I don't care what anybody thinks. David's shirts and jackets will hang in my closet wherever I go.

And that's another problem I face. I don't know where to move.

Baby steps, baby steps I remind myself.

Caravan Day

This is the day real estate agents come to inspect the house. I had cleaned and shined everything to perfection. Fresh new towels hung in the kitchen and bathrooms. Sinks were spotless. I had opened every window in the house to let in fresh air, and sent the cat outdoors, out of the way. And then I went out. I could not stay and watch all those people walking through our home. I could not listen to their comments, whether professional and pleasant or rude and careless. I did not want to face anybody.

I had some errands to run in the village anyway, so left the house early. And then I remembered that the bank wasn't yet open. Darn! That was to be my first stop but now I'd have to start at the end and work backwards.

My last stop was supposed to be at Tim Hortons, where I had planned to pick up a coffee and bring it home to share with the house. Well, not really share it with the house, but just stand in the kitchen, soothing coffee in hand and feel the energy after the agents had left. Was I really doing the right thing in selling? Would I be leaving some of David behind? Would some nice family move in and treat the house kindly?

Or not?

Silly thoughts, but I had them anyway. A house is just a house I had to remind myself.

A year ago, David would have been sitting in this kitchen

waiting for me. We'd started this mid-morning ritual way back in our early days. In those days, after gardening or biking or whatever, we'd stop in at Dunkin' Donuts (Tim Hortons hadn't arrived in Hudson yet) and order coffee and doughnuts. Those were happy days. We were in love, we had an abundance of energy, and the whole world looked rosy.

When it got to the point where David couldn't leave the house, why I'd pick up our order, plus or minus doughnuts and bring it back home.

"Why don't you just make a pot here?" asked David's younger son who had been visiting at the time.

David explained that we liked our daily jaunt to Dunkin' Donuts. It was a change of scenery, the coffee was always hot and fresh, doughnuts deliciously decadent, and it gave us a feeling of being out on a date. By the look on Josh's face, he must have thought it was a boring place to go for a "date".

So as naturally as water running downstream, we continued with our mid-morning ritual while David was in hospital. It gave him something to look forward to during those dark, uneasy days. And it was something I could feel good about at a time when there was little else. I could not cure him, I could not even bring him back home, but I could bring him a good fresh cup of coffee. You learn very quickly to value the ordinary things in life, particularly a life that is coming to an end.

The Drive-Thru was empty at this hour; my coffee served efficiently with a cheerful, "Have a nice day!" Since it was still rather early, I decided against taking the highway back (which would have been my normal quick route) and chose to meander along the river road towards the village, grocery store and bank.

Driving leisurely along the lakeshore is always a pleasure. The open fields and farmhouses typically bring me back to those happy, carefree days when David and I would bicycle that route. I'd peek into people's gardens admiring their pretty flowers, while David immersed himself in birdsong. Through

David's patient teaching, I learned to identify the calls of some common birds in our area: cardinals, blue jays, chickadees, blackbirds, sparrows.

David was the first to hear Canada geese honking as they flew overhead. He'd look up to the sky and point excitedly to that familiar V shape, which told us their migration had begun.

Every fall we'd say good-by to "our geese" and every spring we'd welcome them home. Canada geese held a special place in David's heart and the artwork in our home reflected this fondness. The natural world was important to David and he paid attention to all her signs of changing seasons, and listened as she spoke.

Cool, fresh air poured through my open car window, and as bright morning sun warmed my face I began to relax. The road was rather long and winding with no traffic to speak of, so I took my time. The landscape had changed over the years. New homes were under construction on the waterfront, sadly taking over the agricultural part of the land. Cows grazed in the fields next door, making for a strange hodgepodge of granite and grass. Cheerful spring flowers scattered lawns and sprinkled over into ditches. I found myself being pulled along, pleasantly lulled by the song of the river.

Then all of a sudden I was looking into a soccer field that dipped down towards the river. Oh my goodness, Thompson Park! I had not thought where this road would take me; my only thoughts were on the end point – reaching the village. Thompson Park, the place where we had scattered David's ashes nine months ago. Well, not in the park, of course, but in the lake. I might have driven right past, if not for the geese. Canada geese, here in the park! I'd never seen Canada geese here before.

I quickly pulled over, parked the car and sat there with a big smile on my face, as if I'd just found a pot of gold.

"David, you did it again! You sent these geese to me as a

comfort. You knew I was nervous about people going through our home and you wanted me to know you were here, by my side, supporting me. Ha! And you even made sure I'd had my coffee with me too!"

Good thing nobody was around to witness this weird lady talking to the geese (or herself, which is probably worse!).

Perhaps, I've given you the impression that David was perfect. Well, I can assure you, dear readers, he was not. He was a nerd. A geek. More left-brain logical than right-brain creative, and sometimes came across as insensitive – which he was anything but. He wore glasses and sported a Beatles' haircut (about 30 years out of date) when I first met him. I wouldn't have looked twice at this man had I been in my younger years. In fact, I'd walked right by him when I was 25 and worked in the ECG department of Lakeshore Hospital. Strange to think that about 20 years later, we would meet again and fall in love.

He never threw things out – our basement was a testament to that. The car he drove was an old, beat-up Mazda, which should have been replaced, but David "liked to get good value for his money." Nothing wrong with that philosophy, but he could well afford to buy a new one. A typical Aries, he was stubborn as a goat.

"David, we need a new answering machine," I said to him one day shortly after I'd moved in with him.

"Why? What's wrong with it?"

"It's old, it garbles the messages, I don't understand when people leave their phone numbers."

"Well, you know all your friends' numbers, don't you?"

"Daaaavid!" We ended up getting rid of that old machine and subscribing to the telephone company's answering service. Much better!

Springtime, a few years down the road, and as I cleaned and freshened up our home, I took a critical look around the living room. We'd already moved some of our Robert Bateman prints from one room to the other – just for a change. Our furniture was fine, except for the sofa and love seat.

"David, we need some new sofas."

"What's wrong with the old ones?"

"That's just it – they're old!"

"Well they're functional – they work."

"But they're old and crummy and falling apart." I exaggerate just a tad; they really are comfortable, merely worn looking. He just shakes his head as if I'd asked him to fly to the moon. We never replaced them.

Another time, after COPD, I was cleaning the countertop after breakfast. I noticed some rust shavings that had fallen from our space saving "under the cabinet" coffeemaker.

Ewwww.

I quickly wiped them up and inspected the coffeemaker. It was coming from the metal base.

"David, we need a new coffeepot – there's rust coming out of it." Now if this was pre-COPD, I'd have just gone to the store and bought one. But at this stage, we were joined at the hip. There was no more "her area of expertise and his". We did everything together.

"It still tastes good and there's no rust in the coffee."

"Well, I hope not! Otherwise, we wouldn't be drinking it!"

"So, what's the problem?"

"The problem is," I say with exaggerated patience as if to a child, "it's old. Finished. We need a new one."

"But I like the coffee in this old one."

To make a long story short, I went out and bought a new coffeemaker, fully expecting David to toss the rusty one away.

He did not.

He stored it in the basement, like you would do with a child's outgrown teddy bear. I rolled my eyes as I watched him carefully package it up and carry it downstairs.

Puleese, I thought to myself. It's just going to sit there collecting dust.

Turns out, this snazzy-jazzy, bells and whistles new one was a failure. The coffee was lukewarm and plastic-tasting. No matter how many times I washed it, that awful taste would not go away. As if that wasn't bad enough, the finish started peeling off the burner or warming plate where the glass carafe sat. It was almost as if they painted the burner black instead of coating it with a proper finish.

I e-mailed the company with my complaints, and they asked me to cut off the electrical plug and send it to them in the mail. Once they received it as confirmation of their defective product they would send out a brand-new one.

It would take only six weeks. Six weeks! Without a coffeemaker? What the heck are we supposed to do in the meantime? Smiling triumphantly, David fairly pranced down the stairs to rescue our old one. With a silly flourish, he slid it back in its under-the-cabinet spot and immediately plugged it in, ready to go!

The new one did arrive. Eight weeks later and it was fine, thank goodness. And yes, the old one went back into the basement. Just in case.

Chapter 23

Changes

Changes. I feel changes within. I am not the same person I was nine months ago. I go to financial meetings and sit at the head of the conference table now. I take pride in arriving well prepared, with my portfolio and a handful of pens. I focus on what is being said and try to comprehend graphs and projections, instead of blanking out and letting David handle everything.

And I have learned when to end the meeting. At first, I would sit back and wait for my advisors to gather up their documents, pocket pens, close files – clear signals that it was time to leave. After all, they had busy schedules, they knew what had to be discussed, decided and acted upon. This was their territory – not mine.

But the last few times, I've sensed a shift, a subtle change in the air. I surprised myself by choosing to sit at the head of the table one morning, rather than shrinking timidly into a corner. With an unaccustomed air of confidence, I strode into the conference room and sat. It was then up to the advisors to take their places on either side of me.

After the accounts were sorted out and papers signed, my advisors sat back. I waited. Nothing happened. I commented on the weather. They commented back. I looked around for guidance.

Everyone looked normal, smiling, chatting as if we were in a restaurant eating lunch. It finally dawned on me that they were waiting for me to end this meeting.

This appointment was to discuss my financial situation, my portfolio. They were working for me. Yes, they had the knowledge and expertise in sorting through the endless paperwork and particulars relevant to estate management, but this was my life, my future, my concern. It was up to me to adjourn this business meeting when I was ready.

So, I cleared my throat (why do we always clear our throat before changing direction or covering up?), attempted a kind of a "wrap up" or summary of the proceedings (to make myself look professional), stood up and extended my hand (to really make myself look professional, rather than a grieving helpless widow). And after a few more sessions this became my new normal.

This year for the first time, I had the unpleasant task of sorting through and preparing all the documents pertaining to my income tax return; and sending it out to our accountant. David was the one who always looked after this. Finance was his specialty. He loved working with numbers, balancing checkbooks, following the stock market, keeping an eye on tax laws and fluctuations.

I did not.

Now I have to make decisions in areas that are foreign to me. I don't even know if I've sent off the right documents, tax slips, and receipts. Have I missed anything? Will I be fined by the government if I forget anything?

I was nervous about this whole process. My boundaries are definitely being tested, my comfort zone is no longer comfortable. I've had to break out of that little cocoon in which I'd been hiding. I'm not quite ready to spread my wings and fly yet. In fact, I don't even know if I have wings, but amidst all the uncertainty and confusion, I am beginning to feel the first stirrings of pride, of tentative accomplishment as I gain strength and learn to stand on my own two feet.

How do I feel about all this?

Strange?

Yes. I'm changing and it feels odd.

Sad?

Of course. David should be here to share in these changes,

however weird that sounds.

Blessed?

Yes and no.

Yes, because it is better to have loved and lost, and our love was so deep and so strong and so utterly divine.

And no because, who wants to be in this situation anyway?

Does any of this make sense?

I had a dream. I was leading a healing circle once again. Haven't done that in years. In trying to figure out who I am or what I want to do with my life, this dream came as a pleasant surprise. I was actually happy, doing something I loved, and connecting with people once again.

I made up my mind that very day to seek out a Healing Center and test the waters. I wanted to be part of a spiritual community where yoga, tai chi and guided meditation were taught. But where to start?

Meditation. That seemed like a good place to begin. Low-key, short session, no commitment. Tailor-made for me at this point in my life. I had to start slowly. I could not commit to weeks of anything. One class for now.

Luck was on my side that day as it turned out there was a Yoga Center in my community that accepted "drop-ins".

Good. That was perfect for me. The first session was free.

Even better.

I took the plunge and entered the semi-dark, quiet meditation area.

As it happened, the owner of the center was to be our guide this morning in this healing meditation. I knew Inge through her writing, as she contributed weekly to our local newspaper. She exuded positive energy on paper; in person it was even better.

The meditation session was not quite what I wanted, what I expected. It was too general, but then it was a short session. One could not get into "find yourself on a forest path...", the kind of guided meditations I used to lead quite a few years ago.

However, the experience as a whole proved to be a good one. It gave me an opening to tend to my own healing at a pivotal time in my life. My mind had been whirling with decisions and "what ifs" and I sorely needed the kind of calmness you can only get from meditating.

At home in the early mornings, I would make an attempt to meditate by lighting a candle and gazing into the flame. But invariably my mind would wander off somewhere or the cat would jump up on my lap or I'd decide that now was the time for a cup of tea or a bathroom break. In other words, it didn't work.

Inge, a very welcoming and empathetic soul, took some time after the session to get to know me in a genuine and supportive manner. I found myself pouring out my heart to her, as clients swirled around us, either coming or going. It didn't really matter, as I felt safe here; no one was going to judge me for crying in public.

Besides leading guided meditations, Inge is a yoga teacher and holds classes at the Center.

Yoga doesn't hold much interest for me. It seems too static. I need movement, not fixed postures and tai chi is better at filling that need.

Tai chi is an ancient practice, a moving form of meditation consisting of specific poses (like Sweeping Lotus Petals in the Wind, or Embrace Tiger, Return to Mountain) with smooth transitions between each. In Chinese philosophy the circulating of "chi" or life force throughout the body enhances one's health and vitality. Stress is relieved by the slowness of movement bringing peace of mind, balance and harmony to a person's life.

I like the slow, graceful, yet sometimes challenging positions of the practice, which I know are also strengthening my muscles. To me this is far better than working out at any gym. Realistically, I know it's not possible to gain the same kind of muscular strength, but that's fine with me. I much prefer the gentle, tranquil nature of a tai chi class. Flute music, soft and sweet, rain falling in a tropical forest, or the refreshing sounds of a flowing river enhance the atmosphere and always put me at ease.

Tai chi classes were held in the evening, Inge informed me, once a week on Wednesdays. I told her I'd think about it. I don't like going out in the evening, but this class started at 6:30. Definitely not too late, so maybe I'd give it a shot. I had nothing to lose.

Chapter 24

May

In 2005, after graduating from nursing school, I took a trip to the Bahamas. For as long as I can remember, I've dreamed of swimming with dolphins. Not in captivity, where they are taught tricks to amuse the public, but out in the open ocean, where they swim wild and free.

I found WildQuest by searching the Net. It was a Retreat located in Porgy Bay, a friendly fishing village in North Bimini, one of the smaller, less populated Bahamian islands. Yoga was offered in the mornings along with meditation. The beach was a short walk away and available any time. Meals were vegetarian, served buffet style. In the evenings, healing circles were held as a way to relax and wind down after a full day's events.

Every afternoon, weather permitting, the guests were taken out on a sailing catamaran to swim and connect with dolphins in their natural environment.

It was a fantastic experience. Once in a lifetime, I'd thought. Well once was not enough. I wanted to go back. Longed to put my feet in the ocean again. To jump with wild abandon into glorious waves and enter the underwater world of sea creatures.

Before even boarding the catamaran, our group was given an overview of dolphin behavior. For example, we were instructed never to approach a dolphin in the wild, but to allow them to come to us. The ocean is their territory, their home and our innocent actions might be misinterpreted as aggression. At the very least we'd frighten them away, and we didn't want that!

Luck was with us on that trip, for the dolphins did come. They swam under and around us in circles. It was absolutely divine.

And now something was pulling me back there. It could

have been my impatience for summer to arrive, or the desire to immerse myself in the warm Caribbean ocean and let the healing waters soothe my soul.

Or, maybe it was because I subscribed to WildQuest's weekly e-newsletter. Definitely a bad idea, as they posted the most captivating videos I'd ever seen. Sparkling turquoise water surrounded the catamaran while dolphins raced alongside, occasionally breaking the surface and jumping in sync to the delight of those on board. There were underwater shots of swimmers coming face to face with spotted or bottlenose dolphins. Magic surrounded this Retreat and everybody seemed to be in love with life.

I longed to go back to that place where bliss was the norm, where I could be part of a group of happy, carefree people even for a little while.

The program for Summer 2011 looked varied and interesting with a different theme or focus each week. Sound healing, animal communication, living your dreams, creating dance, music and art were some of the themes. As well there were workshops on kinesiology, quantum light breathing and specific yoga techniques. A full moon ceremony sounded intriguing.

One theme drew me, as if beckoning. Actually two. Anna was to lead workshops on crystal healing and vibrational therapy. Well that would be a good fit – I could use all the healing I could get.

Dawn was a wildlife biologist who specialized in marine mammal behavior and communication. I wondered how someone could communicate underwater with dolphins and whales. How do you "speak" to them? How do they "speak" back to you? I was a little skeptical, but after all, wasn't I communicating with my husband in the Afterlife? What would people think of me if I told them?

But could I do this? Did I have the money? I'd already been

away twice this year, in January and March, and now it was May. Could I continue spending at this rate and still have money left for important things like food and clothes, car and home maintenance?

It seemed like I was always struggling to find balance in my life. I'd read comments like "live in the moment, live in the now" or "money is just energy – the more you put out, the more will return to you". Could I really live like that? Did it even make sense?

My legal fees to settle the estate were substantial, so why shouldn't I take just as much, if not more for myself? This rationale was flawed, but it was how I justified taking money for the trip out of my retirement fund. The more logical part of me would argue, "Keep spending and you'll go broke."

On and on went the struggle. Left brain, right brain. Enjoy the moment, spend money, it will come back to you. Break away from old negative patterns that say, "You're not good enough, you shouldn't spend money, you need to save for a rainy day."

Aren't these all rainy days? I've certainly cried oceans of tears.

Save, invest, be frugal. Frugal? That was the last thing I wanted to do. How is that going to make me feel better?

Well then, how about sensible?

Okay, define sensible. What is sensible? Ahh, that would be the "balance thing", exactly what I was trying to accomplish or achieve or figure out.

I spent the entire weekend flip-flopping with this issue. And to complicate matters, there was another component to this whole thing as well.

Was I running away?

Overwhelmed with feelings of panic, I wanted nothing more than to escape, to run to the ocean. Was this avoiding the pain and grief? Did this mean I was turning away from my problems instead of facing them?

How in the world would I know?

Every step I took seemed to stir things up, bringing more questions and inner turmoil, rather than the progress I was hoping for.

Do I go or do I stay? All the "signs" pointed towards me going on this trip. My babysitting days were looked after, the affirmation cards I drew supported my going. Family and friends told me David would want me to be happy; he'd want me to go on this trip. And yet, I couldn't take the plunge. I could not book it. I sat at the computer researching the best and cheapest flights to Fort Lauderdale. But in the end, I just could not take it to the last step. My credit card sat on the desk, waiting for me to either use it or tuck it back into my purse. I decided to sleep on it (the problem, not the credit card). In the morning everything would look better.

Next morning everything did. The way was clear. Book the trip.

But I did not.

Was I slipping back into "cautious mode"? Was I afraid to enjoy life? Was I allowing fear to rule my life? Probably. I don't know.

Finally, I just gave up. If I was having this much trouble booking the darn trip, it wasn't worth it. Something was wrong. I was not meant to go there, even though "all the signs" were favorable. Forget it. I was done. I give up. Sorry, I could not break these "old negative patterns" that were holding me back from life. Too bad. Maybe next time.

A local Bereavement Support Group met every Friday morning for coffee at Java U, which was located in Fairview Shopping Centre, Pointe-Claire. This group was different than the one I had started to attend back in January. I had dropped out of that one because I was not ready to break free of my protective cocoon and face the world, even though "the world" was just a handful of other people. Besides, it was held in the evening and I hated driving in the dark.

This Friday morning group was organized on a "drop in" basis. No commitment was necessary and that suited me just fine.

Last week was my first session and I thought it went well. There were almost as many men as women in the group and most seemed comfortable in this setting. Ages ranged from younger people having lost a parent or other relative to elderly ones grieving the loss of a spouse or a child.

After we were settled in our chairs, the facilitator started off with a bang.

"Last week Wendy made a comment that I'd like to draw your attention to." All eyes turned to me and I sat up in my chair, anticipating what would surely be a sage piece of advice or deep insight I'd shared with the group.

"Wendy said, 'Life sucks.'"

Ouch! I felt a stab of guilt and immediately shrank into my chair. Did I really say that out loud?

I had to think for a minute, but yes, I remember saying this to a man who was sitting next to me. He had been so overcome with grief while telling his story, that speech became impossible. Tears poured down his face and sobs shook his body. I felt sorry for him and reached over to place my hand on his shoulder in a gesture of comfort.

"Life sucks sometimes, doesn't it?"

I wanted him to know I understood his feelings and it was okay to cry. I certainly did not think this commiserating comment would be discussed at our next meeting.

Facilitator looked around the room and continued on, "Do you feel that life sucks? Or are you using tools to get through this time of grief?"

People shifted in their chairs, took a sip of coffee, a bite of cake, fiddled with pens or coughed politely. Nobody wanted to begin.

Facilitator chose the lady sitting next to her. "Mary, would you like to start? Where do you stand on this?"

As I listened to each person talk, it became apparent that many agreed with my statement, but most were quick to add that they were "counting their blessings", as if it was better to sweep negativity under the rug. Or they might have felt it necessary to show everyone that they were moving on with life.

I figured I'd better do the same. My turn came and I did just that. I said how blessed I was to have children and grandchildren and how fortunate we were to be members of this support group.

Then something inside me rebelled and I said in a louder voice, "I still need to validate my feelings. Life is not very nice right now!"

Nervously, I looked over at Facilitator to judge her reaction, but she merely nodded as if this outburst was customary and moved on to the next person. I took a small sip of coffee and wondered if I'd just made a further mess of the whole situation.

Another few people spoke up and then it was Lisa's turn. "Life sucks!" she stated boldly. "I hate this life! I'm overwhelmed. I'm sad. I feel horrible no matter what I do. I'm alone in the world now, as I have no family and I'm really having a rough time!"

Yes! I thought to myself. That's exactly how I feel right now! Why I didn't I have the courage to say that? Why didn't I have the guts to stand up for myself and let my real feelings show? Never mind counting my blessings. I really did not feel that way a few moments ago when I spoke, so why did I throw in that goody two-shoes attitude? Because I wanted to be liked by the group. Because I was following the crowd – just like I did when I was a teenager. It was Facilitator's fault. She made me, so I got mad at her.

Not to her face, of course. In my mind.

All day, I went over and over these feelings, this interaction at Java U. Didn't she think we had the right to hate life, the right to our feelings and emotions, no matter how awful they were? Was this group all about being sugary-sweet, nicey, nicey, let's think positive? Well, then I'm not going back! This group is not helping me at all!

As the day wore on, however, I came to terms with the whole situation. How could I get angry at the facilitator? She was just doing her job, which was to bring us from sorrow to comfort. She was not telling anybody what to feel or how to feel. I was the one responsible for my own feelings and reactions. I was responsible for feeling guilt at first with my famous "life sucks" comment, and then anger afterwards at covering up my real feelings. How could I blame somebody else for my actions?

Strangely enough, it became clear after my tai chi class that evening. I hadn't practiced tai chi in a group in quite a few years, and was looking forward to getting back into it.

The Yoga Center was empty. Day classes were done and Inge had gone home. I waited alone for the tai chi instructor, feeling uneasy.

Who was this teacher? Was he any good? Would there be a full class of students, or not many? Would they have taken years of tai chi together with this teacher and be more accomplished, than I? Would I feel awkward and clumsy?

It wasn't long before the other students arrived. I saw open smiling faces, and immediately felt relieved. The teacher was young, but looked competent enough and welcomed me as a new member of the class.

The class lasted only one hour – not nearly long enough for me, but even in the first few moments, I felt my spirits lift as remembered movements such as "White Crane Spreads its Wings" flowed throughout my body, waking up every cell. I had been too long away from this soothing practice, one in which I could actually feel a sharpening of my senses. An awakening of something in my soul.

It's not as though I don't practice tai chi at home. I do.

Sporadically. On the beach it's a given. Wherever I am on holiday, tai chi is part of my morning routine. It's a grounding way to begin each day and leaves me feeling connected to the ocean, sky and my surroundings.

However, being with an instructor proved to be far more effective and surprisingly refreshing as he guided me to learn new moves. "Cloud Hands", probably one of the most well-known and easiest moves to do, was taught this evening using unfamiliar hand positions.

As you sweep clouds through a pretend sky, your whole body fills with light and air. Visualization is part of the practice as moves are nature themed. Your sky could be serene and blue, or stormy or velvety black with stars weaving through your fingertips. You are free to create whatever you want in your mind.

I was not prepared for the changes I felt just by changing hand positions. Perhaps it was because I had performed "Cloud Hands" in the same way for so long it had become automatic. With different hand movements, I felt an internal shift as new sensations flowed through my hands and fingers. The energy was gentle, yet strong and left my palms tingling.

Since a good part of my concentration went into my hands – the drawing in and circulating of fresh chi (life force), I had missed the more subtle energies rippling all through the rest of my body. It was only afterwards, once the class was over, that I became aware of feeling energized, totally and completely in every part of my being. I felt good about myself.

I felt powerful!

As I mulled over the day's events on the short drive home, I came to an understanding about the support group issue. I realized that by not giving voice to my true feelings, I was not living my authentic self. I was living for others' expectations.

And hadn't I been doing that for most of my life? School children in the 50s were expected to conform and not voice an opinion at all. Answer questions, do not question answers.

I was a "good girl" at school and continued on in that pattern into adulthood.

Well it's obvious that pattern doesn't fit any more.

I was angry at the facilitator initially, but then at myself for falling into that trap of suppressing my own feelings; that knee-jerk reaction of nodding, smiling, wanting to please and be liked. Of wanting to be one of the group.

And now in recognizing this does it mean I'm growing? Am I growing? Making progress, evolving even in the face of grief?

Or especially in the face of grief, as it continues to erode the person I was, or the life I assumed would go on forever.

I did not go on that dolphin trip. I felt good about my decision to live within my means. To not just fly out the door and run away to the ocean. I was much more responsible than that. I could handle my finances. I could hold back my childish impulses. Wasn't I good?

It was May after all, a good time of year to be at home. May, a magical month of metamorphosis, where tender green shoots poke up from the earth to embrace the warm sunshine. Fresh new leaves suddenly appear on tree branches where tiny buds had previously shivered in the cold. Drab brown gardens explode with color as blossoms unfold and perfume the air. Once April rains give way to warmer and sunnier skies, I itch to be out in the garden, tidying and prettying it up with gnomes, faeries, butterfly solar lights, and stepping stones. Why would I go away in May?

I continued on for a few days patting myself on the back. Every once in a while my mind would stray. I'd look at my watch and say to myself, if I'd gone on that trip, I'd be in the ocean right now, or participating in the full moon ritual, or a learning about crystal healing, or vibrational medicine.

Never mind, I'd made my decision. I was on track with life. Besides, an evening of mystical sound healing was scheduled at the Yoga Centre this week that I didn't want to miss. It promised to be spectacular with Tibetan singing bowls and crystal gongs – definitely out of the realm of ordinary, and something new to experience.

Monday evening, the night of the concert. I had not registered to go. I would just go and buy my ticket at the door. How could I commit ahead of time? How do I know if I'd be feeling all right, not too tired from babysitting or whatever?

I hemmed and hawed with this decision, almost as much as with the dolphin trip.

Should I go? It cost twenty-five dollars. Not much, but what if I didn't like it?

An hour before the performance I thought I'd call to see if there was any room for me – maybe it was all sold out.

"Oh yes come!" enthusiasm flowed through the phone from the voice at the other end. "There's always room. We'll just pack everyone in. Bring a blanket and pillow. Come in your pajamas if you want to! It's so much fun and sooooo relaxing!"

What? Pack us in? Forget it. I can't do that. I'd feel trapped. Squished. Unable to breathe. How could I enjoy this? I love music, especially music with a healing vibrational quality to it, but sitting on the floor (I assumed), wearing pajamas?? No way. Not a chance in hell!

Now don't be silly, I scolded myself, it will be fine. I'm sure not everybody will be wearing pajamas, after all we have to drive or walk home. Ha! Imagine walking down the street in your pajamas? I think not.

To clear my head and settle my nerves (yes, I felt a rush of anxiety and pressure in my chest after that conversation over the phone), I went for a walk. It was a nice warm May evening, the kind that brings everybody out of doors and into their yards, their gardens or around the block for a stroll. I listened to birds singing high up in the trees, took some deep breaths of fresh air and argued with myself.

Go, it will be worth it.

Don't go, you'll feel trapped and then have wasted twenty-five dollars.

Go, you have twenty-five dollars. You can always leave if you don't like it.

Don't go. I don't *have* to go. Nobody can *make* me.

On and on and on.

Finally, I decided not to go. Sorry, I can't do this. I just can't. If I've lost another opportunity to break away from old limiting habits, well so be it. I've failed again. Too bad.

Next morning, I got up feeling strange and a little queasy. Something was going on deep inside me. I did not feel well. There was nothing I could put my finger on, just a vague feeling of depression. The sun was shining brightly, which should have boosted my spirits, but didn't. I felt uneasy, as if something was missing in my life.

Looking at my watch once again, I thought to myself, too bad I didn't take that dolphin trip, I'd be getting ready to go on the catamaran now. Everyone would be gathered on the dock, excitedly milling about. I could picture sunscreen being passed around, towels and snorkeling equipment sorted through, happy conversation flowing, and anticipation spicing up the air.

"Then why didn't you go?" a tiny voice whispered in my ear. "Why don't you do things that make you feel good? That's not running away from life's harshness.

That's healing.

This is the first year after David's death. The wound is still raw and fresh. Next year, hopefully, the pain will have softened, become less bleak, less traumatic, but if you don't look after healing this wound it will dehisce" (that's medical speak for burst open).

As I look back to those vulnerable days right after David's death, I can see how far I've come all these months later. That paranoid, totally confused and fearful person doesn't exist anymore. She's left paranoia behind, swept confusion out the door, but fear is still lurking in the corners of her mind and heart.

I don't want to be afraid of life. I want to live. I don't want to worry about every little step I take. I remember how good it felt a few short months ago when soaking up the sun on the beach in St. Maarten. Why not invite these feelings? Why not travel if that's what it takes?

So with one smooth click of the mouse, my trip was booked.

It turned out to be everything I'd longed for – and more. I booked a direct flight to Fort Lauderdale, which was scheduled to leave Friday, mid-morning. So much better than getting up in the middle of night to be at the airport super early! Yes, it cost a little extra, but what the heck? I'm travelling in comfort now. My timing. My way.

This time I drove to Brenda's home, left my car there and let her take me to the airport. Last time I'd parked my car at the airport at four o'clock in the morning. I'd been afraid to park too far away at that lonely dark hour, so ended up in a zone that charged exorbitant fees, because it was closer to the terminal.

Well, not any more. I have family. They want to help me. I need to learn to accept their help. And this was to be a recurring theme on this trip.

Accepting help. (Just when I think I've learned a lesson in life, I seem to slide backwards and have to relearn it, all over again.)

The three-hour flight was fine. Yes, there were couples and families travelling together, but it didn't tear at my gut like it did back in March on the charter flight to Sint Maarten. I landed in Fort Lauderdale, found a taxi and was whisked away to the Bahia Mar Hotel. After checking into my room, I dumped my suitcases on the floor, kicked off shoes, pulled on my bathing suit and slipped into flip-flops, grabbed a towel, then dashed out the door. I couldn't wait to walk in the soft sand, to stand at water's edge and let salty waves lap at my toes.

A catwalk led from the mezzanine part of the hotel over the busy street and onto the public beach. How convenient, I thought adjusting my sunhat and wishing I'd remembered my sunglasses, which were tucked neatly in a side pocket of my suitcase.

Squinting in the bright sunlight, I flip-flopped along the catwalk as cars whizzed by on the street below.

I was about halfway over when a monarch butterfly surprised me by flying right across my path. The rich orange of its wings glowed coppery gold in the afternoon sun.

"Hello, David," I called out as it fluttered away. "That was fast. I didn't expect a sign from you so quickly!"

That monarch was the only butterfly I was to see for the duration of my trip.

My weekend in Florida passed quickly. I did the usual fun things: swimming, sunbathing, shopping, eating out. On Sunday night as previously arranged, our group was to meet in the hotel's private dining room to get acquainted before heading out to Bimini the following morning.

When we were all seated around the table, the group leader stood up to introduce herself. Celia was an energetic women in her 40s. She had the right personality to put everyone at ease. After all, we were meeting for the first time and would be spending the whole of next week in close company at the Retreat.

I listened to my fellow travellers as each one stood up to introduce herself. We were all women, about 18 of us. Some were retired, one was an accountant, several were office workers, a young lady with purple hair claimed to be a healer. And then two ladies stood up and introduced themselves as hospice nurses.

Oh no, was my immediate thought as my heart sank. There is no way I want to talk about death and dying. Forget it! I'll just ignore them and concentrate on the others. I turned to the lady sitting beside me.

"What do you do for a living?" I asked by way of making conversation.

"I teach thanatology." Her eyes scrutinized mine, waiting for a reaction.

Searching my memory banks, I came up with nothing.

"What is that?"

"The study of death and dying, grief and loss."

"Oh," I managed to squeak before turning quickly away.

"Quite the conversation stopper."

Her voice had an edge to it and she also turned away, evidently used to this kind of reaction, but still not comfortable with it.

Feeling caught off guard and embarrassed at being rude, I kept my eyes on my plate and made myself busy by buttering a dinner roll.

And then I got angry. This trip was supposed to be about healing my sorrow, not reinforcing it. I had come here to escape tears that wouldn't stop, to shrug off that suffocating shroud of heaviness that wouldn't leave me alone. I was sick and tired of staring at his vacant chair, cuddling his bathrobe in bed at night instead of his warm body, talking to the empty house, and eating meals alone.

What was I doing in this group? I twisted around in my chair and glared at everyone.

I couldn't believe my ill fortune. What are the chances of me running into three people in a group of this size, whose occupations revolved around death? I decided then and there that I would figure out a polite way to stay away from them. Completely.

Early the next morning, we boarded shuttle buses that

would take us to Fort Lauderdale Executive Airport. From there we would take a small plane for the 25 minute ride to our destination in Bimini.

Our plane was scheduled to leave at 9:00 a.m. and as per instructions, we arrived just before 8:00. We poured out of the buses and entered the terminal, chattering excitedly, eager to get underway.

Our plane hadn't arrived yet, so we sat down to wait. One hour went by, then two, then three. Apparently there was a mechanical problem that needed sorting out, forcing us to wait some more. Still no plane. Lunch was ordered for us.

By this time we were getting antsy and crabby. All we wanted to do was get to Bimini and swim with dolphins. Some of the ladies had booked this trip months in advance (not last minute like me) and instead of serenely riding the waves in a turquoise ocean, here we were in a small cramped airport, growing impatient as precious time floated away like petals on the wind.

The afternoon wore on. It was frustrating to experience such a long delay, but as time passed, I noticed that friendships were beginning to form. I could feel bonding within the group as I watched people open their suitcases and pull out travel pillows or blankets to share with complete strangers. All of us had been up before dawn, so understandably some wanted to sleep. People scrunched up on cramped couches or stretched out on the bare floor. Not the best of circumstances, so it was nice to see everyone pitching in to make their travel companions as comfortable as possible. Hot tea, cold drinks, bottled water, and munchies were fetched from an adjoining room where a table had been set up specifically to accommodate our needs.

Wanting to stretch my legs, I stepped out of the terminal and onto lush green grass out in front. I didn't want to be cooped up inside, where the air was cool. I wanted warmth, I wanted sunshine. I wanted to be in the outdoors, in the tropics, on vacation. It was annoying to have to wait so long.

After a while I went back in again. Was this plane never going to arrive? I could sense an energy change; people were becoming restless, politeness had given way to apathy or boredom, some were angry, others resigned to letting events unfold as they were meant to.

I was in the latter category. Since the problem was mechanical, I felt it better to wait until the plane was ready and reliable.

Finally, finally at 3:30, the plane arrived. Euphoria rippled over us like waves and we clapped and jumped around like school children. In good spirits once again, we boarded the plane with anticipation and quickly took our seats.

Twenty minutes later (give or take a few), we landed on Bimini Island. Crew members from WildQuest greeted us as we disembarked. The air smelled like seaweed and fish with a soft moistness not felt further inland.

A quick bus ride took us to a water taxi, where an incredibly large middle-aged Bahamian fellow greeted us with a captivating smile. His dark eyes twinkled as he extended his hand to help each of us step down from the wooden dock into the boat.

"How ya doin', Lovely? Got a date tonight?" He winked at all the ladies while continuing to flash that irresistible smile. "Lookin' good, Shooga!"

Everyone laughed.

It was nice to be welcomed to the island in this warm-hearted, devil-may-care fashion. Back at home, he'd likely be reported for flirting while on duty.

By the time we arrived at the Retreat, the afternoon was drawing to a close, but we were still anxious to get out on the water. Unfortunately it didn't work out that way. The wind had picked up making for very choppy seas. Safety was the issue here, so we stayed off the boat and settled into our rooms.

The next day we were eager to begin our adventure. After a quick briefing on dolphin behavior we were ready to board the catamaran. DolphinQuest is a Lagoon 410 sailing catamaran, built for cruising the ocean. Two hulls provide stability in rough water and there was plenty of room to walk around or stretch out on towels and sunbathe. There was an interior cabin with a small kitchen, and a marine toilet located below.

As instructed, we slipped off sandals or flip-flops and left them on the dock. Towels and water bottles were provided by the crew and stowed into a waterproof chest permanently affixed to the boat. Everyone had brought sunscreen and we took turns slathering it on to each other's backs. In no time, we were off! The air buzzed with excitement and smelled like coconut oil.

Sailing out to sea was a breeze. The water had calmed down during the night for which I was thankful. There was an area of mesh on the floor of the boat where you could look right through to the ocean below. I stretched out on my stomach to take a look. The water was so clear I could see down to the sandy bottom. Schools of tropical fish rushed beneath me, caught up in the movement of the boat.

We followed the coastline for a while, but before heading out into deeper waters, the captain dropped anchor in a small secluded bay where we could start right in with snorkeling.

Those new to the sport were given instructions on the basics in a calm and relatively shallow area. I couldn't wait!

Excitedly we slipped on long froggy flippers and one by one slid off the boat into a warm turquoise bath. At last!

I had a bit of trouble with my mask at first, but once sorted out, I could relax and take a good look at what was swimming underneath me.

Tons, or should I say schools of vividly colored fish swam here and there, playing at games of hide-and-go-seek, or fish tag. They were dazzling to look at, as if all dressed up for an evening gala. Rocks and plant life were clearly visible on the ocean floor and I was delighted to be part of this underwater world. A battered wooden boat lodged in a sandbar was almost completely covered in weeds. Evidently, it must have sunk quite some time ago.

"Have you seen the shipwreck?" a couple of snorkelers called out, eager to share their find.

"Shipwreck? It's more of a dingy!" someone else sputtered, laughing.

As insignificant as this "shipwreck" was, I felt excited just to be a part of this discovery. It was fun to watch lively fish milling about the wreckage as if they were school children touring a museum. No doubt we were upsetting them and adding to the general chaos with our slippery flippers and bubbly breathing.

Moving away from the shipwreck, I decided to stop thrashing about and just float for a while. I wanted to see if by calming the water around me I could entice more fish or other creatures to appear.

A nurse shark swam into my line of vision, gracefully weaving its way along the ocean floor. It wasn't very big, as sharks go, but I felt a little nervous anyway.

"Harmless," I was told. Still, I was glad when it swam away.

A mound of porous rock which I presumed to be coral loomed up ahead. It's strange how one minute you're swimming along, scanning the area from side to side in an effort to see everything at once, when quite suddenly something new and unexpected floats or swishes into view.

That's what happened with the coral. It seemed to be coming towards me rather quickly, and yet I was the one moving.

I was just thinking about turning away in case those rocks were sharp, when I felt a firm pat on my left calf. Surprised, I stopped floating, pulled off my mask and looked around. Nobody was close to me.

Did a clump of seaweed hit my leg? Or a fish?

No, there was nothing.

I scanned the immediate area again, then a little further away to where my fellow snorkelers were busily snorkeling. All was as it should be.

David, was that you? Nothing of course. No answer and no more playful pats. Hmmm.

The sun shone down hot and strong on my face. Oh, it felt good to be here. Nothing to do but drift lazily along with the warm currents and watch as "stories from the bottom of the sea" unfolded below.

A particularly pretty yellow and purple fish caught my attention. I wondered if it was teasing me as it darted right in front of my mask and then flashed away to hide amongst the rocks. It was extraordinarily beautiful with its vibrant colors and quick, supple movements.

There were dozens more I discovered much to my surprise. They must have been waiting in the reef, until they felt safe enough to come out. I watched, enchanted, as they skillfully swam in and out, here and there, seemingly in random patterns, but somehow I had a feeling they knew exactly what they were doing, and I felt privileged to be witnessing this elaborate underwater choreography. It was I who was out of place with my fake costume and random movements.

Back on the boat, I was eager to learn the identity of my exotic fish. Opening a reference book of sea life in and around the Bahamas, I found out that my purple and yellow friend was a butterfly fish. I was amazed! I did not know butterfly fish even existed!

Coincidence? I wonder.

Coming back, the seas were very rough; a turn of events the crew had not anticipated as weather patterns had been stable earlier on, and the sky clear. Without warning the wind picked up, with a strength that was unsettling.

Some of us were seasick, myself included. It was awful. Normally, I just crawl into a hole and hide when I feel sick, but on this trip, there was nowhere to hide. It was obvious what was happening to me as I sprinted to the back of the boat and heaved over the side. However, I was not prepared for the attentiveness of my fellow passengers.

Somebody put a reassuring hand on my back while I vomited. Somebody else brought me clean paper towels to refresh myself and a glass of water to rinse my mouth.

"Empty your stomach completely," the crew advised, "you'll feel better."

I did.

Looking back I think this had been a long time in coming. I needed to purge, to get rid of the layers of grief that were still weighing heavily upon my soul; grief that I wouldn't or couldn't let go of.

Once back on shore, I headed straight for my room and a hot shower. Supper was out of the question, as I could not even think about putting anything in my stomach. Several guests knocked on my door to see if I was all right. I was touched by their kindness, but told everyone I just wanted to sleep.

The next morning, it was apparent that several others had come down with a stomach virus. So it might not have been just the stormy seas that caused my upset yesterday. I really did not feel well and decided to remain on shore that day. I could not face another day of motion, rough waters, or rocking boats. Some other people stayed behind as well.

As the day unfolded a strange and wonderful aura crept in and took over our little camp. The bonds of friendship begun earlier in that small Fort Lauderdale airport evolved as those of us who were healthy looked after the sick ones as naturally as if we'd been doing it all our lives.

Everywhere I turned, somebody was performing a healing treatment on somebody else. Caring hands placed on shoulders, wet cloths fetched to place on foreheads, feet massaged in an effort to soothe and relax. The healer with long purple hair was heard chanting to somebody in the privacy of her room.

Someone else performed hands-on healing to anyone wishing a treatment. We all looked after one another until the virus ran its course.

It was an incredible experience and totally unexpected.

Usually when fellow travellers become ill, one feels empathetic, but uninvolved. You stay away and go on with your own activities, leaving the sick to recover.

This went beyond empathy and polite concern. And ran as smoothly as a symphony with people weaving in and out of the kitchen bringing sweet herbal or nasty-tasting medicinal tea to those in need, extra facecloths, something to read, or cool fresh glasses of lemon water.

Really, I should not have been surprised, for in a Retreat setting with its focus on healing, people would naturally reach out to help one another. But it still made an impression on me as we were virtual strangers, having only just met.

Believe it or not, I made friends with the hospice nurses. We shared stories, feelings, and heartaches. I told my story over and over, which I've learned is another way to process grief. Nobody turned away; nobody grew restless with my telling. On the contrary, they gave me their full attention, as if what I was saying was important.

I felt validated.

I felt relief.

I felt supported.

"I felt so alone." My voice quivered at the memory and tears stung my eyes. Nurse Caroline leaned in to listen.

"What happened?"

Taking a deep breath to steady myself, I continued. "I felt totally abandoned by the medical profession once David went into his coma."

Nurse Caroline didn't say anything. She waited for me to go on.

"The regular staff were off since it was the weekend and nobody told me what was actually happening to my husband. They were all walking around with closed faces. No one looked me in the eye. It was as if they knew something and I didn't. I wanted to ask what was going on, but something held me back. Every time someone new entered the room, I wanted to take them by the shoulders and shout, 'What were you told? And by whom?'

But nobody said a word to me. Didn't I count? Didn't I deserve to know what was happening to my own husband? Was he dying or would he wake up?"

Nurse Caroline put a compassionate arm around me and offered a tissue. I had been wiping my nose on my towel without realizing it.

"And just where was David's doctor?" I could hear my own voice rising sharply but was powerless to stop.

"I had to waylay her the evening before! She was just leaving the hospital and I wanted her to order round the clock medication to keep him comfortable. As it was, he had awakened late in the afternoon, unable to speak. He had pointed to his head, which I knew was aching. His legs were shaking too. I was appalled that the doctor hadn't come in to see him, after the initial early morning visit. And now she was leaving!"

Chest heaving, I clenched my fists so hard my nails dug into my palms.

"You must have felt neglected." Caroline's arm tightened its firm grip around my shoulders.

"Yes, that's right! As if nobody cared!" Choking back a sob, I allowed myself to be rocked by this sympathetic woman. Someone I barely knew.

After a few moments I let out a sigh, my anger dissipating like air going out of a balloon.

"Looking back now I can see that all this was meant to be."

Caroline waited for me to explain. Minutes went by. I looked out over the ocean. The water sparkled with thousands of diamonds, waves were gentle – not a dolphin in sight.

"All the turmoil, the unfamiliar nurses, the doctor who left, my mistrust of everyone because I didn't know them, nobody staying with me – all that cleared the way for my daughter to come. She was meant to be with me. She sat with me. She knew what to do. She was the one who guided me through the process – those last moments of David's life, when I was completely frantic. It was her compassion and experience that got me through. And I will be ever grateful to her for this."

I inhaled deeply. I was done. Almost...

"But, there is something I have to tell you that's been worrying me."

I try not to squirm as if my body language would somehow give my thoughts away. But should I really tell her? Should I spill my guts to this kind woman? Will she judge me? Will she tell me I did something horrible?

Taking a deep breath and looking down at my hands, I continue with my story, "I took his oxygen mask off before he'd stopped breathing." Quickly I look up to assess Nurse Caroline's reaction. She waits placidly for me to go on. There is no look of horror on her face.

"I could see his chest jerking up and down, and knew his lungs weren't working any more... Something was telling me to get rid of that clumsy mask – it was useless now and the oxygen flow was hurting his nose... and yet I was so scared..."

I shudder at the memory, guilt heavy in my chest.

Someone walks by.

I take another second or two to compose myself, buying time. But I know there is no turning back. I have to know. I have to ask.

I shade my eyes from the sun and peer into her face hoping irrationally that she will answer my question before I ask. That I won't have to voice it.

A pair of calm blue eyes with crinkles at the corners, watch and wait.

I look away, gathering my resolve. Look back, then take the plunge.

"Did that kill him?"

Instantly, I avert my eyes – so dreadfully afraid of her answer.

"No, not at all," soothed Nurse Caroline. "In hospice, once the dying process is fully engaged, we suggest to the family to remove the oxygen, as it only prolongs what nature is trying to bring about. Don't worry, you did the right thing."

Tears of release streamed down my face and I let them come, as Caroline put both her strong arms around me in a big bear hug. I cried and cried. I don't know if anybody else was watching us, but it really didn't matter. I needed this comfort, this watershed of grief to flow.

Hours later, I was sitting with Dawn, the marine biologist facilitating this Retreat. I was fascinated by her stories of whale interaction in the Pacific Ocean. Apparently her research crew turned up a lot of interesting facts, not only about whales, but other ocean mammals as well. What a thrilling profession she'd chosen!

Then it was my turn to talk a bit about myself. I told her about losing my precious husband. I was in tears once again, but she didn't shy away. She looked me right in the eye and said,

"He's here, you know."

"What?" I blinked. This coming from a scientist?

"Yes, I can see him over your left shoulder. He's smiling."

I couldn't believe my ears. Was he really here? And why did he show himself to Dawn? I looked deep into her eyes to see if she was sincere. Did she genuinely sense David? Or was she just trying to make me feel better? A shiver ran down my spine when she did not look away. Her eyes shone with truth.

I think I'm finally beginning to "get" this healing part of the grief process. I could not understand, way back in the beginning why social workers, nurses, doctors, and all the literature I'd read linked those two words together.

Healing and Grief.

In my mind like fire and water, they just did not coexist. Grief is painful. It hurts! Who wants to grieve? Who wants to feel sorrow and despair? Who wants to wake up every morning, longing for the contentment of an old life that will never be? Grieving, in my opinion, is devastating to the soul. How can it possibly heal?

Healing, on the other hand, soothes and calms like the soft flow of water over parched skin. Healing is synonymous with hope; hope that the pain will eventually diminish to the point where we can sit up and take notice of our surroundings and begin to engage in Life once again. Hope can help to change our focus from that awful void, that ache in our heart to perhaps a teeny bit of enthusiasm for a new life just beginning to emerge, somewhere at the end of that dark tunnel.

Healing through grief, I've discovered, is a process. It takes time and pain and tears. But if you allow those tears, if you sit with your pain, if you acknowledge where you are in this life (not where you want to be – life is not lived looking backward), you will eventually come to a place of healing.

Chapter 25

Transitioning

"Surreal," murmurs Dawn at my elbow.

Surreal, I thought, liking the sound of that word as I gazed all around at endless blue; blue sea and blue sky; where only a thin line defined the horizon.

It was a strange feeling, as if there was no world beyond our boat. We were all alone here in this blending together of ocean and sky. I felt wrapped in a protective bubble or as if I were floating around in a dream where time was nonexistent. In fact nothing existed beyond this sea and sky, our boat, the other guests and a few birds. There were no houses or trees, no cities or roads, no airports or shopping malls, just a soft gentle ocean breeze, endless serene blue, rhythmic back and forth rocking in the waves as fish swam in the depths below.

What day was it?

What time was it?

Did it really matter?

I could feel myself being lulled, pulled into a state of drowsiness while cradled in the arms of Mother Ocean.

Surreal, I thought, surrendering to the extraordinary feeling of journeying in another world, of sailing away into openness and nothingness.

The rhythm of the boat carried me forward, yet I could see no progress towards the elusive horizon. It felt like we were going nowhere. There was nothing to hold on to. The old familiar world had slipped away.

Where do I go now? What do I do? I need to keep moving forward; the boat will take me wherever it is meant to. No thinking, no planning, no control.

Is this what it feels like to Transition?

Immediately my head snapped up. Where had that thought come from? Reflexively I looked around, looking for the source of that thought, as if somebody had been whispering in my ear. Nobody was paying me the slightest attention. The lady beside me had her eyes closed in repose. Some of the others were staring over the rails of the boat, scanning the seas in hopes of being the first to catch sight of a dolphin. Still others were lying on towels, soaking up the sun.

Is this what Transitioning feels like? To sail quietly and serenely through the warm haze, through gauze as soft as angels' wings? To slip out of your body and allow that eternal blue to absorb your essence? To totally and completely surrender to the gods, the heavens, to whatever will be?

Suddenly, four flying fish popped up out of nowhere and zipped off in different directions, as if on cue, startling me out of my dream-like state. It was fascinating to watch these quick silvery little fish skim over the water like dragonflies and scatter to the four winds, or back into the ocean, out of sight.

Was there a meaning to this?

David was born on the fourth day of the fourth month. Four fish, four directions. Was I reading too much into this?

"Hummingbirds of the sea," observed Tasha with a smile as she turned to see who else had watched this extraordinary performance.

Oh, I liked that vision, that concept. Hummingbirds of the sea. Could they also be butterflies? No, that wouldn't fit. Butterflies fluttered, danced and swooped. These finned creatures shot out in a straight line, more like tiny birds with whirling wings.

The next day the dolphins appeared. Swimming, frolicking, rolling and tumbling, they seemed only to live for the spreading of joy. We saw two of them swimming alongside the boat, then four, then the whole pod! It was as if they were greeting us with shouts of glee, "Welcome to our ocean. Come on in! The water's fine!"

Eagerly I donned my snorkeling gear. One by one, we slid off the boat and smoothly entered the water, not wanting to make a huge splash and frighten them away.

At first I couldn't see anything. Impatiently I swam around silently calling out to the dolphins to come and play.

Dolphins, where are you?

Tendrils of seaweed waved their long fingers at me as I scanned left and right, searching for these gentle creatures in the clear waters.

I heard shouting from the boat and looked up to see the crew pointing to a pair of spotted dolphins only a short distance away. They were tumbling and whirling around each other reminding me of kittens or puppies at play. I was so excited! This is what I'd come here for! Please come a little closer I begged the dolphins.

They did not. Instead they flipped their tails and swam further away – presumably out to sea.

But there were plenty of others around permeating the water with their distinctive humming energy. Maybe if I pretended to be part of the ocean, like a piece of algae or a sea sponge and not some strange-looking creature in a froggy mask and flippers, maybe then the dolphins would come to me. If only I could get close to them!

And then it happened! Right underneath my belly! Two huge dolphins were swirling to dance music that only they could hear, turning and twisting and showing off their white bellies, as they teased within inches of me. They were so close I could have reached out to touch them! Reflexively, I sucked in my gut so they wouldn't plough into me. I needn't have, for they wouldn't have touched me, but my reaction was instinctive.

I was enthralled. I was ecstatic! I nearly burst with pride and something else I couldn't even name. My body was rocking to the rhythm of pure dolphin energy.

"Breathe!" I reminded myself, "Through your mouth – not nose." Ha, it wouldn't be the first time I'd inhaled a nose full of saltwater in my excitement.

It was so easy to lose myself in this magical moment and just absorb the sensations coursing through my body, in the vibrations of wild and free dolphin energy in this vast ocean playground. We were free, we were dancing, we were one, breathing in sync (or so it felt in that moment). We were sharing a world of incredible, playful joy. And it all felt euphoric and so surreal. As if we were in a realm so out of the ordinary, it could not even be described in ordinary terms.

Life under the ocean and above were two very different experiences. And I was thrilled!

How grateful I felt to have plucked up the courage to listen to that inner voice, the one that encouraged me to let go of fear and embrace life. To break the cycle of despair and run to the ocean if that's what I felt like doing. To get on the plane and just go!

How fortunate I was to have chosen this Retreat, as it turned out to be a place where I was completely immersed in an atmosphere of healing, not only in the sensational energy of dolphins, but also in the people who came into my life.

I met the most nurturing and empathetic souls who listened with compassion, as I poured out my heart, who picked up my heavy burden and smashed it on the rocks. Never did I think that total strangers could so easily understand my innermost feelings and effortlessly alleviate my fears.

I actually made friends with the thanatologist, the woman who I'd rudely turned away from at that first "get acquainted" dinner in Fort Lauderdale. We had some heartfelt discussions about caring for the dying, about grieving in our society, and on a larger scale, about environmental and ecological grief – her life's work.

Did I feel David with me on this trip? Certainly. From the monarch butterfly when I'd first arrived in Florida, to the pat on my calf while snorkeling; from the butterfly fish playing in the deep to sensing his actual presence on the boat, David was with me the whole time.

As these experiences strengthen my belief that Spirit communicates through our natural world, I know others share this view as well, for I've read their accounts. So this is not "news" to the world, but it certainly was to me in the beginning of this journey.

Does that mean that when I see a butterfly, two herons, or a pair of ducks is it always David? No, not always.

But it's always in the timing: a pen in the grass as I wonder how I'm going to survive without my husband, or a heart cloud in the sky, sent to dry my tears. The cardinals and rabbits appearing on my birthday – my first lonely birthday without David.

The impeccable timing of the sun coming out from behind clouds just as I arrived at the lake last Christmas. I know it was David welcoming me, saying hello, spreading his special love and warmth all over me.

Along with uncanny timing (almost as if Spirit could read my thoughts), there must be something that sets these signs apart, a behavior they wouldn't normally engage in – like the butterfly calmly waiting to catch my attention instead of fluttering away, or the utter stillness of the silvery white moth in Sint Maarten. A hawk appearing in my backyard the week before David died was clearly out of its territory. So was the bat with wings of silver that seemed to change shape before my eyes.

Friends of mine, people in my Internet Widows Support Group describe strange occurrences that have nothing to do with animals, plants, or our natural world. Weird happenings inside their homes, like a Christmas decoration appearing mysteriously in the bathroom, before anyone had even thought about bringing up boxes from the basement, favorite songs suddenly blasting from a CD player, that had been turned off, hall lights spontaneously turning on in the middle of the night. I was reminded of my own flickering kitchen lights in those early weeks after David died, or the pens nobody could find at the notary's office.

There was a woman from Kentucky who had lost her only pair of glasses. Since she couldn't afford new ones, this was a huge problem for her. She looked all over the house, even in the closets and came up with nothing. About a week later, she went into her bedroom closet to get her purse. She stepped away from the closet and placed her purse on the floor right beside her feet. Then she heard something drop behind her. It was her glasses. There was nothing for them to drop off of. She was standing away from the bed, away from the dresser. "It was as if they were thrown at me. Very strange," she said.

There was another woman from California who had lost a very precious necklace her husband had given her for an anniversary. She had been out to lunch with friends and discovered it missing when she got home. Immediately she retraced her steps back to the restaurant. As she crossed one of the streets along the way, there it was lying intact in the middle of the pavement. Miraculously, her treasured necklace had not been run over, not walked on, not picked up by somebody else. It was as if her dearly departed husband had kept it safe until she found it once more.

Stories like these warm my heart. I am not the only one receiving messages from the Other Side. Other people do too and some of the signs are really quite astounding.

Actually, my own mother received a message from her mother who had died about a year or so earlier. Mom had been going through a rough period at that time in her life, when one afternoon, a kindly neighbor popped over for a visit. Mrs. H had baked fresh apple muffins that morning and brought some along to savor with their tea. As well, she was eager to share photos her daughter had taken a couple of years ago while on holiday in beautiful British Columbia.

There was a postcard of a peaceful garden scene slipped in among the pictures. It was taken in Stanley Park, a well-known sanctuary created in the middle of Vancouver, a bustling city in BC. Lush, green foliage framed a pond where ducks floated about or nibbled at something in the rushes. Elegant swans gliding over the water added grace and charm to the tranquil scene. Summer flowers in shades of deep pink, creamy white and violet grew in abundance along a winding foot path. Off to one side of the pond stood a huge red cedar tree. An elderly woman was sitting on a wooden bench beneath that tree, resting in the shade.

All of a sudden my mother's face blanched. Without a word she handed me the postcard. I looked at it. And then I looked again. My grandmother was sitting under that tree!!! How did my grandmother end up in a postcard? And how did it happen that this postcard was picked up by the daughter of my mother's neighbor? My grandmother didn't even live in British Columbia. She lived in Manitoba, but every summer travelled to Vancouver for a visit with her brother and sister-in-law.

At the time, I didn't know what to think. My grandmother appearing in a postcard was a mystery. It was my sister who intuited that our granny was sending Mom a message of comfort at a time when she needed it the most.

Chapter 26

Walking His Last Days

June. Eleven months. I feel like I'm now in countdown mode. Four weeks to go and then it will have been one year. One year since you passed away, my sweet Love.

What was happening this time last year?

It was a beautiful time of year – early summer. Your days in Palliative Care had fallen into a routine. There was a level of comfort in your surroundings, despite the "elephant in the room".

And yet, even though I tried to deny it, I could sense your energy depleting, going somewhere I couldn't follow. I could see you moving towards that profound tiredness described in the pamphlets for Caregivers as one of the clues that their loved one is truly slipping away.

We spent time in the Healing Garden. It was a respite, a sanctuary, somewhere we could go and pretend that everything was fine, that we were out in our own garden at home. The weather had to be perfect, not too hot, or windy, or chilly. You were still recovering from the "mask incident". The time when the nurse found you with your mask dangling over the side of the bed. Somehow that mask had accidentally slipped off in the night. No mask meant no oxygen, and for how long?

Nobody knows.

But you didn't die then. It wasn't your time. You can't imagine how grateful, how tremendously relieved I was to find you alive, sitting up in bed reading the newspaper. I was terrified you'd be gone by the time I arrived at the hospital.

June. Once again I made my pilgrimage to Thompson Park, where we scattered your ashes. I did not expect to see any signs this time. There was no pen lying in the grass like that time two weeks after you'd died, no herons, no spring robins pulling up worms in the grass or Canada geese to signal your presence. I did see butterflies flitting among the wildflowers, but they seemed to be going about their normal activities and I expected to see a few monarchs or fritillaries at this time of year.

The lake was calm on that hot sunny afternoon and the sky a serene shade of blue. It had been cloudy and cool earlier in the day, with a heaviness that played on my emotions, and I wasn't sure if it was worth the effort to go.

But after parking the car and walking down the green slopes toward the water, the sun came out and I felt a sense of peace envelop me. I was glad I'd come.

It was a Sunday that day. Not quite the anniversary of the eleventh month of your passing, but a day or two later wouldn't make any difference. There were people all about. Families picnicking and some small children playing soccer. I noticed the water level was higher than the last time I'd been here.

A loud buzzing noise caught my attention and I looked instinctively upwards. A motorboat was speeding towards me from the middle of the lake. What an awful racket! Before my brain could process that this was way too fast for a motorboat, it took off up into the air. A seaplane! I hadn't seen one of those since I was a child! Was that you flying, David?

I remember those long ago days, when your eyes would light up with such enthusiasm as we watched airplanes flying low overhead, either just taking off or coming in for a landing.

And even further back in time, when we were happy and free and travelling to tropical islands, David would watch out the window of our plane as it raced down the runway. In the seat beside him, I'd be squeezing my eyes shut and clinging to his arm as we lifted off and plunged headlong into thin air (well that's what it felt like to me). I was not a happy flyer. David was.

Not quite ready to head home yet, I thought I'd take some time to walk along the shoreline. It had been a lovely day and I was feeling mellow. I was glad to be able to come here and not feel that gut-wrenching searing pain of last summer; that shivery black loneliness that would steal over my soul as I watched sailboats in the distance. It seemed like David was in those sailboats, sailing further and further away from me, sailing on to another shore. I was supposed to feel happy that he was out of pain, not sick, but all I could feel was the separation, the space between us growing ever wider as time went on. Oh where are you, My Love?

Time and tears had helped to close the skin over that gaping wound in my heart. It would never heal completely, I knew that intuitively, but I was learning to adjust to this new world without David.

Something was moving in amongst the reeds. I waited quietly to see what would emerge. A pair of mallards, one male and one female waddled out of their hiding place and into the water. I was thrilled! A pair of ducks! I hadn't expected to see anything today. Not really.

Ducks, I remembered, meant comfort and protection and these looked to be the very same pair I'd spotted on my front lawn a couple of weeks before David was admitted to hospital last year. Oh, I know that's unlikely, but I wanted them to be the same messenger ducks, as if they somehow remembered me.

We'd never, ever seen ducks on our front lawn before. There was no water, no garden pond, not even a rain puddle to attract them, but that morning when I looked out the living room window, there they were. David was already feeling his illness tightening its grip, and I knew that if Spirit had chosen to send us ducks, our path, our way ahead would be anything but smooth.

Confusion and unrelenting sorrow had taken over my life this past year, on a scale far worse than I could ever imagine. Unbelievable as I look back, how I ever survived, particularly in those early weeks and months. It was as though half of me had been ripped to shreds by some savage monster, whose teeth left a gaping hole in my being.

One day at a time became my mantra as I struggled to hold on to my sanity. Sometimes I could only manage things moment to moment as huge tidal waves of grief suddenly and unexpectedly crashed over me. I felt myself drowning, spinning out of control as if in a giant bottomless whirlpool.

Every morning I awoke to the fresh shock that David was gone forever. It was like being punched in the stomach or slapped in the face.

He's gone, came the echoes from every room in our home.

His absence became palpable. He was not in bed beside me, not downstairs putting the coffee on, not sitting at his desk in the den writing out checks or figuring out the budget. How many times over the years did he jubilantly cry, "I've balanced the checkbook!"

"Good," I'd affirm with a smile, sharing in his enthusiasm and loving to watch his eyes light up with satisfaction. Meanwhile I'd be thinking, of course, you always do a good job with our finances. No surprise here.

I miss him.

As I move towards the second year of this journey-that-nobody-wants-to-be-on, I wonder what it will bring. I am trying to get back on track, but the tracks have all disappeared. Nothing is the same as it was. Not even something as simple as eating breakfast. One slice of toast goes into the toaster instead of three. I brew coffee for one instead of a whole pot. I eat quickly and move on to something else now, instead of enjoying a leisurely breakfast for two.

In summers past, hummingbirds would gather at the feeders just outside our kitchen window. Tiny, sparkling jewels, their wings beating so fast that all we could see was a blur. It was delightful to watch them hovering, sipping and then darting away.

Squirrels entertained us in winter as we watched them digging in the deep snow, trying to figure out where they'd buried last season's acorns. Hardy little chickadees hopped and chirped in the hedges. We could actually hear those chirps through the closed and frozen kitchen window.

In the mornings, David would share interesting news items from the paper as he scanned the pages; providing food for discussion along with our breakfast. We'd plan our day. There was no rush; in fact David could not rush once he became ill.

His lungs would not allow it. So we learned to go with the flow and move at a slower pace.

There were days when the slowness irritated me. I wanted life to be more energetic, more active like it used to be back in the days when he was working and I had friends to visit and oodles of activities to look forward to.

Now as I eat alone, I wish with all my heart to have that slowness back. To have David back. Is that selfish? Yes, decidedly yes, for that would mean David would still be sick. So I have to take those thoughts back, push them away.

Life has changed (get used to it, I'd scold myself). Simple everyday activities that constitute sharing a life are gone.

Our evenings consisted of quietly reading together or watching television.

During the day he would carry out his rehab exercises faithfully, while I'd go for a walk, practice tai chi, or take an aqua fit class. We'd shop together, eat out, take trips to the library, pharmacy, bank. Later, as his illness progressed, I'd go alone on these errands. But David being David would still want to be a part of the excursion. He'd make out "to-do" lists for me, so I wouldn't forget anything. I should have kept those lists; hung on to those bits of paper with some of David on it, those smiley faces at the end and always, always his signature: "I love you."

Now it feels like my world has been cut in half. There is half the amount of laundry to do, half the groceries to buy, half the cooking. I hardly bake anymore. David so enjoyed my desserts. Now I don't bother. Besides, how do you bake half a pie? Half a cranberry loaf?

There is less than half the amount of books to be picked up at the library. David was an avid reader, almost right up until the end; he had to make the switch to audio books when reading became too tiring.

I hate going into the library these days. I quickly choose my own books and leave, closing my eyes as I pass the "new book" section. David always kept up-to-date with his favorite authors and watched for their latest books to come out. Picking up a brand-new book by Robin Cook or James Patterson was like Christmas morning for him. He couldn't wait to get home to lose himself in the plot.

I rarely go into the pharmacy anymore, as there are no medications to pick up. There are no more deliveries of oxygen, no home care nurses or therapists. No doctor making a house-call.

My house looks empty. Most of the furniture is gone as I prepare to move. There is nobody to talk to about my inner feelings. My world has shrunk and I feel like I am contracting into myself (maybe this is why I constantly feel a need to run away to the ocean, to get away from this shrunken world, this half-empty house. I need to open up, breathe deeply and thrive, to socialize, to have people around me, especially at mealtime).

And the worst of the worst is trying to get used to living not just alone, but without David. There's a difference. Living alone is solitary, but whole. Living without David is lonely, fragmented, as if I'm only half here. I've been sliced in two.

It feels strange. I feel strange.

Certainly not the same person I was, and never will be again.

I miss talking to him about nothing. I miss talking to him about everything. All the important decisions I have to face are on my own now without his intelligent, sensible, and well thought-out advice. Issues such as: house renovations, investment strategies, retirement plans, legalities and real estate decisions, and most important anything and everything of a medical nature.

He was a whiz. Knew everything.

In fact, Brenda called him a walking encyclopedia.

I've picked up another virus. This whole year I've been sicker than I have in the past 10 or more. Having just gotten over a stomach virus, it seems I've picked up a chest cold. I wake in the night coughing. Early mornings are bad too, until my lungs clear. During the day I can function, go about my daily routine, but I'm tired.

It struck me. Am I walking in David's footsteps? The last weeks of his life? It's as if I'm walking a religious trail or some path that has specific stops along the way.

Now it's June. David has less than four weeks to live, if we go back a year. In my head, I return to that vulnerable time we spent together when he was in the palliative care ward. Had he started his end-of-the-road downslide, his final descent? I don't remember the exact date in June. And I didn't write anything down. A little voice in my head kept urging me to write so I'd remember this unfolding journey, but I just didn't have the strength. It was stressful enough worrying about David being so sick, so close to the end of his life and being so far away from me.

Every night just before leaving his hospital bed, I'd look deep into his eyes and tell him how much I loved him.

"I love you more," he'd reply with a brave smile, the trace of a shadow flickering across his face.

"Oh, no, I love you even morer."

"Impossible! I love you mucher, morer and even mostest!" We were like kids, playing a silly game, but it felt good.

And then I'd look longingly at him, absorbing every little detail of his being, as if I could take all of him into my body and keep him safe with me forever.

Would this be the last time?

Would I get a call in the night?

I hated to leave him looking so pale and thin in his hospital bed. I hated to go home. Home was wherever David was. It was not that big empty house we once shared with such love.

Two weeks to go before the anniversary of David's death. I am drawn once again to Thompson Park. I spend an hour or so in the pleasantly warm sun, walking the shoreline, surprising probably the same two ducks I saw the last visit. Thinking back to that tearful ceremony of scattering his ashes, I look out over the water to try and locate the exact spot where David's boys and I stood that beautiful summer day to perform our morbid task of emptying their father, my husband's remains into the flowing currents of the river.

There is not much of a breeze today and the lake is smooth. No boats are in sight, but I take a few moments to scan the horizon anyway and drink in the sounds of early summer: droning insects, gentle lap at my feet, piercing cries overhead, and just as I'm turning to go, a quiet sailboat slides into view.

Ah, at least there is one sailboat today. The day we scattered his ashes, there were a few, I remember. Watching sailboats in the distance always brings memories of a lesson I learned in one of my Bereavement Support Group meetings:

A cluster of people are standing on the edge of a seashore, watching a sailboat depart on its final journey.

"She's gone," they mourn huddling together for comfort as she sails out of sight.

But then a great cry is heard from the opposite shore where we see another group of people excitedly waving and cheering as they

spot the boat sailing into view.
"Here she comes!"

This scenario is intended to change perspective, to bring hope to those left behind. All is not lost, merely shifted as their loved one is transported to the Other Side and welcomed with open arms.

Back at home, I put on the kettle. Not that I really need a cup of tea, it's comfort I crave and somehow the simple act of sipping tea soothes the spirit and gives my hands something to do. Taking my tea outside on the deck, I pull David's garden chair into a warm sunny spot and sink into it. There are many trees in my backyard; too many I think, too much shade and not enough sun. It seems I'm always moving my chair, as if chasing patches of sun to sit in.

Our backyard faces south, but the sun rarely reaches the grass, which has all but withered away. Moss carpets the yard and weeds poke up from the earth with free abandon.

A baby squirrel races along a tree branch and into the safety of its nest. Another follows and then another and then one more. Four young squirrels in all. New life, a new season, life moving on.

How can this be? How can the world keep turning without my true love? How can life go on, how can *my* life go on?

By simply changing the focus.

Oh really?

And just where did that thought come from? It was probably something I'd read earlier on, a technique I thought sounded worth trying. Did it work back then? I don't remember. Could I really just shift the focus of my thoughts enough to turn my life around? To pull myself up and out of this bog of despair before I sink right down to the very bottom?

Leaving David behind while I go on with my life is a concept my brain cannot accept. It's called Moving On. How could I possibly do that? The last time I saw him he was in that cold hospital bed. How could I leave him there, all alone? No that's not me. That's not the kind of couple we are. We are a good couple, a happy couple, a married in-love couple. We are two halves of a whole. We don't leave each other no matter what. I cared for him for years. How could I abandon him in the morgue, or in the funeral home, or even in the ashes scattered to the elements? How could I pick myself up, dust myself off and walk away as if all was well. How could I ever turn my back on him when he needs me the most?

It makes no sense at all.

And yet my rational mind knows it makes perfect sense.

He's gone.

It knows his body is no longer in the hospital, morgue, or funeral home. I will not drive to Mount Sinai Hospital, ride the elevator up to the third floor and peek into "his" room. He will not be there.

Oh, I've been tempted over this past year. Once or twice, I've wanted to do just that. But I restrained myself. I knew it would only bring on heartache. Driving that familiar route, entering the parking lot, smiling at the attendant (would she be the same one?), putting out my hand for the ticket, looking for a parking space, walking through those heavy glass outer doors, riding the elevators or rushing up the stairs to Room 1316?

Would the same nurses and volunteers be there? Would they recognize me and wonder what on earth I was doing back here?

Months later?

Would I go into the kitchen and watch as somebody heated up coffee or food in that microwave for their loved one? The same microwave I'd used months before? How would I react when looking into "his" room? No, I did not want to go down that path.

But I had thought about it.

Just to make sure. Just to make sure there hadn't been some

terrible mistake and he was still there, sitting up in bed, oxygen mask on, waiting patiently for me to come and wrap my arms around his frail body.

My David. My Forever-husband.

How to change my thinking, change the focus? How to turn away from that deep pit of despair, that swamp of heavy emptiness long enough to take a breath? Why should I shatter the illusion that he is still alive somewhere either back in the hospital or on a long unplanned trip? (You can see how strong and protective the role of denial plays in the grieving/healing process.) How will I ever transform those stark feelings of terror and betrayal into hope, courage, and peace of mind one day?

Slowly. Gradually. Increment by increment, degree by degree until the focus shifts ever so slightly away from profound and excruciating loss.

Away from heartache and tears.

Never mind for the moment just where you are going.

Focus on the moving part, the steps. And as you take this first baby step, leave behind the guilt. Leave behind those feelings of abandonment that churn around in the pit of your stomach. Those awful feelings as if you've just stepped into a lifeboat, safe and snug, while leaving him behind to drown. While leaving him to go down with the sinking ship.

Let go of betrayal. No one has betrayed you. We are not in control of Life and Death.

And since we are now moving, we have to go somewhere. Our road has changed, the old path gone, like the one that was swept away by the "broomdog" in *Alice in Wonderland.*

Where do we go?

Just for an instant, we take our focus off that deep wound Death has inflicted to look ahead, to search for a new road. And in that instant the bleeding slows and light begins to seep into our consciousness. As we reach for that glimmer of Light and hang on tight, the terrible darkness recedes and a soothing ray of hope streams in, encouraging us to surrender and begin to walk the Path of Acceptance.

That horrible "A" word we did not want to know back at the beginning of this journey-that-nobody-wants-to-be-on. After all, Acceptance means we approve, we agree, doesn't it?

No, not at all.

David Kessler says in his book *On Grief and Grieving,* "Acceptance is often confused with the notion of being all right or okay with what has happened. This is not the case. Most people don't ever feel okay or all right about the loss of a loved one. This stage is about accepting the reality that our loved one is physically gone and recognizing that this new reality is the permanent reality... we learn to live with it."

In other words, Acceptance means we've come to a place of peace. We are learning to live with a situation that simply cannot be changed.

Ever.

As I stop looking for bits of him all over the house, I am changing my focus. As I stop opening drawers just to gaze at his underwear, or go into the medicine cabinet and smell his toothbrush, as I stop visualizing him at the kitchen sink, or filling the coffee maker or raking leaves in the backyard, as I stop listening for his breathing in the night, his key turning in the front door lock, I am changing my focus.

Gradually.

From what was to what comes next. From how things used to be with all the love, commitment and devotion of our blessed marriage, to "I wonder what the future holds for me?"

A hint of curiosity, a wee bit of anticipation are clues. I'm not stuck in that swamp of sorrow and lethargy any more. I want to get moving.

Somewhere. Anywhere.

I begin to understand that I *have* changed, life has somehow intervened and changed me when I wasn't looking. Through all the pain, tears, regrets, unhappiness, grief, somehow, little by little, the insides of me have transformed.

Who am I now?

Certainly not the same person in that loving, happy, fulfilling relationship when David was alive. Certainly not that same sorrow-filled, confused, paranoid, out-of-control Widow. Unhappily the Loving Couple is gone. Thankfully, the Out-of-Control, weeping at the drop of a hat, feeling betrayed Widow has gone too, but who am I now?

As the focus changes from what was to what will be, I begin to look forward.

Moving On – such an emotionally charged concept.

Moving On – am I leaving my beloved behind? But where is he? How can I leave? These early questions were agonizing, they tore at my soul and distorted my thinking. But they do fade slowly, not only with the passage of time, but in the process of letting go. And that's the beginning of Acceptance.

Moving On. I still don't like that expression, so I'll change it to Moving. Moving On still flickers with betrayal. Moving, on the other hand, is growing, is evolving, is going forward, like walking or swimming or riding a bike. We need to move, we have to move or we become stagnant.

So I'll walk, I'll swim and I'll ride my bike. I'll grow and evolve. But I'll never leave him behind, because David will always be in my heart. I won't stand at his grave and weep forever. Nor would I want him to stand at mine. Life flows and I will learn to flow with it.

The last week of June and David's last days here on earth. I remember taking him out in the Healing Garden, where he could savor a bit of sunshine on his face. Could he actually take fresh air into his lungs? Breathe it in like someone without lung disease would do naturally?

I don't really know as he was wearing a mask that covered most of his face ensuring he would receive as much pure oxygen as possible. But at least he could feel the freshness of early summer air caressing his skin and watch as goldfish swam around in the pond. It was such a peaceful Healing Garden, bittersweet in its serenity.

I remember his good days and his bad. When did his final decline actually begin? I think it was a couple of weeks before he died.

He had not been feeling at all well and looked it. He was feverish and coughing more than usual, making us think it might be a virus or cold. What worried me most was that profound tiredness I'd read about that comes at the end of a life. It seemed to be creeping over David, stealing his energy.

And his glazed eyes. I hated it that the spark had gone out of his eyes.

The doctor looked in on him and prescribed antibiotics. I did not know they prescribed antibiotics in Palliative Care. However, one thing this journey continues to teach me is to never give up hope. You don't stop treating the patient because the End is near. You do whatever it takes (within reason) to keep the patient as healthy and comfortable as possible.

As time goes on, it feels like a sort of a "countdown", as if I'm Walking The Path of His Last Days. I am drawn to that time last June and can clearly visualize David in his hospital bed in the Palliative Care Ward. I can hear his voice as we converse together. I look at the kitchen clock in the morning and remember that at this hour, I was packing up a lunch to take with me to the hospital. In the early evening, I look at the time and know that I was helping David get ready for bed before leaving to go back home. It feels like I'm reliving that whole experience, as if we are taking this journey towards its inevitable ending once again.

Only this year I'm alone.

David lives only in my memory.

My activities are different now too. Our house is up for sale, so I have to spend more time than I normally would on upkeep and maintenance. I am journaling and writing in my blog, whereas last year I did not have the strength. I attend sessions at my Bereavement Support Group. I travel now, seemingly at the drop of a hat.

My time is spent on me.

I'm not a Caregiver any more. I babysit more frequently than I did when David was home and needing me. The youthful energy of my grandchildren helps to anchor me in the real world.

This virus will not go away. My body is feeling tired, sore and nauseated. The coughing is getting worse. Am I taking on David's symptoms at the end of his life? Headaches and nausea were common in his last few years, more so towards the end of his life. I don't feel hungry most days. David's appetite diminished over the years, but particularly in hospital. And I've stopped exercising. I'm just too worn out, and the dolphin energy, the glow from my last ocean trip is gone. I no longer practice early morning tai chi.

As I go through yet another coughing fit, I wonder. Is this how he felt over the last months and weeks of his life? Coughing uncontrollably and gasping for breath?

How frightening!

When his mask accidentally fell off, did he panic? He must have. Did he feel frightened? Most certainly, particularly once the breathing treatments stopped working and he began coughing up blood. I think we both knew the end was close, but neither one of us wanted to give that thought power by speaking it aloud. We both hoped for a miracle, but intuitively knew that this time, there would be no reprieve.

The Lines between us are blurry...

Words are not necessary, and only drain energy away from David's waning body. Besides, I know instinctively how he feels.

"Do you feel strong enough for a turn in the Healing Garden, sweetheart?"

"Yes, I'd like that .. but if it doesn't feel good..."

"we'll come back right away," I finish for him with a reassuring smile.

I bring his wheelchair over next to his bed. Hook up two giant oxygen cylinders to the back of it. David sits at the edge of the bed and waits until his breathing is comfortable.

There is no rush.

When he is ready, I help him transfer from the bed into his wheelchair. We wait a few moments more while he catches his breath. I have gotten so used to seeing him this way, so extremely short of breath that it hardly makes an impression on me anymore.

This is David. This is where he is here and now. COPD has robbed him of his energy, his mobility, his day-to-day functioning, and soon also his very life. I can only imagine how someone who happened to walk into the room would react to seeing this middle-aged (not elderly) man struggling for every breath with every movement. They would probably think his life was over. Well, he's not dead yet. He still has some good moments to cherish, some loving slices of life to savor.

Once I've carefully unhooked his oxygen line from the wall and hooked it up to the portable cylinders, we are ready to roll. Out of his room and down the hall. It must feel strange to be whisked away from the safety of his private room, his refuge. There were weeks in the beginning when he was too fragile to leave his bed, much less the room.

We take the small elevator down three floors to the main level. I hold my breath all the way down, trying not to think of what might happen if the elevator malfunctioned and we got stuck. With a reassuring thump, like the safe landing of an aircraft, we're down. Out of the elevator, down another hall and into the cafeteria. Sliding doors to the Healing Garden open automatically as we approach.

And we're outside! Clean fresh air on our faces, warm sunshine washes over us. I push David's wheelchair over the stone paths, past the fish pond towards a nice shady spot. Pretty flowers grow in abundance along the walking paths. There are lots of others out and about as today is Sunday. Families come to visit.

Some patients stroll with the aid of a walker. Some are being pushed in a wheelchair. One thing they all have in common – the need for oxygen. There are portable cylinders and nose hoses on every patient. I saw only one other full oxygen mask, on a tired-looking rather petite woman. Her husband was by her side, looking completely overwhelmed. I smiled at them as we walked by, but nobody smiled back.

John, David's eldest, came to visit. It was good to see him; good to visit in the fresh out-of-doors, rather than upstairs in the hospital room.

Twice more we make the trip down to the main level, through the cafeteria, and into the sanctuary of the Garden. We've never been able to do that three times in one day, but the weather was so nice, it did David the world of good. I watched him tilt his face to the sun, and let out a small sigh of contentment. I was grateful that he was able to relax a little bit in this healing atmosphere. And this was to be his last time outside. His last time in the Garden. His last Sunday on Earth.

A shimmer, a glimmer in the summer sunlight; very subtle, very slight, just enough to catch my attention. The sun reflecting on something with wings. Something enormous with wings.

"Oh look," I called to the grandchildren, "come and see."

Resting on the grass close to the house was the biggest butterfly I'd ever seen. Its wingspan must have been a good six inches, large enough to fit on a tea saucer.

We moved in for a closer look. The butterfly sat very still and did not fly away, even as we approached. Its wings flickered a little, but it held fast to the twig or leaf where it rested.

"Be careful," Brenda warned the children. "Don't touch it, let it be."

Brenda had called around the animal rescue centers and Insectarium but got nowhere. They did not do butterfly rescue, nor did they give any advice on how to help. The Insectarium people just kept referring her to others, and my daughter did not have time to sit on the phone. Instead she e-mailed them a picture and they were able to identify Annie.

Annie is a hyloper cecropia, a moth really. And I found out via the Internet that this was the biggest butterfly/moth in North America! Strange that I've never seen one before. But then perhaps not so strange, as their life cycle is really only seven to 10 days. They mate in early June; the female lays about 300 eggs and then rests in a state of torpor for the remainder of her life. The male goes on to mate with as many as three females and then he too succumbs.

The adults do not eat.

End of June, David's last days on earth. The last two days of his life, he spent in a dream-like state, in a coma. He did not eat.

And then I found out by the size of its antennae, that Annie was not a female after all. She was really a He. Annie died on day seven.

"I've brought pictures from my trip to Paris," said Dr. Q to David one evening. Unusual, I thought, but rather nice of her. When do doctors have the time to bring pictures in to show their patients? Or was it because David is a doctor himself and she felt a special kind of bond?

David was tired all the time. I could sense it, could see it in his eyes, which were glazing over now and looking inward. Oh how I missed that twinkle, that sparkle in his eyes as we shared a smile, a joke. That spark meant life, and I wanted to ignite that spark with my own eyes and hold on to it forever.

But even with David's fatigue, I sensed that looking at carefree

one afternoon, I noticed one of the lady relatives sitting outside the patient's door. It was not a good sign. It meant that there was something serious going on within the sanctuary of that sick room. I could hear bursts of crying from within, but this lady met my eyes with a smile on her face. I was rather surprised and thought that perhaps I had been wrong in my assessment that one of her relatives was either engaged in the dying process, or had just died.

I smiled back then looked away, but a moment later, couldn't help looking at her again. She looked so composed, so calm and quiet. Yet this time as I looked a little more closely, I could see clearly the tired lines around her eyes; the sadness that was concealed behind her sweet smile. I was touched by her peaceful persona, her calm acceptance of this terrible situation, and wondered if her family member had been very old, or had suffered dreadfully and was now at peace. And then they were gone too.

This is what happens in Palliative Care. You see new people arriving. Nod in the hallway as they become familiar; perhaps chat a bit in the patients' kitchen while using the microwave or making coffee or tea, and then one day they're gone.

And you know.

Is Annie's death symbolic of a final good-by? Will I stop seeing butterflies and moths in the Second year? Of course I'll see them, but will I see significant ones, ones with messages from the Other Side?

As I learned earlier on, ancient people believed butterflies to be a powerful symbol of transformation, of metamorphosis. The transition from cocoon (death) to winged butterfly (rebirth) brought hope to surviving relatives. Their loved ones had "survived" the journey into the Unknown and were returning with the message that all was well.

Will Nature continue to be Heaven's messenger, to be the conduit from David's world to mine?

There were other strange occurrences I couldn't explain. A sudden flickering shadow at the edge of my vision disappeared the instant I turned to look. A few chosen flowers in my garden glowing with an ethereal light on a cloudy day. Why some and not others, I have no idea.

I received unexpected thought messages from my mother the night before she died: memories of myself as a young child, Mom taking my hand as we walked to school that first frightening day, Mom's soothing voice and gentle touch as I retched over the toilet bowl, Mom teaching me how to pick wax beans in our garden, pull up carrots and tease raspberries off their hull – only the ripe ones! Mom singing as she carried my birthday cake into the dining room where our family waited expectantly and I wiggled around in my chair, barely able to contain my excitement, for it was *my* special day.

I remember receiving nauseating waves of anxiety that could only be coming from my father as he suffered a fatal heart attack at home – alone. I had no idea why I was feeling so distressed, until we found Dad stretched out on the floor in the upstairs hallway.

Sometimes out-of-the-blue, I feel as if I'm somewhere else, lost in space or hovering between worlds for a few moments. This doesn't happen often – very rare, in fact, and I don't find it frightening or weird. It's the same feeling, same soft, cottony sense of timelessness I experience when I open myself to the world of creativity. As I lose myself in writing, singing, or working in the garden, those gentle, not quite of this world feelings envelop me.

It must be like channeling; information sent from one world to another; from Across the Veil to Our World.

One woman I know tells me she "channels" her dead husband's humor. She never had a sense of humor. He did. And now it seems as if he has passed his on to her. Who knew?

Will everything stop now as I prepare to enter the Second

in his chest. Could it be just an infection? Would he respond to the antibiotics and breathing treatments ordered? Would he, please God, get better?

"You're really feeling miserable with this, aren't you," said Dr. B, sitting right up next to him on the bed. It was not a question, but a statement.

She knew. She looked into those weary, glazed eyes and knew.

Canada Day was approaching, with celebrations and fireworks to take place in Ottawa, our nation's capital. Peter and Marcela invited Brenda and her family to spend the holiday and asked me to join them.

We were to drive to Petrie Island, a short distance away from Peter's house, where activities such as face-painting, crafts, games, puppet shows, and races were to take place. There would be popcorn, cotton candy and ice cream for the kids. Afterwards, instead of going home, the plan was to have a picnic supper under the trees or right on the beach, depending on how hot it turned out to be that day.

Should I go?

I really don't want to be away from my home, distracted from Walking His Last Days. But the invitation is tempting. Spending time with my children and grandchildren celebrating Life would be a better choice, wouldn't it?

Should I not take part in celebrating Life?

Thursday, his last fully conscious day on Earth. He was weak and tired, but managed with his usual good humor to carry on as normally as possible. We drank coffee as was our custom and ate our meals together. I remember his "last supper" that evening.

"I did not think I could eat it all," he said setting his fork down and turning to me with a look of pleased surprise on his face.

Oh good, I was thinking, maybe now he'll get better.

That evening I sat on his bed and held him close. He asked me to

"None?" I was surprised by his answer.

"Well, just a hawk."

Strange, I thought at the time, now why did he only visualize a bird? No land animals. It was only later I figured it out. He was leaving his body, leaving this earth and the hawk was his guide. According to Ted Andrews, the author of Animal Speak, *"the hawk is a powerful bird that can awaken visionary power and lead you to your life purpose. It is the messenger bird and whenever it shows up, pay attention. There is a message coming."*

His last fully conscious evening and we were so lucky, so incredibly fortunate to have been able to spend this precious time together in this loving and comforting way.

The Lines between us are blurry... and so were our bodies as we cuddled together for the last time that David was fully and consciously alive.

July 1st, Canada Day. I went. To Ottawa. To celebrate with my children and grandchildren. The weather was hot. We went to the beach, had our picnic and a BBQ supper. I stayed overnight and spent the whole next day with my family too. I thought of David off and on, as he lay in his morphine sleep a year ago.

Driving home that evening I let the tears flow. It had been a wonderful couple of days. My heart felt lighter as I watched the little ones playing in the water, on the swings, in the sand. Once again I was struck by the passage of time as I watched my own children being the parents.

When did that happen?

It wasn't that long ago *I* was the parent with small children. The Wheel of Life turns and now they are the ones with small children, and I the grandmother.

Climbing into my own bed that night, I felt a burning pain in my chest. Was it sore muscles from carrying heavy toddlers (which I love to do), or gardening, or is this how David felt the night before he died? Was his heart hurting?

mantel, kitchen table, bedroom dresser and night stands. It seemed I had to light up every corner of every room.

Then I lit them. Every single one. As the morning blended into afternoon, I felt my heart rate speed up. I was back in that dreaded space, Palliative Care at Mount Sinai Hospital.

I could visualize the nurses coming and going, the morphine injections, David's changing breathing patterns, my agitation and helplessness, his brother visiting, the priest's arrival. I remember Brenda calling the nursing station because she could not get through to me. I was not answering my cell phone.

That hovering in the air, like angels' wings, waiting...

Brenda strode through the door. Her calming presence was a balm to my raw nerves. She took one look at David as he struggled to breathe, and knew.

"It won't be long now, Mom."

We sat on either side of his sleeping form, watching... I held his hands, stroked his dear face, and whispered words of love...

Moments ticked by. The sounds of hissing oxygen filled the room. The priest had come and gone. Last Rites had been administered.

I sensed the change in his breathing first before I actually heard it. It was quickening as if in anticipation of something momentous about to happen. There was an edge to the quality of his breathing, almost like a warning.

Instantly alert, I scanned David's face. It remained unchanged.

He looked calm, yet strangely detached. As if he was ready to go.

Well, I wasn't ready to let him go!

I shivered and moved closer to my sleeping husband, as if protecting him, or seeking his protection from a force I was not ready to comprehend or even acknowledge.

The rhythm of his breathing changed yet again. It was coming in short, panting bursts now, reminding me of a woman about to give birth. Earlier on, I remember watching his legs trembling in the bed, reminding me of the time my own legs trembled and shook as I was

I looked at the clock – 3:50 p.m.

I burst into tears and felt my world shatter all over again.

Book II

Silver Dragonfly Wings

Part I

Chapter 1

Year Two

JULY 4, 2011. One year and one day since you vanished.

I am now entering the year of "seconds". What will it hold for me? Can I really continue on without you? Are you still okay, wherever you are?

JULY 22nd, our anniversary. Would I receive a sign from David? This was the second anniversary without him alive and in the flesh.

It was almost sundown. The day had passed smoothly. I started off by cleaning up my desk, or rather David's desk. Paying bills, organizing bank statements, looking after bits and pieces that I'd put off simply because I prefer to write. Or e-mail, or garden, or be with my grandchildren. Anything other than desk work.

"Hmmm, sounds like a David sort of day," was Brenda's astute comment over the phone. And she was right. David would enjoy balancing the checkbook, "getting lost in numbers," as he liked to call it.

I thought about going to Thompson Park, where we'd scattered his ashes a year ago, but something held me back. The weather was uncomfortably hot, but that wasn't the whole reason. I just felt like celebrating life, rather than remembering his death. Death, as we all know, does not go away. You can't "forget" about it. It hits you in the face every day, every waking moment until you forcibly push it aside.

And change your focus.

Today, I wanted to remember the good times. Our wedding day, holding hands, our first kiss –those cherished memories

back of Other Chair, the one that will always be empty.

It rested for a few moments before darting away. But then it was back. Closer this time, fixating me with its enormous eyes as if issuing a challenge. What was I supposed to do?

Dragonflies, I remembered, were ancient symbols of transformation, of illusion, of changes in the wind.

And before I could figure out what that was all about – it was gone. As if spirited away, leaving a silvery trail of rainbows in its wake.

David? Was that you?

I was about to get up and head out for my evening stroll, when a whirring of wings had me turning around in my chair. A shimmering ruby-throat hovered about looking perplexed (if hummingbirds can do that).

Shoot! It was looking for the feeder, which I'd brought into the house a couple of days ago to clean, and left lying on the garage floor. Darn! Sorry, little hummer, wish I could offer you something else.

A glint, a flash and it was gone, zooming up into the trees.

Could this be the "anniversary" sign? Or was it all of the above? A whole bouquet of signs, instead of flowers?

Hummingbirds are symbols of joy. Does this mean David is feeling joy? Can Spirits do that? Or is he reminding me that life needs to be celebrated? That I need to be "in joy" instead of drowning in tears.

Happy with the glimmering magic of tiny wings, I set out for my evening walk with a growing feeling of contentment.

I was afraid I would not receive any signs once that first terrifying year was done. Not that they wouldn't be welcome. On the contrary! Any small wisp of a sign, glimmer of communication would be like a warm hug, a shared secret, an affirmation of a love so strong it could never be broken.

Yet butterflies had been scarce this summer and I worried that David was fading away, leaving me far, far behind (Was

It was growing dark as I neared another wooded area not far from home. Dry leaves and twigs make up the forest floor and I could hear little animals scuttling about in the underbrush, as if preparing for bed.

A tiny light blinked at me from deep in the woods. Oh, it must be a firefly! Those wee glowing faeries that seem to appear in the night as if by magic. How blessed I felt. As if a gift from the heavens.

Shivers up my bare arms. And deep love in my heart.

Hugging myself I headed for home.

I submitted an article for the *Montreal Gazette's* series: *Transformed by Travel*. And it was accepted! I was thrilled! Imagine! They chose my story to print in the newspaper! For everyone to see!

I wrote about my trip to St. Maarten, eight months after David's passing. At that time I felt I was spiraling out of control; relentless pain dominated my days and I could not make it stop! Taking a trip seemed ludicrous at the time, as if running away could change the fact that I was a widow – that dreaded "w" word.

But go I did – and was surprised to feel a stirring of happiness, a shift away from the heaviness of grief.

Immersed in warm Caribbean sun, gentle breezes, cheerful voices, and easygoing contentment of Island people as they went about their daily activities, lifted my spirits, blessing me with hope. To say the experience was transformative was a given; I came home sun-kissed, hair in beach braids, ragged edges of my soul soothed for however long this glow would last, and above all else – with a longing to embrace Life once more.

The editor of this series of articles was David Johnston. My husband's name was David John. Coincidence yet again?

With this small publishing success spurring me on, I drove out to Thompson Park to inspect a willow tree I'd noticed growing by water's edge. It was time to get started making a

unsuspecting swimmer into its treacherous depths. Nausea twisted my gut and sweat trickled down my neck. I stopped the car and sat for a minute taking in huge gulps of air. I did not think I would fall so hard or so deep in this second year.

It hurt.

All my talk of healing, of moving on in life, of focusing on the gifts of our relationship rather than the agony of loss seemed like pure nonsense right about now.

Oh, I know it's a process. I knew I'd have relapses, but I did not think they would hurt as much as they do. The only thing I can say is that now they are familiar. As I feel myself dropping down to the bottom of the well, I don't panic anymore.

I let myself go. I give up. I surrender.

I know I will reach bottom – eventually.

And I also know that this too will pass. I will find my way back up to the top.

Not my idea of a good time, but at least it's not shocking anymore. I don't shiver and shake, terrified that I'll never survive. Instead this pattern of being overpowered by the Grief Wave has become all too familiar.

People tell me the second year is harder than the first. I'm not sure yet. I know that everyone's journey is different. Yes, the searing, burning rawness has tempered to a quiet simmer. But the empty hollowness is still there. The longing for and missing him is still there. Even though for the most part, I have Accepted his death, every once in a while, I turn to ask him something. I hear noises in the night and think he's downstairs in the kitchen plugging in the kettle for tea. I thought that after the one year mark all that would go away.

It doesn't.

You can't just "turn off" a person's essence as easily as clicking off a lamp.

I have a love/hate relationship with my Bereavement Support Group. I don't want to be there. I don't want to be part of a

Soothing, caressing feelings washed over me. Oh how sweet, David, what a nice way to start the day. Now why is he sending me these cards today?

Two days later as I was in the garden, tending my flowers – it clicked.

Time seems to just go! It flows, like a bubbling stream. September 3rd is here already and this time I was prepared.

After breakfast I slipped into the backyard and placed four candles under Grandfather Oak. No one was about, but still, I did not want to contend with nosy neighbors. On to Tim Hortons to grab a couple of coffees, as if we were right back at the beginning.

David's I poured under Grandfather Oak, as if I'd never stopped. The day was balmy, so I took some time to just sit and sip. Relax and pray. David's face appeared in the clouds, as if he were smiling down on me.

The day passed pleasantly enough and by evening I was ready for my usual stroll. Exiting the back door, I circled around the house and came face to face with a turkey feather lying at the side of the driveway.

It was very long and copper/bronze with black flecks. Now I'd never have known that it once belonged to a turkey, except for the fact that I actually saw a real live one.

Right here in our driveway.

It was five or six years ago one warm August morning. Dressed in T-shirt and shorts, I opened the front door, yelled over my shoulder, "Bye, David!" and left for my walk.

Standing on the front porch for a moment admiring the garden across the street, I had no idea a huge bird was pecking diligently at something in our driveway just a few feet away.

What beautiful rudbeckia Susan and Jim have! Why aren't mine as vibrant?

So focused was I on their flowers, I didn't even see Mrs. Wild Turkey until I was almost on top of her!

happy memories close and not give in to sorrow?

I left Turkey Feather right where it was, because it was kind of mangled-looking and rain-soaked. But each day as I passed by, I gave thanks for its important message.

Then one day I changed my mind. Why keep staring at a turkey feather in my driveway? And thanking it as if it were a person? How silly! Why not bring it inside and place it on my fireplace hearth, next to mini pumpkins and autumn candles? Thanksgiving was just around the corner, and it would add a nice decorative touch.

So, I smoothed it down and brought it in.

The next morning, while I was meditating, a different message came to me. The turkey feather was not a reminder of happier times long gone, but a message for now, for the present.

"I am here. Not gone. Here. With you."

Those words just popped into my head as I drew the *Life Everlasting* affirmation card.

Ah, that is a much more powerful and potent message. Thank you, David! I like that!

My house is up for sale. Not a very comfortable time in my life. Yes, I realize it is time to move on. To leave our safe, loving nest. To leave the home we shared with such enthusiasm and bliss. But David is gone now and I don't want to live here alone.

And yet, how can I leave? Leave our bedroom? The one we've shared for the past 15 years? His clothes are still hanging in the closet (well some of them, okay most of them). I can see him sitting at the sink in our bathroom, waiting for me to come and help him wash. But no, I should concentrate on happier days, not on sick days when he was too weak to wash himself.

In happier times, we'd shower together. Run to the bedroom and make love. It seems like such a long time ago now. We had the world at our fingertips, love, happiness, success in our careers, family, good health.

Chapter 2

Autumn

So much is happening these days. It's the end of October now and I am preparing to move. My energy feels scattered. But let me back up a bit.

On October 9th the house was sold. April 9th it went up for sale. A year and a day after David was admitted to hospital and never came home.

A young couple came in for a visit on October 3rd (yes I know – the 15 month anniversary of his passing). They arrived at 8:30 a.m., spent 20 minutes in the house and wrote up an Offer to Purchase the next day. I was shocked! Usually people come back for a second or even a third visit before deciding to buy, but these people knew right away.

We haggled over the price a bit, as is usual, but the outcome was the same. Sold. Conditional on building inspection and their finances being approved for a mortgage.

The building inspection went well, except that an abundance of sand was discovered in the French drains. Not good. Tomorrow the specialists arrive to excavate.

In the meantime, I'm out searching for a place to live. Nothing seems to fit, nothing is as nice as the house I've just sold, even with the outdated (but cozy) kitchen and crummy garage floor.

I check out apartments and condos. Waterfront units catch my attention and have me drooling. Living practically, I should rent something inexpensive. However, I feel the same way I did after my divorce back in 1993, before David came into my life.

At that time, I rented an expensive townhouse (one I could barely afford) because I wanted to make a good home for my children. I visualized a three-bedroom cottage with finished basement, garage, and a decent-sized backyard to sit in and

Startled, I looked over at the employees. Nothing special. Two regular guys stocking shelves, totally oblivious that they were "messengers" from the Spirit World. I wonder what they'd think if I told them. Oh, I was tempted!

"Excuse me, do you have any idea that you're channeling messages from my late husband? His name was David, you know."

I think they'd run – as far and as fast as they could!

At home during the evening the phone rang. It was someone from McGill University Alumni asking for David. Now in the early days and months that kind of call would have sent me spinning out of control. Are they stupid? Don't they update their lists? He's not here anymore! Take him off your list! Don't they realize I wish with all my heart David could be attending whatever function they were calling about?

Of course they don't. It's just a job to them and those calls don't spook me anymore. Time does have a way of smoothing over the rough, sharp jolts of pain that come out of the blue.

Actually I was happy to receive this call tonight. That made the 3rd time David's name was mentioned or seen in one day! What more could I ask for in terms of reassurance? I guess signing that lease was the right thing to do.

David came to me in a dream on my birthday, November 1st. I don't remember the dream, but just that he was there.

November 25th, I said good-by to the house in Hudson and moved into The Condo. The new people would not be moving into Our Home for another three weeks, but I always feel it's better to leave some time between occupants. Nothing I can explain, just a feeling that the house should "rest" or air out or change energy or something. At the very least it would give me time to go back once more and give my beloved home a thorough cleaning.

Condo life, as I'm finding out, is a totally different experience;

Chapter 3

Winter

Frozen water now, with steam rising off the ice on very cold days giving it a ghostly appearance; animal tracks make crisscross patterns in the superficial layer of snow. Where do they go? Why are they walking out over the frozen water? Do they ever fall through or do they have some kind of 6th sense about ice thickness?

Ducks gather in a huge flock at the deepest part of the lake, in the center where a strong current keeps water from freezing. They're so far away they look like one huge black blob all drifting together, but then at some secret signal they swirl upwards and away, becoming a cloud of ducks.

December 3rd. Seventeen months since David's passing. This would be a good day to go back to the house in Hudson for a last look around before handing over the key. I was not looking forward to this, to handing over my house to strangers, but what's done is done. No turning back.

Not having had a chance earlier, I scrubbed sinks and toilets and swiped at cupboards. Lastly I tackled the kitchen floor with one eye on the clock. It was important to me that I leave Our Home looking its best, well-loved and cared for, yet Brenda had invited me to spend the afternoon with family, to be part of their Christmas tree decorating ritual.

Torn, I raced through my chores. I wanted to stay at the house for as long as possible and I wanted to leave. I wanted to savor what had been "ours" and I wanted to be with my grandchildren celebrating life.

In retrospect, I should have stayed longer at the house. As it turned out, I missed the Christmas tree decorating anyway, as I ended up trekking out to Thompson Park after my cleaning

of a gift shop and I moved in closer to have a better look. A faerie ornament, delicate and whimsical hung from a branch of the display tree. Ooohh she was pretty! Dancing and twirling as if alive and beckoning people into the shop.

Opening the door I entered to the sound of tinkling bells. What a charming place! All spruced up with Santa sleighs and candy canes and smelling like a pine forest with a touch of gingerbread. Shaking the snow off my hat and coat, I smiled at the sales clerk then made a beeline for the window display to get a better look at "my" faerie.

She was exquisite, made of porcelain and rather expensive I noticed as I flipped over the tag. I can't recall every paying a lot of money for Christmas decorations.

No need.

With the arrival of Dollar Stores in every strip mall, Christmas ornaments, greeting cards, glitzy wrapping paper, ribbons and bows can all be bought for a dollar or two.

Cradling this wee treasure in my hands brought a rush of warmth, a tingle in my palms, as if she was pleading with me to take her home. It's hard to explain, but she won me over and I decided in the spirit of "gifting" myself and "opening to the abundant universe" I would not turn down this small pleasure because of the price.

Just as I was congratulating myself for my new thinking, another ornament caught my eye. It was a pair of nesting birds – bright red cardinals, looking very regal amongst the traditional Christmas stars and tinsel.

With one swift motion, I plucked it off the tree.

I felt light! I felt free! It felt good to pick out expensive ornaments for immediate purchase.

I like it. I buy it. Ha!

Moving away from the window display, I ventured deeper into the store to see if anything else caught my fancy.

Nope, nothing good. "Just as well," I thought seesawing

undone. Fear of losing my world, the one I'm trying to get a grip on, this new one I'm still trying to figure out.

When we were two, our way of life was routine: grocery shopping, appointments, work, play, friends and family, everything was in order. Everything fit. Whenever there was an uncertainty it would be talked about or just dealt with and let the pieces fall as they may. I felt as if nothing really bad would happen. Wrong choices would be corrected. Everything would turn out all right in the end.

But now everything is worrisome. I have little confidence in myself or my decision-making abilities. Even though I do feel I've made progress, am gaining strength and courage, Fear undermines almost everything I do, as if taking great delight in throwing me off course.

Only half of me exists now and I waver in the wind. I'm learning to put down roots of my own, but the process is shaky and uncertain and I grasp at every little success, every small feeling of accomplishment. Even the purchase of a simple Christmas ornament is a step forward.

Feeling very pleased with myself I hung the faerie near the top of my tree as soon as I got home. It seemed a fitting replacement for the angel I gave away back in those early weeks. It had been David's angel, not a particularly pretty one, but something he treasured. Regretfully it was gone, like so much else I had tossed in a frantic attempt to banish my grief.

A symbol of hope I thought, admiring New Faerie winking down at me from her perch. Hope in accepting our new relationship; coming to terms with he in the land of spirit and me still earthbound.

And the nesting cardinals. What could be more fitting? Cardinals appeared for me all last summer in Brenda's backyard, bringing messages of comfort and hope to this lonely soul.

January, the coldest month of the year, found me spiraling down

whenever I'm in the area, I make a point of stopping by to pick up half a dozen sesame ones. They are so good!

I slid into the left lane and set my signal light to blinking. Partway into the turn, I realized what I was doing and laughed out loud. A few minutes later found me pulling into Sean and Kim's driveway.

I could hear crash-bang noises coming from inside as I knocked on the front door. Kim answered in her dressing gown looking flustered but delighted to see me. The older siblings were at home due to a ped day, and with a full house of children, Kim was more than happy to have another adult for company.

We chatted away as the children played circles around us. Puzzles, trucks and cars, train tracks and Lego pieces littered the floor. With a sweet-smelling cuddly baby in my arms, I melted into the sofa. Happy little voices were music to my ears and when Kim asked if she could run upstairs to shower and dress, I just smiled. She took that as a yes and bolted.

Ahhhhh – so glad I decided to ignore my mind and let Spirit guide me.

Eventually I had to leave. Slipping on my winter coat I reached out to give Kim a warm hug. "Come and visit anytime. I mean it. Don't hold back!"

Smiling my thanks I headed out to my car and kicked up a pile of fluffy snow, just for fun. I turned to see if anyone was watching through the window, but no, the children had all gone back to their play.

I finished up my errands, stopped into the Food Court at Fairview Shopping Centre for a quick bite, then decided I'd better go home and work on my writing. I really would have preferred to stay "out and about"; shopping or visiting or stopping for gas again (how pathetic is that?). There are days I just need to keep moving, but my conscience was poking at me to stop frittering my time away and settle down to do some work. Writing work.

excitement, eyes shining.

"Now, now, that's not polite. Let poor Grandma take off her coat at least!" Brenda tried to look disapproving but failed utterly; there was too much noise and activity for anyone to really take notice. The kids disappeared into the living room as quickly as they'd appeared, back to the other guests. Evan, my son-in-law, stepped forward to greet me and hang up my coat.

The afternoon flew by. I was in heaven! It was pure bliss to share in the little ones' excitement of opening gifts, playing games and stuffing themselves with pizza and chocolate cake. Oh, I remember those days when my children were small. Happy memories of long ago.

But back home again, those feelings dissolved, evaporating into thin air. I was alone again. I hated this roller coaster of emotions. I hated feeling so alone.

"Oh, David, where are you? I thought it would be easier this second year, I thought I could 'get through' all this grief and function without feeling miserable all the time. But it's not happening! Where are you?"

Sunday I took some time in the morning to sit at my laptop and write. I had no expectations and just let the writing flow. And it was good.

Far better than pushing myself to do something because "I should". So from now on, I will commit to being open and allowing the process to flow – or not. There will be days I cannot write. Days when I need to be doing something else, no matter how trivial. I remind myself that "nature doesn't hurry and everything gets done."

I want to live like that.

But, a little voice in my head taunts, you can't just do something whenever you feel like it. What about hard work, diligence? What about reaching for the stars? Success? How can you hope to achieve anything by sitting back and waiting for the muse? Or whatever you call inspiration. You do need to take

Even throughout David's illness, I did not have that feeling. I was stressed to the max by our circumstances, but I never felt that I wanted to shift into somebody else's life. David was my life, my love, a reflection of my soul.

Now he's gone. At least in body. And I need to find my own way out of this jungle.

I thought the journey up the mountain was hard.

It was. We were fighting a losing battle, a terminal illness.

Letting go was even harder.

And I thought the journey back down the mountain would be easier. Just slide down the slope and pick up life once again.

But the slope is no longer there. The mountain has changed into a jungle. And I have to forge a pathway all by myself. David can only guide from above and I need to be quiet to hear his whispers.

My intuition has always been my guide, now even more so, but my head is the computer, trying to sort things out. We are used to thinking our way through situations. Or how else would modern medicine evolve? Mathematics, discoveries, biology, education? I am not one of these people who condemn the brain. Popular talk these days is, "Get out of your head and into your heart."

That always puts my back up. As if our brains are not important. Are no use. Puleeese! How about saying, "Let your brain rest for a while." Let it rest and allow the heart, the intuition to be your guide.

In bed that night sleep would not come. I felt nauseous, sick to my stomach, dizzy as if I'd spent the day riding a lopsided merry-go-round. I knew for certain that I hadn't contracted a virus or eaten bad food. I've experienced this before – it's missing David, plain and simple.

In that hazy time just before falling asleep, I saw an image of David in my mind's eye. I wanted so badly to follow him.

but to be honest, he was already walking that path when we met. He was open and ready for me – just as I was open and ready for him.

"David, I so want to be with you. I so want to follow you wherever you are."

Through blurry tears, I saw him smile; his gentle brown eyes let me know that I had to stay in this world. There was more life for me to live, more to learn, more to experience and most importantly, I had to find the real essence of me – alone.

Sounds strange. I'm a 60-year-old woman – you'd think I would know who I am by now.

But I don't.

All I know is that I want to feel peace in my heart. No more pain. I want the pain gone – forever!

With a sigh, I pulled the covers tight around me as if bundling up against a harsh world. Perhaps in time the answers would come.

I caught a glimpse of Red Fox the other day. In the early morning dimness just before sunrise, he was a shadowy form slinking close to shore. Don't they hibernate in winter? Where did he come from? Did he walk across the frozen lake? I reached for my camera knowing it was useless to capture this moving shadow of a fox, but I tried anyway.

And no the picture didn't turn out.

That night I felt the bed shaking ever so gently, and dreamed that David was alive.

round, dark shape emerged from the water and scrambled up onto the rocks. It had a long tail, almost like a cat. Couldn't be of course, but was it a fox? Do foxes swim?

April 3rd. Early morning I step out onto the balcony just in time to watch as two Canada geese fly by in tandem. They look peaceful, if there is such a thing as a peaceful goose, sailing along in harmony.

I am determined to stop counting days, months. There is no reason to trek out to Thompson Park. David is not there. I prefer to sit quietly, light a candle and think about him. Time has a way of moving on whether we like it or not.

My gaze swept over the lake and I caught the movement of two ducks swimming close to the water's edge. I see this pair quite often and think they are a manifestation of David's and my spirit. Our commitment, our relationship, our love infused into these sweet duckies as they go about their everyday activities, foraging for food, diving or just being.

I met with my Bereavement Support Group in the evening. Yes, I can finally get out after dark and drive to the church without too much inner turmoil. This group is made up of widows only. It wasn't planned this way, somehow it just happened. There are five of us, a small group and it's a much better fit for me. We completely understand the issues of being newly widowed, from not being able to fix a running toilet, to inhaling the lingering scent of him on his hairbrush, to preparing his favorite foods that nobody will eat.

Over the weeks we discussed letting go strategies (which I didn't want to do), sharing our loss through rituals with family (which I don't do. I light candles on my own), learning to move on in life and stand alone (which is difficult to even think of).

But with each session, we become less rigid, more comfortable with each other and more open to discussing raw feelings. Judy surprised me by announcing that she shut the door on her husband's sons after he died. She told her husband as he lay in his sick bed, that nobody was getting anything, no matter what his wishes. The boys would have to wait until she died

Whoah! I was shocked. I had misjudged her fortitude. Obviously the boys did not live in that home, but had their own homes, their own lives. I imagine she was afraid they intended to clean out the contents of their Dad's home, once he'd passed on. I don't ever know.

Martha told a story about raccoons in her attic. She was terrified and called her sister with cancer husband to get rid of them. She was appalled at herself, but so frightened. We had to laugh at the picture of this poor man coming to the rescue of his family, more than likely glad to come to their figure.

...

Cookies were ...

...

patio, my mind slipped back to the day of David's passing. I don't remember much about that day, except feeling wrapped in a fog of shock as I sat here in this same garden. Voices faded in and out punctuated by the sharp chirp of birds. It felt like I was enveloped in a cloud where everything outside of my immediate vision was blurry or nonexistent.

But today, almost two years later, I am greeted by a melody of songbirds as they weave in and out of thick cedar hedges at the bottom of Brenda's garden. A sudden memory of a cardinal, crimson against the backdrop of a blue summer sky, calling out to me with a *cheer-cheer-cheer, purty, purty, purty*; trying to get through to me as if it had an important message to impart.

That was only weeks after David died and I remember feeling rather annoyed at the shrillness of its cry. It was only later while watching a children's program that I understood the importance of its message. *I need to find my wings and fly free.*

Hoisting little Nathan onto my hip, I pointed up overhead to where a whole party of birds swung on a telephone wire, seemingly just for fun. Then without warning they scattered into the neighbor's yard, descending on a crabapple tree that was just coming into bloom.

Sunday afternoon, a day to check out Open Houses. The first one I saw was elegant and charming with a view of the lake, but far too expensive for me to even consider. I did have fun though, peering around each room, opening doors and cupboards, all the while pretending I could really afford a home of this distinction.

The others proved to be disappointing. Older, in need of repairs. Priced to sell, but not to this lady. Who wants to begin a new life by cleaning up after someone else? By gutting yukky bathrooms and outdated kitchens?

Not me. I understand the houses here are older, but the area is respectable, affluent with mature trees, superior city services

this year. Why? I don't quite understand. I'm not good with numbers and calculations and our tax system. Where oh where are you, David? Why can't you still be here with me, ironing out our financial questions, managing our taxes, our budget, our money?

Wealth management was effortless for him, and he enjoyed the process.

I don't.

I find it confusing and time consuming, particularly since it takes me such a long time to untangle financial statements and government forms.

Round and round these thoughts go in my brain. I thought by now I'd have found something productive to do with my life, something satisfying that would bring in a little extra income. It's not happening. Why not? Where are you? I need help, sweetheart.

Restless, I step out onto the balcony hoping that a change of scenery will change my mood. Leaning against the railing, I tilt my face towards the heavens as if answers will magically appear in the clouds. Except there are no clouds. The sky is as clear as clear can be. All I can see are two white trails etching a path across a wilderness of blue, one only just ahead of the other.

Aww, is that you, David? You and me? Making our way across the sky as if following a parallel path? Are you close or are you far? Or does distance not mean anything anymore? Are you telling me we will always be together? No matter what? Or where? Awww, that makes me feel good right down to the bottom of my toes. And who cares if I'm leaning over my balcony talking to airplanes?

With a sigh of contentment I continue to watch as the planes fade away into nothingness.

Hope. I feel hope. A teeny, tiny bit, lifting me up, twirling me around as I dance back into the condo. I can do this. I can sort

out of the building with my need to be back among everyday people, rushing home from work or school or out for a late afternoon stroll.

As I crossed the street, a woman wearing house slippers and a light summer dress rode by on her bicycle. I'd seen her before and wondered whether she was in her right mind. She was older, in her 70s I think and wore heavy clothing in the heat of summer and flip-flops or slippers in the cold. I had no idea where she lived or if she had family to look in on her.

It wasn't quite warm enough for summer attire, and as I was still recovering from my cold, I'd thrown on a pair of jeans and grabbed a light jacket on my way out.

A ripple in the water caught my eye. It skimmed across the lake in a huge V, just like the one I'd seen from my living room window a few weeks earlier. I watched transfixed as something swimming just below the surface raced along to shore.

Was it a huge fish?

Not likely in this lake. Certainly not a duck as I couldn't see a body. Couldn't see a head either, just a rippling of the water at top speed. What was it? I rounded a bend in the path and lost sight of the lake temporarily; tall weeds and hedges obscured my view.

Then quite suddenly, the lake reappeared. A huge brown rodent squatted by the shore, half in and half out of the water. It was fat and ugly with long, sharp teeth. Yet I was thrilled! I'd never seen a beaver before.

There were plenty in Hudson at the Beaver Pond, but I'd never caught sight of one; only their messy-looking dwellings of mud and sticks. And here I was thinking I'd left all the animals back in Hudson!

Mr. Beaver sat rooted to the spot, except for the occasional twitching of whiskers and moving his head from side to side, presumably to listen or maybe smell the air. I sucked in a breath and stood very still; waiting and watching. Oh how I wish he could pull his big flat tail out of the water so I could have a look!

After a while I got tired of standing around and crept forward a few steps. In a blink, he splashed back into the water and swam away. Too bad. As I continued down the path towards the shoreline, I wondered if that ripple on the lake had been Mr. Beaver swimming to shore.

Then one day I decided to take my camera down from the shelf and see what it could do.

Really.

Not as in the occasional birthday or Christmas use, but every day. Now I know why I moved to and Stills, videos. Oh it was wonderful to capture more of life's precious moments day by day. One time more interesting was the swim, a family of Canada geese flying on the shoreline back and forth. Three hidden a little bit of a moment because their drab coloring blended in so well with the surroundings.

One evening I enjoyed another scene of young raccoons. Like a flash of lightning they scrambled to a hidden shelter across the yard right by front door. I watched from the bushes at the side of the road. In a matter of a few minutes I caught their scurry away and ran up a tree and after a bit of it the narrow path, up the road vanished.

The whole episode had been too quick for me to pull out my camera, but now it was in my hand ready to go. The problem was, the raccoons were gone.

A little while later I was rewarded, for there they were, scurrying down on us everything once from the safety of their perch up the tree tree. It was there that not too many people were about and there were enough colour as frighten the little critters.

It's easier to snap and adjust the exposure just once the light was dull. But I was honored, now to my big camera, and I even thought maintaining of things in a lovely the moment. It brought back to my days becoming up so slow and savor ordinary moments: a butterfly lighting on a marigold, someone pointing out a sailboat while bending close to a child, a pair of pileated woodpeckers circling a tree, my very first beaver sighting.

But my proudest moment was when I captured a great white egret outlined in gold as I filmed him against the setting sun. Not having a tripod or even a monopod, I held my camera at eye level and tried my best to keep it still. My hands grew numb and my arms shook, but I really had to film that majestic creature. It looked regal, tall and stately with an elegantly curved neck and pure white body as it gazed haughtily out over its loyal subjects – the common waterfowl.

Over the course of the shoot, I had to lower my camera and give my arms a rest, shaking my hands to get the blood flowing again. Then all of a sudden King Egret would begin its hunter's walk. Cool, elegant, precise steps, its graceful neck leading as it scanned the shallows for a meal. In a flash, its sharp beak shot out slashing the water. A silvery fish appeared wiggling helplessly for an instant.

With a gulp it was gone.

This particular shoot took me about 20 minutes. Airplanes roared overhead spoiling the sound, ducks and seagulls swam in and out of sight like players on stage, but I was enchanted with the whole scenario. I did not know white egrets existed here as I'd only ever seen them in Florida and the Caribbean.

Chapter 5

Summer 2012

June 21st. Summer Solstice. The turning point of day/night balance. Today marks the longest day of the year. I drench myself in the heady warmth and light of the season, feeling energized and open and ready for anything.

Ogunquit

"What? I stopped in my tracks.

Ogunquit, Maine. The Ocean. Ogunquit-by-the-Sea. Ogunquit. The place was so magnetic and fabulous and so uniquely me and I very often wished [I could] to get to that spot because there's more [life/feeling] and I felt safe enough to go.

[I can] imagine myself there, warming myself on the brown sugar sand, slathering of sunscreen, dipping my toes in the bubbling foam.

[...]

[...] very own mirror image of the place where we spend our [...]

[...] I go there, what if it's too much?

Could I really do this? Was I brave enough to immerse myself in memories I could be torn apart with longing? With yearning for what was?

Could I drive the six or seven hours across the Canadian/US border, down the I-99 and on to this beautiful jewel of a seaside spot in Maine, alone? Alone.

And but why would I do this?

Simply put, I love this spot. This pretty seaside town was familiar. The beach, shops, fabulous restaurants. The [...] Pound and Barnacle Billy's, Betty, Dolly, Holly — all trollies that run along Shore Road from the hotels and Inns to the beach or restaurants, the Marginal Way – a picturesque walk along the rocky coastline ending in Perkin's Cove – and the piece de resistance – The Ocean.

Bittersweet, as memories rose up to challenge me. I had to go. I had to make those memories come alive. To bring David back to life again.

I knew he would be there.

In the gleam of sunlight on water, in the sigh of the wind, the rhythm of tides, that first sip of morning coffee, and last glimpse of twinkling stars as I drew the curtains before bed.

I had to walk the path David and I took those heady, passionate times we were here. The Colonial Inn where everything was new, including our relationship, stuffing ourselves with fresh-caught lobster and blueberry pie, Bernard's Bakery where David picked up hazelnut coffee and cherry cheese Danish in the mornings so we could languish in bed a while longer, walking the beach hand in hand.

"We'll walk 15 minutes and then turn back."

"What?" I'd never timed a beach walk before. What on earth? I dropped his hand and turned to look at him. Sunglasses hid his eyes, but I could feel he was serious.

"Yes, that way we won't walk too long," he explained, smiling. "It's easy to get caught up, walking along until you realize you've gone much farther than you intended. Then you have to walk all the way back."

"Oookay, Mr. Logical." Giggling helplessly, I spun around and clomped into the ocean, making sure to splash him thoroughly as I went.

"Hey!" Bending down, he retaliated by scooping up a handful of water and throwing it at my back. I was already wet and didn't care. Happy memories. We were like little kids at the beach.

Could I, would I really do this? Bring back those feelings, those memories of love, of indescribable joy, of giddy euphoria?

Sucking in my breath, I made the reservation. No, not at the Inn where we usually stayed, but another one close by. And two days later I climbed into the car and began the long drive.

It was tough. I got lost a few times and had to turn back, but once that soft sea air poured into my open car windows, I knew I was getting close. That incredibly potent scent of fishermen and mists and ancient legends could only mean one thing -- The Ocean!

The Ocean was near and beckoning; powerful enough, even at a distance, to comfort and calm my jittery nerves.

As I approached the small bridge, I felt my shoulders relax, and the edges of my calm. That bridge was a landmark and now the rest of the way would be easy -- no more wrong turns or missed exits.

I was almost there!

About an hour later, I entered the town of Ogunquit, quite impressed with myself for having made the trip. All on my own...

The most peaceful quiet, allowing for a quiet walk alone and I took all the time I needed to revisit our happy memories. Some tugged at my heartstrings and I had to bite my cheek to keep from crying in public. The 'Gypsy' Restaurant where David proposed, Sea Glass Jewelry where he insisted on buying me a pair of dangly earrings as a special memory of our first trip together, the perch of jagged rock overlooking the ocean where I lost sight of him for a few moments as I stood on the Marginal Way.

We had been walking along when we came to a fork in the path - I went one way around the prickly bushes and he the other, closer to the rocky ledge.

When I got to the spot where I thought he'd be, there was no one. Scanning the rocks and sandy beach below turned up only sea birds and a few sunbathers.

Where was David?

I did not realize that the rocky pathway dipped down to a secluded area not visible from the footpath. For a moment I panicked – thought he'd disappeared into the ocean, but as his smiling face bobbed back into view, I breathed a sigh of relief.

"Where did you go?"

"Looking for harbor seals – did you spot any?"

"No, I was looking for you!"

He pulled me into a huge bear hug and I hugged him fiercely back, breathing in his unique scent of sunlight and spring moss, honest body sweat and salt.

"Let's go for ice cream."

"Sure!" I could always eat ice cream. Some things you never outgrow.

Joining hands, we continued along the Marginal Way towards Perkins Cove, where lobster shacks, restaurants, and touristy beach shops beckoned. The path was full of smiling people on vacation, some jogging, others meandering or taking pics, or resting on the many benches strategically placed just off the footpath where one could admire the magnificent view.

Chapter 6

Year Three

July 3rd, 2012 marked the second anniversary of his death. Two whole years have gone by. Two years without David in my life. It does not seem possible. How could I have come this far? Managed without him?

You do. You just do.

Time marches on, slips by, waits for no one. Life continues on and we can choose to be a rock stuck stubbornly in the muck of the bottom of the river or flow swiftly along with its currents.

It's strange to even put into words, but often I feel things like I had no mind of my own, no decision-making power or free will.

I felt I was caught up in a river and it was dragging me along. It felt different - not the life I had as a child, or a teen, or a young adult or ever - just a different world as if someone had dropped me onto a planet and left me there to stare at a green sky and blue grass or where swarms of people in small white buildings and streets flowed past in confusion.

Well, maybe not that crazy, but totally foreign like arriving in a strange city or country or the feeling you have when you get lost and your surroundings do not match what your mind is telling you.

Family is the same, they talk of ordinary things: what's happening at work, a child's progress or troubles at school, upcoming birthdays or holidays. Friends too. They continue on with their lives, merging briefly with mine, then disconnecting, returning to the stability of their own world.

One foot in front of the other and somehow life around you changes, evolves and you find yourself standing in a different spot, feeling like a different person.

July 22nd – our third wedding anniversary. Third! Wait a minute. I'm in the year of seconds, aren't I? No, that was last year. The second year anniversary of his passing was 19 days ago, which puts me smack dab in the year of Thirds.

Yeeks! What will happen this year? Will I ever learn to live without David? Will I ever conquer this loneliness? This heartache?

I'd like to think so. I'd like to believe that I've made progress in adjusting to this New Life. But I honestly don't know.

It's summertime – a fantabulous time of year, but I hate where I'm living. This should be a season of celebrating life, of inhaling fragrant flowers and biting into juicy tomatoes straight from the vine, of long sun-filled days, of who-cares hairstyles and casual clothes, of street festivals and frappuccinos. Of hot, sweaty days and humid nights. And for the most part I am enjoying the season – summers are short here in the North.

But I so miss our home!

It's hot and uncomfortable in the condo. I put the AC on only in the afternoons when the sun is at its strongest and turn it off at night because I like to sleep with windows open. No point in letting all that cooled air escape outdoors.

The AC system is a wall-mounted unit, efficiently cooling the living room, but leaving the bedroom decidedly hot. Not very effective at all.

Our beautiful home had central air circulation with nice cool air in summer.

I wish I were back in our home, David. With you.

Our old life back again!!

Very early morning and I can't sleep. Coffee in hand, I wander over to the window and press my forehead against the cool glass, trying to see through the morning mists. Are my duck friends up and about yet? Geese? Is the beaver around?

To the east soft fingers of light reach out through the gloom gently awakening a slumbering earth. The lake comes to life with a shimmer – a new day has begun.

A kayak glides into view, then another, then a few more. I watch transfixed as they skim across the gentle waves, arms thrashing with each paddle; reds and yellows and blues painting a striking picture against the dull grey canvas of a cloudy day.

As enthralling as this view is, this glimpse into life on the lake, I long to be a homeowner once again. My own space. Trees, a garden, a clothesline, windows to open on all sides of the house. A quiet street.

Kayakers are out of sight, but now the pace is picking up, buses and cars and cyclists go by my window. People walking their dogs, or walking themselves, it's a busy here; much busier than in Hudson, a semi-rural suburb of Montreal, where I lived for almost 20 years.

But in Hudson I felt isolated. There were times I could go for a walk and not see anybody. Here I feel there is too much activity. Who wants to see and hear buses go by their front door? Not me.

Days are long, I am Miss Observation. Staring out my front window does me little good. I wander, but there is no yard work or puttering around my cozy kitchen, no bird feeders to fill and hang, no next door neighbors to chat with over the cedar hedge.

Caregiving and keeping house for David and I took up the greater portion of my day for a good many years. Back then I felt we were living in a bubble, cut off from the real world. Our little world of medications, breathing treatments, washing, cooking and eating, of restricting visitors for fear of someone bringing a virus into our home. Of only leaving our sanctuary together for doctor's appointments.

I could bop in and out – there were little air holes in our bubble, but each time I went out I worried. Would I be the one to bring home an illness? Something as ordinary as a person coughing or sneezing at the grocery store had me backing away, terrified I'd bring home a killer virus – pneumonia or something horrible that would completely destroy David's lungs. Would I return to find him stretched out on the floor? Gasping for air?

It sounds so far-fetched, so ludicrous to worry to that degree, yet I did. All the time.

That life we were living felt utterly draining. Frightening. Nothing we could do would change the outcome. Frustrating. We could not live an ordinary life: a life of passion, of travel, of social activities and fulfilling work. Yet we held on to each other desperately, with a bond so deep yet so fragile. Each moment together whether monitoring oxygen levels, washing hair or cuddling in bed was treasured, cherished, held close to our hearts, because we knew that one day "this moment" would be our last.

"We're lucky rabbits," David was fond of saying, and even though our circumstances were dismal, I'd have to agree. We were lucky to have found one another.

But now my days are empty. They lack focus, goals, a common thread. Spurts of joy with my family are what keep me sane, bring me hope. But I need to get back on track – to find something worthwhile to do. To look forward to each day.

I need a Life.

"Get a Life," I remember huffing at some marketing person over the phone one day a hundred years ago. And laughing rudely as I hung up. Hmm, now I'm the one who needs to "get a life". Not a very comfortable feeling.

What could I possibly do that would be worthwhile, fulfilling work? Not something I'd have to commit to every day, nor something too taxing. I still want time to spend with family, to take walks, to make a stab at creating with my camera, with the written word. Perhaps I'd learn something new – a foreign language, Zumba or how to paddle a canoe or kayak.

Or maybe I could help out in a Nursing Home. Not with feeding or everyday care – that would bring back too many painful memories, but something recreational. I'm hopeless at crafts, but enjoy singing and tai chi.

Tai chi. That's an idea. With its sweeping movements and heightening of energy. Maybe this New Life is steering me in the direction of energy work.

I can do that! I'm sure if it!

It's not complicated. Energy is all around us – it flows from within and without. And never dies.

Brenda is the Director of Nursing Care in a private Nursing Home. Maybe I should give her a call and try to figure this out. It was evening and I knew she'd be home with her family. Glancing at the clock to make sure she wasn't putting little ones to bed. I picked up the phone and punched in her number.

After a bit of chitchat I got straight to the point.

"I need something to do with my life. I'm bored here in the condo. What do you think about me singing songs with the Residents or teaching them tai chi."

Something about being on the phone, you can pick up someone's facial expression by listening to the tone of their voice. Or the silence. I could hear her turning things over in her mind, frowning slightly, while keeping an eye on the little ones.

"Tai chi?"

"Well, just some basic movements. Nothing complicated."

"Well let's see. Someone comes in Thursday afternoons to play piano and sing all the Oldies."

"Oh, how nice." Darn, forget singing.

"And a recreational therapist every day. We also have students coming in after school to volunteer. Some sit with the Residents and do crafts, others encourage the women to fold towels or clothes."

"Oh, that's a great idea! It must give them a sense of being back home doing everyday tasks. But what about the men?"

"They hand the men simple tools, nothing sharp of course, a flashlight to take apart, or something made of wood to click together, like a birdhouse or toy train tracks. Their hands haven't forgotten these familiar activities, even though their brains have."

"Wow," I was impressed. "But is there room for me?" I felt like a little girl pleading to be included, wanting desperately to be part of the elite social circle. "Do you think they would like tai chi?"

Silence.

I could picture Brenda's eyebrows knitting together as she considered my request. I held my breath.

"Sure, you could give it a try. Every bit of stimulation helps."

And so I began.

It did not go as I expected.

Not at all.

I walked into a room of elderly men and women, all of whom were sitting in wheelchairs.

Seventeen people were asleep.

Two ladies were wide awake and ready for me.

One gentleman looked awake, blue eyes bright and cheerful, but in the next instant he dozed off.

A sinking feeling swept over me. My whole lesson plan flew out the window in the blink of an eye. I had prepared a short talk on the origins of Tai Chi, along with a brief description of this ancient practice, and its associated health benefits.

No one would have understood a word.

I stood in the center of the room, ladies and gentlemen seated all around me, while I moved among the residents, like a floating cloud or a butterfly.

My intention was to hold a class, as in demonstrating tai chi moves in front of a group of people. They would be sitting in neat rows watching and participating as much as possible, taking into account any physical disabilities.

It did not happen that way.

I had forgotten that most people residing in nursing homes were there for a reason. They no longer had the mental capacity to stay alone in their own homes.

Over the previous week, I had researched the Internet and my own memory banks, to come up with a program of tai chi moves suitable for people in wheelchairs. I had practiced those moves at home, over and over until I was satisfied.

It did not matter one iota.

The two sweet old ladies who actually followed my moves, became tired very quickly. I had not considered that, even though I knew the residents were elderly.

As a result, short frequent breaks needed to be incorporated into an already pared down version of my original plan.

But despite all this, I felt the atmosphere was comfortable, respectful.

Serene actually.

Nurses were compassionate and patient, as they glided around repositioning someone here, adjusting someone's blanket. My sweet old ladies smiled. One of them complimented the color of my blouse. "Roses and cream," she said.

The blue-eyed gentleman caught my eye once or twice as I was "sweeping lotus petals in the stream" and I wondered if there was a spark of interest somewhere deep down in the center of his being. In a place normally hidden from ordinary eyes.

Next week, I will go back and try again.

This time I will be ready.

This time I will work with a much smaller group – those who are awake and interested.

This time I will make a point of reaching out to connect with each dear soul, before beginning the structure of a class.

Will Chair Tai Chi benefit this group of soon-to-be-ancestors?

Will it strengthen each tired body, sharpen each cloudy mind and nourish each fragile soul?

I hope so.

Summer has faded into autumn and I wish I was outdoors raking leaves.

Seriously.

All those years of finding it a chore and now I actually miss raking leaves. David loved it.

"It makes me feel grounded," he told me long ago, as he stopped for a moment to lean against his rake. I remember that day as if it was yesterday, his boyish smile, golden sunlight outlining his body, and all those leaves waiting to be bagged.

Personally, I'd rather go bike riding.

Every autumn it was the same: rake, rake, rake. There are a lot of trees on our property and that means a ton of leaves. Not that I hated it, in fact I quite enjoyed being outdoors in the fresh air, piling leaves into huge mounds to scoop into bags, but after a while I wanted to escape and just go biking or shopping or something else.

"Go," David said and he meant it. "I'll be fine."

And off I'd go, some days feeling guilty and others not at all.

I miss raking now, raking and bagging and dragging to the curb; the freedom of owning my own property. To look after it however and whenever I want.

Sometime around my birthday I had a dream, which was not a dream at all. It was more like a "Visitation".

I know David is just on the Other Side. He (in his Spirit Form) can watch me. It must be like looking through one-way glass. He can see me, but I can't see him.

Going to bed that night I thought about feeling his fingers caress my cheek, I thought about our love life and how happy we'd been. The faint smell of cigarette smoke, the soft melody of wind chimes hanging just above my bedroom window told me he was near. He was listening and still part of my life.

The Lines Between Us Are Blurry... And still are.

Sometime in the middle of the night, I dreamed that I had broken through the Veil, the Curtain that separates our world from the world of Spirit. I had the Code. I knew the Password. I could walk between the two worlds and enter...

I trembled with excitement as I got closer. Somehow I think I was flying as my body seemed to be floating and I could see the ground far below. I knew I was being propelled towards David.

And there he was, sitting reading a book or a journal or something. He looked up at me (yes I must have been flying) and smiled.

Now I know beyond a shadow of a doubt what that phrase "a million dollar smile" really means.

That beautiful, brilliant smile as he looked at me was pure Gold.

I had cracked the code and entered His World. And he was there. Ready to receive me as if I was expected.

I was overjoyed! Tears flowed down my face.

No, he did not glow ethereally. He did not look like a being of light or spirit. He looked older, slightly shrunken and dry. He had more wrinkles, but not overly so. Only someone who knew him closely could detect the change in his appearance. His eyes still held that familiar David sparkle I knew and loved so well.

I held out my hands to touch him. We did not embrace, which seems strange, but I do remember stretching out my hand to meet his. Our fingers touched.

Something we always did, even when making love was to entwine our fingers. Holding hands came as naturally as breathing to us – even while driving the car. I was impressed when I first met David that he could drive a standard shift car and hold my hand at the same time. When he switched gears, he'd let go of my hand, make the shift and then pick up my hand again.

We interlocked our hands as if he were alive again. His felt like paper, thin, as did the atmosphere I found myself in. I felt paper thin too. Not of body. Just the surrounding air, the environment.

We went somewhere. I don't remember much anymore. I wish I'd made myself write it all down in the middle of the night when I woke up.

But it was all so clear at the time. I was really there. It did not feel like a dream at all. So, of course I'd remember.

Well, of course I did not. What I did remember was that exhilarating feeling of having broken through the Veil, of finding the key or cracking the code and knowing I could Visit any time I wanted to.

David was not coming to me in a dream. I was coming to him – in the world of Spirit.

I fell back into the dream that was not a dream. Somehow I knew in the depths of my soul, that this was real. I was elated to find I could reenter that world and continue the adventure or story we were creating. Just the two of us.

But I don't remember the content of the story. I don't remember what happened, except some vague impressions. His body seemed to become heavier as the dream or visitation progressed. It was more substantial and as this happened, he became less real and less happy. Even the atmosphere was growing heavier, almost suffocating and I was having difficulty drawing a breath. It was beginning to feel as if something awful were about to happen.

Don't ask me to explain, as it didn't really make too much sense. And I still have that vague feeling of myself floating above, rather than completely involved.

I hear a dog barking as I drift in and out of sleep. Is it morning already? Or is someone walking their dog outside my window in the middle of the night?

A few days before Christmas, I popped into Tim Hortons. I had
spent most of the morning shopping and needed the sustenance
of a quick coffee before continuing on.

People were smiling, chatting together while waiting in line.
The air was alive with anticipation of the holiday and everyone
seemed to be in a good mood.

The shop was all decked out for the season. Evergreen
wreaths danced in the windows twinkling all over with frosty
lights. Scintillating streamers of deep red and gold looped their
way across counter tops and display cases drawing the eye to
where delicate sugar cookies and doughnuts oozing with cream
lay in wait. Even the lowly carrot muffin was dressed to the
nines in garish green frosting and rainbow sprinkles.

Employees called out a cheery "Happy Holidays" to one and
all, their red floppy hats with white trim making them look like
Santa's helpers.

The line, which had been moving briskly before, suddenly
slowed down. I looked towards the cash to see what the problem
was. A woman seemed to be having trouble with her debit card.

"It worked at Zellers a few minutes ago!" She was starting
to get embarrassed. Feet shuffled behind me. I waited a few
minutes to see if the problem would resolve.

It didn't.

I looked away and then looked back. No change. She was still
trying to get that card to work so she could pay for her order. I
looked at the screen to see what she owed. $3.38. Hmmm.

Boldly I stepped forward waving two toonies at the cashier.

"I'll get this and have a Merry Christmas." I smiled at the
flustered woman.

"Oh, thank you," said the woman her face turning red,
"that's very nice of you but they said they'd pay for it if my card
doesn't work."

The cashier looked at me and nodded.

"No, no, it's okay, it's on me." I said grandly thrusting my toonies in the cashier's face. I wanted to be the good guy. I wanted to give to a stranger in a random act of kindness (and speed things up so I could have my coffee). But nobody wanted my money.

The cashier just smiled.

The woman continued to fiddle with her card. And I started feeling like an idiot.

"Oh," I said pocketing my toonies and stepping back in line.

Just then the card worked. The lady paid her bill, thanked me again and left. The cashier smiled and asked for my order.

"Small coffee to go."

I gave him the money, then stepped aside to wait for my coffee. One of the servers handed me an extra-large, extra-hot coffee! Wow! No way could I drink all that, but I smiled and thanked her anyway. Perhaps that was their way of acknowledging my offer to help.

"Would you like a free breakfast sandwich?" called out another server. He was busily preparing food, but must have overheard our conversation at the cash.

What the heck? What's going on? I thought to myself. Oh well, just go with it.

"Sure."

"Bacon or sausage?"

"Bacon please."

"Biscuit or English muffin."

"Biscuit. Thank you very much."

I walked out of the restaurant feeling light. Somehow good karma was swirling around Tim Hortons that morning and it felt wonderful.

I got into my car and pulled the door closed. After depositing the oversized coffee in the beverage holder, I carefully unwrapped the breakfast sandwich.

It was sausage on an English muffin! Not what I'd requested! Laughing, I took a few bites anyway and started the car.

"David, is that you joking around?"

His breakfast sandwich order never changed; it was always sausage on English muffin.

Always.

And I remember bringing home an extra-large black coffee in those last years of his illness, for us to share. Made more sense economically and it became our new ritual. I'd pour half the black coffee into his special mug and hand him the cream and sugar.

My mug was a rich forest green. I liked to add a hefty amount of whole milk and heat it in the microwave. Almost like a latte.

Bittersweet memories.

Yet just now I felt good. Not sad, so maybe David's message was, "Hey! I'm still here!"

February 2014 found me in Orlando at the invitation of Peter and family. We stayed at Hilton Grand Vacations at SeaWorld, the same resort as in January 2011, six months after David's passing. I clearly remember the rough, sandpaper-like pain tearing little bits of my skin away – my inner skin, my feelings, my heart, as I yearned for David's presence. Yearned to hold him close to me. To feel his arms wrapped lovingly around my body, his gentle kiss on my neck.

Now at the three year and seven month mark, I feel as if I've made significant progress in living without David. Days are softening, the journey not as harsh. I'm beyond yearning for "proof" that he still exists somewhere, that he's not stamped out of existence (a horrid thought) I know he's here, in the sun, in the air, in my heart. And always will be. There is no fear anymore; just a comfortable "knowing". Like when you're in love – you just know.

I still look up at the sun and wish him Good Morning,

knowing that he's "up there" beaming down on me. It's a feeling of contentment. I hug those feelings close to my heart. Turn and go on with my day now, rather than aching, willing those beams of sunlight into me as if drawing David down from the sky into my body.

Unfortunately, there was more rain this week in Orlando than sunshine. We got off to a good start with one glorious sunny day. Then rain moved in for the next few days forcing us to seek indoor activities. We made the best of things by shopping and eating out, visiting Legoland and Disney stores and finished up with a trip to the science museum. Then it was back to sunshine. Tropical weather I expect, but early mornings were misty, making my ritual of watching the sun rise and greeting David impossible.

But on that last day I was delighted to see that the mists had evaporated. I had a clear view of the sun as it rose, sliding out from behind some trees. "Good Morning, David," I spoke softly, smiling inwardly, remembering those teary days on my last visit. Three years ago.

At that time, I was walking along the paths just beyond the pool area, trying to take in all the warmth and feelings of summer. It was January back home in Canada and bitter cold. As I stooped down to caress some deep purple bougainvillea edging the pathway, a sharp memory brought sudden tears to my eyes.

David standing under a bougainvillea bush, smiling into the camera.

It was on one of our vacations long ago, somewhere in the Caribbean. Those hazy days of magic and lovemaking, of dipping our toes in the ocean foam as waves splashed about our ankles.

How were we to know those happy, carefree days would come to a grinding halt? Like all couples in love, we thought they would never end.

Bougainvillea grew everywhere; huge bushes of show-girl pink, sweet coral or deep magenta. They were a delight to the senses, not being native to Canada and as I stood under a particularly profuse bush, inhaling their magic (no they don't have a scent, but I liked feeling tropical and exotic and wanted to keep that feeling with me) David snapped my pic. Well! I grabbed the camera and pushed him under the bush. Then I took his pic! Ha. Thought he would duck away or make a face, but no, he just smiled his gentle good-natured smile. The one that turned my insides to jelly. And then a kindly stranger stepped forward and offered to take a pic of both of us.

Blinking back those all-too-familiar tears, I plucked a blossom off its stem and rubbed it against my face. Inhaling deeply of its essence I imagined that the memory alone would reach up to David-in-Heaven, and he would appear on the path before me.

I squeezed my eyes tight, as much to shut out my tears as to hold on to that wish, and as I did so, the words of a song became clear through the drone of overhead music.

I will remember you. Will you remember me? Don't let your life pass you by. Weep not for the memories...

Sarah McLachlan's voice.

On this last morning in Orlando, it struck me that I was sitting on the same bench as I had three years ago. At that time I was watching for the sun to rise, believing as I still do, that David would beam down on me with his love and blessing; a fitting start to any day, but particularly on the last day of vacation.

Idly I wondered if there would be a message for me today. What else could he send me? The sun was enough. David was in the sun, the strongest and most powerful star in the universe. I was content to watch it rise, giving thanks in my heart for another beautiful day.

Ahh, but I had forgotten how creative Spirit was, how inventive, how playful. Two red cardinals popped out of the bushes in front of me. They appeared to be playing as they tumbled about, almost like young squirrels. Pecking for berries, then chasing each other, it looked like they were having fun.

A male and a female? How sweet. Thanks, David. He always told me to look for the mate. If you see a cardinal or a blue jay, the mate will not be far away. But wait a minute, these cardinals were both red, both male. How could that be? The female is always a dull brown – not as vivid as her partner.

Oh and then I really had to laugh. David and I always talked about what would happen in our "next life".

"In our next life I'm coming back as the man," I'd tease. "You be the woman and bear our children. We're having four at least!"

"Ha – that's what you think! I'm going to be the man."

"Well you can't. You're the man this time around. Next time, you be the one to get pregnant, lug the little ones around in your belly for nine months, go into excruciating labor and then have them hanging on your boobs for another nine months or more."

At this point, he'd turn a little pale and shake his head.

"Nope, no way."

"Ha – yes way – it's your turn!"

"Well, then, we'll just have to be gay." I laughed so hard I nearly wet my pants the first time David came up with that answer. And it continued to be a joke ever afterwards.

Watching those two male cardinals (they must have been youngsters at play), I couldn't help but smile, then chuckle, then I had to get up and walk away before someone saw this old lady sitting on a bench, laughing at apparently nothing more than birds frolicking about in the bushes.

Well, David, I thought to myself. You've done it this time,

for who would "think" of something so creative? So normal to nature, the interpretation of which only I would know. Ha-ha. Spirit sure is clever.

David – I love you!

Part II

Chapter 1

Moving On

It's been almost five years. And I've Moved On.

Not in the sense of finding a mate, a partner, a husband. Moved On as in Acceptance.

Moved On as in coming to terms with his death, his absence in my life.

Moved On as in living every day solo; accepting with grace all the frustrations, struggles and poor decisions that inevitably occur in life without a partner to bounce things off of.

Moving On as in searching out, reaching up, catching hold of and embracing the smallest feeling of joy: a balanced checkbook, hanging clothes on the line to dry in the sunshine, a warm smile, a helping hand, the first green shoots of spring, the aroma of freshly brewed coffee, curling up with a good book, an unexpected lunch invitation.

Moving On as in choosing to survive, to face my fears and grow stronger in spite of them (or because of them).

Moving On as in seeking out and capturing Peace of Mind if only for a little while.

In Accepting that Peace of Mind is possible without guilty strings attached.

Not that it's been a smooth ride; on the contrary – it's been rough.

Waves of grief still envelop me, but I've learned to ride those waves when they appear, sometimes at the slightest of triggers. A song, a smell, a dancing butterfly in an unexpected place.

Someone who looks like David.

Yes, that happened a few times in the Second Year.

Silver Butterflies turned into Silver Dragonflies that second year, and I saw plenty.

"Dragonfly is the essence of the winds of change, the messengers of wisdom and enlightenment..." according to my Medicine Card Deck (Sams and Carson, 1988).

Well, I don't know how enlightened I became, but I knew I was growing spiritually and with more sensitivity to the goings-on around me.

Signs and messages I used to question now became my new normal. 4:44 on a digital clock made me smile, as did 11:11 or 3:33. The deep throated mating call of a cardinal not only flashed a memory of David's playful side, but also sent the undeniable message that a new season, a new cycle of life was here and now; not in the past or imaginable future, but now. Today.

Life was constantly flowing, changing and I'd better move with it or run the risk of being left behind. With this heightened perception I began to seek out and embrace patterns in our natural world that would bring me to a place of deeper meaning.

There were times when nothing happened. Months would go by without a hint, or a whisper of his essence and I'd begin to worry. Other times, a whole cluster of signs would appear and I wondered if David was warning me of something.

One crisp autumn morning as I was dressing for the day, I decided it was high time I took a shopping trip to Burlington, Vermont. Time to do something different, something daring. David and I always made this trip together; I'd never done it on my own.

Without stopping to worry, to analyze, or talk myself out of it, I took the elevator down to the parking garage, got into my car and zoomed up the ramp out of the condo and into the street. Turning left on Lakeshore Road, I headed south -- towards the Champlain Bridge.

Rush hour traffic had thinned to a steady stream and the

first half hour of my trip was uneventful. However, as I neared the Canada/US border I began to feel uneasy. What would the Customs Officials think of me travelling alone? Would he believe me if I told him I was shopping?

Cross-border shopping is an event. Women plan for this and head out together anticipating bargains, sales, and outlet pricing. They make a whole day of it with giggles and gossip, restaurant food, lots of chattering and nothing else to do but let loose.

Nobody goes on their own, do they? There's safety in numbers – was I being foolish?

My mouth was dry, but I was afraid to reach over for my water bottle in case taking my eyes off the road for an instant would cause the car to swerve and hit another car – or a tree, as I was driving through some heavily forested areas now. Sweat made my hands feel clammy and I found myself nervously glancing in the rear view mirror. Why, I don't really know. I think I was hoping to catch sight of a friendly police car.

Normally, you hope not to encounter police en route, but if it happens, you automatically slow down, whether you're exceeding the speed limit or not.

Today, however, I needed some reassurance, needed to know whether my decisions were impulsive and dangerous or spontaneous and adventuresome. Was I actually jumping into life and fear be damned? Or behaving like some crazy person, taking off at the drop of a hat?

Many women travel alone, many women live alone, but this had not been my experience. I admire those courageous souls who simply go about their lives, sometimes their whole lives all on their own. Do they flip-flop in fear as I do? Do they worry about every little decision?

Flickering thoughts of turning back had me tightening my grip on the steering wheel. Really, I didn't have to make this trip. But if I turned around now would this count as another failure? Would I once again run back home to the safety of my cocoon? Couldn't I even drive two hours down the road to a cross-border mall without ambivalence?

But, I reminded myself – I'm much stronger than I was that first trembling year. I can go out at night even in one of the deepest, darkest coldest winter evenings. I still don't like it, but I can do it.

A car abruptly swung out to pass me in the left lane. Startled, I immediately took my foot off the gas. It was pure reaction, like stepping back to put some distance between us. Who was at the wheel of that car? Was he some weird character, or just in an awful hurry?

Instinctively I glanced at the license plate (in case I had to report a drunk driver) and did a double-take.

It read DAVID. Simply DAVID, no numbers or other letters. I let out a sigh of relief and knew right then and there, everything would be okay.

There were other signs those early years that I did not mention before. Not quite two weeks after David died, Little Nathan pointed to the ceiling in our living room and asked, "What's that?" Brenda and I looked.

There was nothing.

"What's that?" he persisted. Brenda knew intuitively that it was David hovering. I was trying not to think of his absence in our home. It was all so fresh and painful, so I pushed that thought away and walked into another room.

In February of 2012, Brenda, her family, another one of my grandchildren and I went to Fort Myers for a winter escape. We stayed at the Pink Shell Resort, a beautiful hotel right on the beach.

One morning about halfway through our vacation, we were on our way to breakfast.

"Who's Missing?" asks five-year-old Jasmine as we step into

the hotel elevator.

I was taken aback.

Heads swivel around as we check each other out. There are six of us. Grandmother, Daughter, Son-in-Law, and three of my grandchildren.

"Nobody's missing, Jasmine."

The elevator doors whisk open and we step out into the hallway and on towards the dining room. A huge buffet breakfast is waiting for us and we're hungry.

Another day. Palm trees sway in a lazy breeze and a strong sun warms and nourishes my winter weary soul. Every morning I rise early and walk the beach. The sand is unbelievably soft and powdery underfoot and I revel in its smoothness as I head straight for the ocean. Waves lap at the shoreline with a rhythm of their own and I take my time wading into the shallow, cool waters. Shells crunch under my bare feet here, but I don't mind.

Looking up, I see a V-formation of brown pelicans flying quite close to the water. Suddenly one of them dives headfirst into the ocean, no doubt to spear a poor unsuspecting fish.

Back at the hotel, the family is waiting for me. I quickly change out of my beach clothes and into a summer dress. We leave together for the breakfast feast. All six of us step into the elevator.

Jasmine turns to look at me. "Who's missing?"

Once again, I'm taken aback.

Once again, Brenda and I look at each other, then glance swiftly around, although we know everyone is here.

My daughter bends down and looks her daughter right in the eye.

"Nobody's missing, sweetie."

A strange feeling comes over me and I shiver a little.

"Could it be Vincent? Katie? Lara? Stella?"

Jasmine shakes her head.

Having eliminated her playmates, I try for cousins. "Is it

Simon? Ryan? Owen? Adrian?"

"No."

Light is beginning to dawn on me, but I decide to keep quiet.

Weather here in Fort Myers, Florida has been absolutely perfect. There is a kind of serenity, a warmth and peaceful feeling to the air as we spend our days walking in sunshine under clear tropical skies. It's such a relief to leave bulky winter coats at home and slip effortlessly into sandals and flip-flops, kicking them off with careless abandon to walk barefoot in the sand or around the pool.

The children were delighted to spend each day splashing about in the Resort pool, or making sand castles and sand mermaids on the beach. Twice during our trip, we watched a pair of young dolphins swim so close to shore we could almost touch them.

It was a welcome change for me to take a vacation with my family, rather than going alone.

It was good for my family to take a break from their work and school routine. Although we'd had a mild winter this year, there seemed to be a lot of viruses going around. Everyone had been sick off and on since before Christmas. It was definitely time for a change of venue.

All too soon our vacation was over. This was to be our last day. The children were eager to get back home to familiar surroundings. They missed their pets, toys, and friends.

We'd had a wonderful time and were ready to go home. I think we were all getting a little weary of restaurant food (with the exception of those sumptuous breakfasts).

The elevator seemed to be slow this morning, but we didn't mind. This was a day to take things easy, to savor our last moments here in Florida.

Finally it arrived. Doors opened with a whoosh and the children surged in – all wanting to "press the button" for the appropriate floor.

Jasmine turned to look at me.

"Who's missing?" she asks yet again.

Mother makes a decision. It's time to get to the bottom of this.

"Is it a boy or a girl?"

"A boy," she replies.

I take the plunge. "Is it David?"

"Yes."

Acceptance. That terrifying word we didn't want to think about way back at the beginning. That hateful word we thought meant agreement with the tragic event. That annoying word that has finally transformed, mellowed, evolved.

It simply means to stop resisting, stop wishing for things that can never be. It means to live in the present moment. To make peace with whatever nightmares we are trying to deny. Or run away from.

For the first four years, I continued to run away. I sold our home, moved into a condo, then bought another house and moved again. I was restless. Unhappy. Walking, biking, swimming, constantly fleeing grief.

One day, with nothing better to do, I decided to check out the Houses for Sale online, hoping to see My Old Home back on the market. I settled into the sofa with my laptop, clicked on the appropriate link, squished my eyes shut and held my breath as the For Sale page loaded. I must have looked silly, eyes closed in front of my laptop, but I was hesitant to face the truth, whatever it may be.

I took a quick peek. Nothing. Darn!

Ah well, the new family hadn't been there very long, just under the two year mark. They would probably be there forever. Discouraged I put on my coat and went out into the damp and dreary afternoon to kick up some late winter snow. I turned up the street towards the park. Even though it would be deserted in winter, just looking at the play area with its swings and structures, surrounding hedge and huge soccer field was soothing. I could imagine carefree and happy youngsters playing once spring finally arrived.

Back home I took off my outdoor clothes and headed for the kitchen to plug in the kettle. Cranberry tea in hand, I settled into my spot on the living room sofa with laptop and figured I'd try again, just to be sure. Nothing to lose.

I didn't bother holding my breath nor squishing my eyes closed, but watched as the Houses For Sale page loaded. Clicking on my old neighborhood in Hudson, I got the shock of my life. There it was – My Old Home – For Sale!

I was overjoyed! I was heartbroken. Could I possibly move back into Our Home?

Oh why didn't they tell me before putting it on the market? Back when I was living in the rental condo and looking to purchase a house? I could have bought it back then – even without a Real Estate Agent and have saved myself the cost and upheaval of moving into this house that I never really liked in the first place.

The only saving grace here was a duck pond, just down the street.

I had settled in St. Lazare, a community not far from our Old Home, still unsure if this was what I really wanted. Originally, I had thought to move closer to my children, closer to town. But I seemed to be pulled back to the countryside where David and I had shared our lives; the abundance of trees, fresh air, gracious homes and sweeping lawns, oodles of space out here with horse farms and apple orchards practically around the corner. I was remembering what it was like to live in a smaller close-knit community, where neighbors called greetings, discussed remedies for lawn grubs over the garden fence, shared recipes for apple crumble or strawberry rhubarb pie, and as often as not handed you a slice fresh from the oven. Garage doors were left wide open if you had to pop out for a while and people generally looked out for one another.

I missed this life. Our life.

I missed Our Home.

And now I'd only been in this new home for five months. Could I resell it? What about all the money I'd poured into it?

I thought I was done with renovations earlier on when I had to get Our Home ready for sale. But this new house had more. I was in shock! Extensive electrical work had to be undertaken, new garage door installed, fireplace completely rebuilt, landscaping (I foolishly bought in winter and did not know the deplorable condition of the backyard), new sump pump installed, and on and on.

What to do, what to do? Was this a fantasy of mine? Did I really want Our Home back or was it Our Old Life that I longed for. I knew if I could sell my new house and buy back my old one, I'd be losing a lot of money. Would it be worth it? Would I leave myself financially in a hole?

Flip-flip, flip-flop, I felt as if I was back in that first confusing, vulnerable state of Year One.

I let the winter go by. I needed time. But it always came back to, "I want Our Home back." I became obsessed. I pictured myself sitting in our sunny kitchen, watching chickadees hopping from clothesline to cedar hedge, their distinctive "chickadee-dee-dee" ringing out true and free. I saw myself wandering out onto our back deck, down the steps and over to my beloved Grandfather Oak. Dear God, I hope they didn't chop him down! I imagined myself sleeping in our bedroom once again, showering in our bathroom. Was I crazy? Or could this really happen?

Finally, at the end of March, I had to make a decision. Winter is not a good time to sell a house here in Montreal, but come spring, the market changes drastically. Time to get going and either sell this new house or forget my fantasy.

I called a Real Estate Agent and booked a visit to my Old

Home for the following day – Monday morning. There was a good chance the homeowners would be at work. Actually I was counting on this, because for some reason I felt uncomfortable; totally embarrassed as if I'd made a terrible mistake in giving up my home in the first place.

Mr. Agent and I were to meet in front of the house. He was already there, car running to keep warm as I pulled up to the curb. Even after all this time, it felt strange not to be pulling into the driveway – their driveway now.

Deep snow still covered the lawn, but the walkway was freshly shoveled and we could see bare paving stones beneath our feet as we made our way up to the front porch.

"I remember the year David and I had those Unistones put down to replace the old slippery railway ties. Imagine making a front walk..."

Before I could finish, the front door opened wide and The New Owners' Agent stood there smiling at us.

"Come on in."

"Still cold, isn't it?" We chatted politely to cover the awkwardness of slipping off winter boots, careful not to step in the melting snow left on the mat.

"I'll just be in here if you have any questions." She smiled pleasantly, turned and walked into the living room, settling herself on the sofa.

Both excited and a little nervous now that I was finally back inside my home, I sucked in a breath and took stock of my surroundings. The front hall where we were standing looked the same, except that they'd changed the light fixture. It was more elegant and modern than the one "we" had. Okay, I can handle that.

Living room – nice furniture, nice vibes, except the dining room table was placed diagonally in a far corner of the room. Whatever.

Dining room – same chic light fixture here as in the hallway, but instead of traditional china cabinets, table and chairs, they'd turned this space into an office. It looked rather cluttered with papers strewn about. An assortment of pens, paperclips, boxes of labels and other junk littered the surface of an office desk and printer cables hung over the side slithering into a coil on the floor. Hmm.

I tried to absorb this "modernization" of traditional living space, of squashing the dining table in with the living room furniture. Not much room for big family gatherings. And who wants to stare at office paraphernalia while eating Thanksgiving dinner?

Still mulling this over, I continued on into the kitchen – my kitchen.

Ewwww, they'd removed my beautiful tiffany ceiling light! It fit so well in that space, softening the country kitchen look with its rose and jade floral pattern. Its warm tones illuminated our kitchen table every day, as if blessing our food.

This new fixture was very plain. Not nice at all.

The Bay window stood out as proudly as ever. Ah, it was beautiful! Magnificent with its sweeping view of the back garden and neighboring homes. But where were the windowsills? Those pine shelves David had installed years ago where I proudly displayed potted plants and a few knickknacks for contrast. They were gone.

And what was that huge recycling/garbage bin doing in the middle of the kitchen?

What on earth? Where was the love, the character, the coziness of a real kitchen? The very heart of any home? I nearly cried. It was just so different!

On to the TV room where David spent his last weeks in this house. My mellow sage green walls had been painted a boring beige. They'd added dark bamboo shades to the patio doors and taken down my beautiful curtains. Why did they keep my curtains if they didn't want them? Normally, unless you have something very expensive, you leave the window coverings for the new owners as a courtesy. But really, if they were just going to trash them, I'd have taken them with me!

The brick fireplace looked grungy and old. And the whole room appeared smaller than I remembered. I was beginning to feel queasy, anxious and wanted to keep moving.

Around the corner and on to the garage. I opened the inner door and looked into a room that was extremely dirty. Yuk! And the laundry tub was missing.

What the heck?

Why remove a perfectly good laundry tub? And just where were they dumping the dirty wash water, if not down that laundry tub? Some people dump it down the toilet, but then you have to clean the toilet. In the laundry tub, all you have to do is rinse it. I used to scrub my flowerpots in that tub as well. It was convenient to go from garden to garage, clean the pots then store them for the winter. And the painters would wash their brushes in that sink in the garage as well. Rather that than in my kitchen sink!

Breathe, breathe, breathe, I chanted silently. Abruptly, I spun on my heel and let the garage door slam on its own. The basement stairs were on my left and I took a moment.

To pause.

At the top.

What would be waiting down in the depths?

Sliding my hands nervously over the banister, I began my descent, into what I thought would be an old familiar space. That worn-out part of the house where the treadmill stood, where hubby would diligently perform his exercise routine in an effort to keep COPD at bay.

Solid Ikea shelving units lined the walls where old books settled in between odds and ends. There was a box of discarded hardware, hinges, and brackets and whatnot, some well-loved but shabby toys from eons ago that I held on to for my grandchildren, and yes, our old coffeemaker rested front row and center on those shelves – just in case. They might have been a bit dusty and tired looking, but at least those shelves kept a dark basement space neat and organized.

"Functional," David would say.

One winter, I planted up pots of bulbs: lilies and rock tulips and hyacinths and placed them under the sunny south-facing window, on one of those shelves. They never bloomed.

I came to a halt at the bottom of the stairs, sucked in a breath to fortify myself, pushed open the flimsy pressed-wood door and walked into the most beautiful room in the house!

"Oh!" Startled, I didn't realize I'd made a sound, until Mr. Agent turned to look at me, eyebrows raised.

"It's so different!"

Luxurious carpeting hugged the floors in a becoming shade of Dove grey, a warm inviting grey, that made you want to slip down into its softness and linger for a while. Wall units and shelves were gone. Artwork brightened the walls changing the basement/storage dullness to a place of leisure, clean and modern and yes, I had to admit – happy.

An old macrame lamp I'd left hanging in a corner was gone. Instead a more subdued recessed lighting softened the area. Large screen TV, comfy corduroy sofas and beanbag chair, proper stand-alone bookcases and a whole array of colorful toys echoed the joys of a young family.

But my joy was short-lived when we entered the sump pump room. The electrical panel door was hanging open, dangling wires clamped at the ends. How dangerous! What had been going on here since I left? Didn't these people know how to look after a house? The discarded laundry tub sat on the bare cement, cracked and broken. Old pieces of metal and other junk littered the floor with careless abandon.

A feeling of dizziness swept over me and I leaned back against the door frame for support, willing my thumping heart to behave.

Don't be ridiculous, I scolded myself silently, wiping sweaty palms on jeans. This is their home now. Not mine. I'm just looking.

Seeing the expression on my face, or perhaps sensing my inner feelings, Mr. Agent tactfully suggested we go back upstairs. I nodded, but instead of waiting for him, marched on ahead. Nobody had to tell me where the bedrooms were – *I* knew the way.

The master bedroom was located in the north-east corner of the house, at the end of a long hallway. I practically flew up the stairs in my eagerness to be back in "our room" once again. To immerse myself in the space David and I had shared so intimately; to recapture that intimacy, if only for a few moments.

Awk! I nearly fainted. It was completely different! To see the disrepair of a basement utility room was one thing, but to run face-to-face into the complete and total transformation of *our old husband-and-wife bedroom* nearly finished me.

Not even recognizable.

Intellectually, I knew this was a perfectly natural thing for the new owners to do. In fact, I had insisted we redecorate when I moved in with David back in 1996. But we made it pretty! We made it sensual. This was our Love Nest and we made it come alive!

I remember crying when I took down our beloved "Arizona" wallpaper with its sunset colors and teal border as I was preparing the house for sale. We had special ordered that wallpaper after looking for-seemingly-ever to find something that fit us perfectly. I had the bare walls painted a shade of soft vanilla cream that I thought would appeal to someone buying my house.

But these people had painted over that dreamy color; it was a shade of blah or beige or mushroom or whatever that nondescript color was called and there was absolutely nothing of "us" remaining at all. Blinds were the same dark bamboo as everywhere else in the house, nothing special or personal for this most intimate room.

Instead it was completely mundane with plain bedspread, one small dresser with no mirror and no lamps. Not a knickknack in sight or pictures on the walls – not even a bottle of perfume!

Who lived here?

David's study was next door and I was almost afraid to enter. I held my breath and squeezed my eyes shut for an instant, hoping against hope that when I opened them, I would find everything unchanged.

Of course it was all changed. Really. Did I think it wouldn't be? Sunny yellow walls, sheers in a rich cream, and chocolate brown carpet had all vanished. Instead we were engulfed by that lifeless neutral decor that was beginning to give me a headache. Where was the spirit, the zest, the character in this home?

Foolishly, I hoped I might sense a wee bit of David's presence lingering in this room, begging me to come back. His den, his study where he spent a considerable amount of time, sitting at his desk balancing checkbooks and looking after all of our financial matters, turned out to be disappointing. Nothing but dull, drab, non-energy if that makes any sense. Clearly there was not even a trace of my spirited husband in here.

Thoroughly discouraged we took our leave. Our beautiful, loving home which I relinquished to this young family in the hopes that they would love and cherish it as we had, proved not to be the case. At all. Tears threatened, but I held them in.

The final straw came as I walked around to the backyard. Snow covered our deck, and when I looked for the familiar greenery of surrounding hedges, they were gone. Our chickadees' playground had been mercilessly dug up and tossed away.

Quickly I looked to Grandfather Oak. In my dreams and fantasies I was once again embracing that special place where my cherished rituals were performed; rituals I prayed would reach David in the Afterlife. I imagined myself sighing with relief as I poured coffee down his roots to welcome him back into my life.

But the new people had severely trimmed his branches! He looked like a lifeless barren pole. Where was my wise old friend? The one who whispered compassion and bore witness to my grief? The one I could count on for connection and warmth, comfort and hope?

And Lady. Our beautiful shade tree whose long slender branches and wispy leaves formed a silvery/green canopy over our back deck.

What had they done to her? I can't remember what kind of tree she was, only that her trunk was like a braid, three trunks woven together. That's why I called her Lady; her triple trunk represented the triple Goddess: maiden, mother, crone.

But one of her trunks had been chopped! Off! Right down to the base!

How could they do that?

She'd never survive such an amputation! She who was such a solid loving presence in our backyard. Cool, calm, offering tranquility and shelter from hot afternoon sun. Periwinkle grew affectionately at her roots. There was absolutely no way I could restore any of this home to its former self.

I thanked the agent, jumped into my car and drove home crying all the way. I did not even stop to pick up a coffee. I just wanted out of there.

As March melted into April and the earth warmed, I turned my attention to my new garden in my new home. I knew I had to let go of the past.

Chapter 2

Testing My Wings

Something unexpected happened around the four year mark. I began to notice men. If someone good-looking passed by, I'd notice. Hmmm. In the years leading up to this point (and the point was rather vague) I must have allowed myself to open up. To stop shrinking into myself, hoping no one would notice my tousled hair and lack of makeup.

Hoping no one would notice me.

I didn't care what I looked like all that first year. But during the second year, a tiny trickle of well-being or vanity kicked in and I began to take an interest in keeping my hair and nails styled and polished.

Honestly though, I was far too busy packing, cleaning, moving and trying to adjust to this new life to give a fig about my appearance.

And I really didn't care. The thought of someone else in David's shoes made me shudder.

No, I would not go there. I felt totally dried up and asexual. There was no place in my life for a romantic relationship.

And I didn't care. Really.

It must have been on one of my travels. It's hard to travel alone, especially when you're not used to it. Couples travel together. They dine together and dance. Stretch out on the beach or at the pool in twos or with children. Did I really want to live out the rest of my life alone?

No.

I wanted a relationship again, wanted someone to share my life with, someone to talk to, eat and sleep with.

Then I had to open my mind to the possibility.

That's how I begin anything that seems like a dream,

something that is so far in the future as to be unobtainable. I start by imagining it to be true.

But, I'm not ready! a knee-jerk reaction, a voice echoing in my brain sounding exactly like David's retort after the "mask incident" five weeks before he died.

Before even thinking about a life with someone else, I had to let go of that blocking voice.

Patiently, I changed that thought to:

I *am* ready.

A quick catch in my breath, a twist in my gut, then slowly, consciously, exhaling; letting my breath go and relaxing enough to embrace that new feeling. A feeling that was strange, disloyal at first, but with practice (who knew talking to oneself required practice?) I managed to not cringe or recoil when whispering those words.

Saying them out loud.

Making them real.

As time went on and with the help of my online Widows Support Group, I began to change. Some other widows a few years ahead of me had gone on to forge new relationships. They were happy once again. Happy and passionate about Life. Oh they would never forget their lover, their soulmate, their best friend; the one they had vowed to spend the rest of their lives with, raised children with (in some cases), worked and played, nursed and protected throughout a devastating terminal illness, or suffered the shock of a violent or untimely death. No, they would not forget, nor stop loving, but this new relationship was different, almost like living on another plane.

How could that be?

How could you love someone intimately right now, and still love the one who'd passed away? How could you divide your heart, your feelings that way?

The whole concept seemed foreign to me. I couldn't understand or make sense out of it, but then I had to trust those who were walking the path before me.

And they all said the same thing. Unthinkable at first, but then it happens.

First things first, and for me that meant opening my mind to the *possibility* of being in a new relationship.

What I remember reading time and time again on that site was that we survivors are here. Our life is not over yet. Why throw it away on sorrow forever?

Would our husband/wife/lover want that?

I think not.

As I move towards the five year mark I wonder – what will life hold for me now?

I did manage to sell my home in St. Lazare, after living there for only two years. It was not a hard decision to make at the emotional level, as it never really felt right. But in practical terms, it was absurd.

Moving again. It seemed as if I was continually throwing money out the window on moving costs and agent's fees. Not to mention the expensive renovations and hard work I put into that home even before moving in. I was trying to make it into a "perfect house" (which it never was anyway). As I look back I wonder if this insistence on "perfection" was really a control issue. Nobody can control death. I can't bring my husband back, but I can control my surroundings.

I am reminded of that frantic need to clean out after David died. To rip up carpets, renovate the powder room, paint the house from top to bottom. Of course I was preparing to sell, but what if I'd taken my time, changed things that needed to be changed – slowly. Enjoyed the process of rebuilding my life instead of tearing it apart? Would I still be living in Our Home?

Probably. Yes, most certainly, but I was not in the right frame of mind to rebuild. I was hurt, shattered, trying desperately to erase the all-consuming grief through frenzied activity. It was all about pushing away, running as far and as fast as I could.

Not, "Oh well, time to move on."

No, I'm glad I'm not back in that space. Yet my problems are far from over. I have to move. Once again. But where?

It's mid-May 2015 now and after two months of looking, I still haven't found a place to live. Time is running out and with three weeks left before I have to vacate the St. Lazare house a decision has to be made.

What is happening to me? Am I destined to fail at everything? Will nothing "nice and suitable" turn up? Am I crazy switching houses all the time?

Impatiently I pace the floor, open and slam cupboard doors mentally assessing whether I have enough packing boxes. I check the online realtor sites in case the perfect house has finally surfaced. Yes, My Old Home is still on the market, but I don't want it any more.

I can't go back.

Open the fridge. Close it again. Not much in there as I've stopped cooking altogether – and I don't really care. It's much easier to plop a slice of bread into the toaster and smear it with peanut butter and jam.

I will not cry. I will not feel sorry for myself. Others don't have a roof over their heads and are forced to live by the side of the road. Others don't have Internet, a car, family or friends.

Finally I come to a decision. I'll have to put my furniture in storage and move in temporarily with Brenda and her family. I realize how blessed I am to have this opportunity; how fortunate to have a daughter both willing and able to accommodate me for a short while, but that means I'll be moving twice.

Boxes are strewn all around, packing partially done. I'm dismantling this part of my life – yet again.

For the millionth time I ask myself, "What am I doing here?" I've moved twice in the past four years and am getting ready to move again.

It's disorienting at 63 years old to be going through constant upheaval in my life in terms of where to live. Nothing feels right and I'm so tired of putting things in boxes, of throwing things away, of cleaning out and cleaning up. Maybe I need to purge once again. But I haven't even bought proper bedroom furniture yet. Could not find anything I liked. So why this paring down, this decluttering, when I feel I'm already slim and sleek?

I wish, I wish, I wish I'd never sold Our Home. It had plenty of space. It had character. It had David. Now I cannot go back. Perhaps that's just the way life is. I need to remember to put one foot in front of the other, head up and looking forward. Walking straight into the wind. Not wavering.

Summer with my daughter and her family was wonderful. The children were at camp during the day which gave me time to myself. Mornings I'd go for long walks in the neighborhood or hop on my bike and pedal down to the lake. In the afternoon I'd relax in the backyard with a book and a cold drink or run errands or shop. Dinner was always a time of lively conversation with everyone wanting to talk about their day. After washing dishes and cleaning up the kitchen, I couldn't wait to snuggle up with my grandchildren on the sofa and watch whatever was on TV.

Summer eventually faded into autumn. Children went back to school. I became restless. It seemed everyone had something to do, had something to occupy their time. Brenda and Evan had their careers, children were at school, what did I have? This wasn't my home, no matter how good it felt to be here with family.

Winter arrived full force with its paralyzing blizzards and long dark nights. Animals hibernate, birds fly south and people spend more time inside, shutting tight windows and doors against harsh cold and snow. It was January, the beginning of another new year and I felt a need to fly south as well.

A friend of mine suggested I take a cruise. She was a widow

also and preferred travel on a ship surrounded by people.

"You don't have to pack and unpack as you would on a land tour," she explained, "and each port of call has its own character. There are soooo many activities, you'll never be bored or lonely and meeting people is part of the fun. Everyone takes time to chat. Oh, and the food! It's out of this world!"

"Really?"

"Yes. There is such a variety of dishes and they never run out. You can eat as much as you want."

Hmm, I hadn't even thought about that. Running out of food or anything else on a cruise.

Well why not? Might as well go for it – I have nothing to lose, really. David and I had never cruised before, so this would be another "first".

I booked my tickets and off I went. A seven-day Western Caribbean cruise sounded about right. Not too short, not too long. Seven days would be plenty for my maiden voyage and I hoped I wouldn't get seasick. One always hears stories of this happening to ruin a vacation. Or of people sailing through the Bermuda Triangle never to return. Shivery goosebumps ran up and down my arms. Really! I was scaring myself. Time to put these silly thoughts out of my head!

The flight to Fort Lauderdale was short and sweet and I arrived in time to hop on the airport bus. As we headed to the docks in Port Canaveral a welcome feeling of release, of reckless abandon flowed through the open window on a fragrant tropical breeze, ruffling my hair and making me feel like laughing out loud. I didn't of course, but turned to my seat mate to share some of my sudden enthusiasm, my joy at being on this adventure. Turns out she was quite a bit older than I and completely comfortable travelling alone, which gave me a boost of confidence. Others could do it. So could I!

Arriving at the docks, we poured out of the bus and into the rapturous heat of a January sun. Oh, how delightful to leave the winter behind in Canada and warm my bones here in Florida!

Norwegian Spirit was the name of our cruise ship and it loomed far above us tiny humans standing in the parking lot. People were milling about on the pavement, greeting one another with hugs and kisses, taking pics, or heading for the long lineup waiting to embark. I quickly joined the line and nervously looked about. I had no idea what to do, what to expect. Others had their passports in hand, ready to show the officials, so I did the same.

I made my way up on deck and drank in the beautiful sights surrounding me. So caught up was I in the process of boarding and finding my cabin that I hadn't realized how the day was slipping away. A mellow sun hung low in the western sky, its soft hues of butter cream and orange having a calming effect on sea and sky, as if preparing for a long dark night. People on shore were waving a final good-by before driving away or walking towards the buses. Small boats anchored close by bobbed up and down in the waves, looking very much like toys from my vantage point.

A fishy-smelling breeze sprang up just as I felt the ship beginning to move. Excitement rippled through my body and bubbled up into my throat. I felt like singing! We were off!

Yet in the next instant a stab of anxiety, of worry tightened my chest. Would I be seasick? Would the ship sink? Would I absolutely hate cruising, spending a whole week with all these strangers?

Or, I sucked in a breath determined to turn those betraying thoughts around, would I have a total and complete blast? Would I be thrilled, elated to be riding the Ocean for seven days? Imagine – being a part of that magnetic pull, that powerful Ocean spirit that goes beyond mere water or even playful waves.

Hanging on to those feelings of elation, I left the deck and went in search of the dining area for a hot cup of coffee and to check out the dinner menu.

The first full day on board took some getting used to. It was the constant motion of the ship; that side-to-side almost drunk feeling underfoot that felt so unsettling.

Early morning sunlight woke me out of a sound sleep and I peeked out the window to see where we were. Ha! How could I tell? It was sea and sky with not a bird or other vessel in sight. Breakfast was a quick affair as I was eager to explore the ship. Coffee, scrambled eggs and strawberries disappeared from my plate and off I went promising myself to return for a mid-morning snack (pastries, melon, yoghurt, muffins were calling me, I swear!).

All through that first day I was consumed by dizziness to the point where I had to sit down a few times or I'd fall. It was unnerving! I felt loopy, off-kilter and wondered if anyone else was feeling this way. People strolling about seemed to be unconcerned, nobody appeared ill or unbalanced. But perhaps those feeling under the weather had taken refuge in their cabins.

My cabin was small but adequate with a good-sized picture window. I absolutely had to be able to see beyond the ship, to look out over that vast expanse to the horizon, to touch base with the sun, that reassuring presence in my life, that David presence, constantly beaming down from the heavens.

A room with a balcony would have been even better, for I could be that much closer to the elements, a part of it all. Unfortunately those cabins were already taken when I made the booking.

No matter, I wouldn't be spending much time in my room anyway.

Feeling strangely out of place and a little frightened, I wandered around from floor to floor, settling in the Atrium which was located in the heart of the ship. It served as the hub where announcements, entertainment and various exhibits took place.

A display of glittery bracelets drew my eye and I stopped to admire the amethyst and ruby sparkles, the intricate handmade designs. Fine platinum and rose gold necklaces were richly draped in purple silk under glass and a little further along I could see broaches, earrings, and expensive-looking men's watches. Seemed like there was something to suit every taste.

Turning to my right I noticed a line of people waiting to speak to an official stationed behind a desk. I assumed this was for all manner of passenger inquiries. Along the adjacent wall stood a counter with a sign overhead "Shore Excursions". Towering palm trees reaching up to a brilliantly blue sky tempted from huge posters plastered all over the walls. Sugar sand beaches lay below where sunbathers stretched out on long chairs soaking up the sun. Another poster featured platter-sized manta rays floating lazily about in the aquamarine waters off the Caymans.

"Come swim with us," they invited.

How could one resist?

Or for those landlubbers, trolley or train tours were offered through historic parts of town with scheduled stops to shop or taste local cuisine. Anyone longing for more adventurous pursuits had plenty to choose from: windsurfing, rock climbing, open Jeep rides up through the mountains, zip-lining, forest tours and on and on and on.

On the far side of the Atrium a quaint-looking Cafe nestled in a corner and a little further along, a noisy 24-hour restaurant was busy serving up pizza, hamburgers, French fries, sodas and ice cream. Definitely something for everyone on this cruise ship.

I made my way over to the Cafe. Here was a place I could seek refuge. Coffee Corners were familiar places, safe and cozy where one could sit all day and not feel threatened. Nobody paid attention to those sipping coffee, writing in notebooks, working on a laptop, alone or with friends. And as I was definitely alone and feeling ill at ease on this cruise, I did not want to draw attention to myself.

I ordered a cappuccino which was served up elegantly in

a real china cup by a smiling young lady. Oh, this was nice! We chatted pleasantly for a few moments and I felt myself beginning to relax.

After an hour or so of people watching, I left the Cafe, wandered idly around and eventually found myself at the entrance to The Theatre. Might as well see what's going on I thought, slipping quietly into an empty seat close to the door.

It was a performance of acrobats, which turned out to be rather entertaining, but nothing really special. I did wonder how they could keep their balance as the ship swayed and bumped quite frequently.

After the show I retraced my steps to the Atrium where someone was playing the piano. The music was pleasant enough, something popular that I couldn't place. Continuing on, I found myself in front of a staircase which led to an upper deck. A game of "trivia" was in full swing with guests calling out answers at random. I did not know if I should excuse myself for traipsing through, but nobody paid me any attention, so I just kept going.

Further along was a tiny room made into a corner store where snacks were available for purchase, along with designer clothing and purses, makeup, jewelry, watches and pharmacy goods. That's where I was headed to see if I could find something to relieve this dizziness.

I scanned the shelves, uncertain. I must have stood there for long time deliberating. "Try these," urged a creaky voice to my left. Startled, I turned to look into the crinkly eyes of an older gentleman all dressed up in a suit and tie on this very warm day. Briefly I wondered what he could possibly want with me.

Leaning against the counter for support, he pulled back the cuff of his shirt to reveal an elasticized bracelet. Ah, I had heard all about these special bracelets. They were designed to press on specific acupressure points along the wrist to relieve symptoms of seasickness.

"Works for me." He gave me a wink and a nod, picked up a packet of breath mints and drifted away.

Well, I had to try something and it might as well be harmless bracelets than an ingested substance for which I'd be sorry later on!

There was a bit of a lineup at the cash, but I didn't mind. When it was my turn I plunked down the package of bracelets and smiled at the cashier.

"I hope these do the trick!"

She smiled in return. "Oh yes. I'm sure they will!"

With a lightness in my heart and bounce in my step, off I went in search of dinner.

Mouth-watering aromas wafting from the dining room greeted me as I stepped off the elevator and suddenly I was hungry. There was so much food here: tempting fall-off-the-bone prime rib with roasted potatoes, a whole salmon garnished with lemon wedges and sliced to perfection, healthy-looking stir-fries with pineapple chunks or fresh green broccoli, savory black beans and rice and tons of crunchy salads, rolls and butter, soup, sauces and on and on! Everything was beautifully presented and served with a smile. I picked up a tray and chose some delicate pink salmon, wild rice laced with mushrooms and green peppers, a scoop of mango stir-fry and a grainy-looking salad that must be either couscous or quinoa. There was way too much food on my tray, but I wanted to taste everything!

It was heavenly! Melt in your mouth salmon, tangy and fresh stir-fry, all was good, but far too much. With a twinge of guilt, I left about half of it and headed for the dessert table.

When I returned to my spot with a slice of key lime pie and chocolate cake (oh what a glutton I was turning out to be!), my half-eaten supper tray had vanished; the staff here were extremely competent and as I looked around could find nothing out of place. People were eating in groups or alone with no messy empty trays in sight.

Later in my cabin, as I was turning out the light, I wondered if this whole cruise experience was overrated. There were so many, many people aboard, floating in the middle of a vast ocean and what would happen if the ship were to catch fire? Or sink? How on earth would we all get out? I am claustrophobic by nature and these thoughts were far from comforting.

I heaved a sigh and turned over to try and sleep. My stomach felt a bit queasy and I couldn't get comfortable. Quickly I reached up to click on the lamp, then shifted around to stare out the porthole.

The night sky was velvet with pinprick stars glowing like tiny beacons of hope. Lights from the ship brightened the sea just below my window enough so I could watch the churning, frothing waters as we cruised along in utter darkness.

Mesmerized by the movement I was overcome with awe by the seemingly endless depth of the ocean and the rhythmic power of her waves.

What was it about the ocean that called to my soul, pulling at the center of my being and drawing me deep. Filling me with a longing that no words could define. Gooseflesh rippled over my arms and I hugged myself in a tight embrace, looking away, breaking contact.

But I could not stay away. And once again Her magnetic pull held me close like a lover until I wanted to melt into Her and become Her, despite the fear of being pulled into the deep, dark Unknown.

I slept well in spite of my misgivings and the next morning resolved to turn this cruise into something enjoyable and fun. After all – I was here on vacation!

I fluffed up my hair in the tiny bathroom mirror, put on a dab of bright pink lipstick and off I went, breathing deeply as a reminder to focus on happy thoughts. Fun thoughts. Vacation thoughts. Now what do I love to do when on vacation? Run to the ocean. Be there, right at the edge of the water in time to catch the first golden rays of a rising sun. And flow with my tai chi practice.

So that's exactly what I did. Took the elevator up to the dining area to grab a smoothie for some calories (I could eat breakfast later) and then bopped up some stairs as high as I could comfortably go. Oh it was glorious up here! I could see for miles and miles and miles! A few early birds were milling around, some holding coffee cups, others with a camera expectantly pointed to where the sun was just beginning to appear on the horizon.

A huge wave of joy swept over me and through me. I stood in awe allowing the anticipation of a brand-new day, of pure ocean goodness to sink into my body, mind and spirit. What absolute delight in watching the sun slowly emerge from its nighttime retreat, magically washing the sky in a rosy golden glow.

Taking in a deep breath of fresh, crisp ocean air, I began the soothing movements of tai chi.

Ahhh, yes. This is what I came here for!

This early morning ritual of witnessing a sunrise, drawing cool refreshing air into my lungs and moving my body in time to my own inner rhythms.

I felt light. I felt free.

I felt happy and at peace with the world once more. I could totally relax in the moment, feeling connected to Source and completely in the flow of Life.

This is where I belong. At one with Nature.

And when I turned around to leave, I noticed a man watching me. He had a huge smile on his face, a smile of genuine pleasure as if he understood what I was doing, what I had been through or where I was going. Or – perhaps he was contemplating joining me.

I quickly covered up my surprise with a smile of my own and walked over to chat. As my eyes held his, I felt a ripple of recognition pass between us, although I'd never seen him before. A little embarrassed, I took my leave after only a few minutes.

Strangely enough, whenever I happened to bump into him we both smiled as if sharing a secret.

I felt a clear connection, as if we'd met before. Perhaps this was a soul connection of sorts. I don't know, but the whole encounter lifted my spirits and I began to feel a tingling of hope.

Hope that one day I will find someone special to share my life, someone as wonderful as David.

Chapter 3

Full Circle

At the six year mark – I moved.

Out of my daughter's home and back into Our Home.

Yes Our Old Home.

The home I was so desperate to leave after David died. The home that had been so completely transformed I thought I could never live there again.

But it was Our Home. The Home that David and I shared, the Home we lived and loved in. I knew in the depths of my soul that this was where I belong.

I could always change it back. I could liven it up once again and make it sing, make it beautiful. I knew it would not be an easy process. It would take time and more money than I had right now. But this was Our Home.

And that's where I belong.

Author Biography

Wendy Willow is an intuitive palm reader, numerologist, workshop leader and published writer who has given readings at Psychic and Alternative Health Fairs across North America.

Following the urgings of her soul, she began writing articles to elucidate the role of the Palmist, stressing the healing or guiding aspect of the craft. Education was her goal and she became a regular contributor to the *Journal of Alternative Health, Purple Pagan, Waxing & Waning,* and *Ever-Changing Magazine.*

Her need to read people, to search the depths of the human soul for the truth, to encourage and empower the individual clearly defines her purpose in this lifetime. Whether reading or writing, her focus remains the same.

Her studies at The Palmistry Centre and the Institute of Natural Health, Montreal, Canada provided the groundwork for her palm reading/healing career. She opened a bookstore, The Sunflower, in Montreal in 1994, where her palm reading and writing became firmly established. Her first book, *Reading Between The Lines,* was proudly displayed on the shelves.

She now resides in Tulsa, Oklahoma, where she gives online numerology readings and continues with her writing. Tai chi, singing, biking, swimming, gardening, lunching and coffeeing with friends or walking in the woods turn her days into joy. Travelling too, as much as possible.

You can find her at: http://www.wendywillowauthor.com.

Previous Title

READING BETWEEN THE LINES
A Peek into the Secret World of a Palm Reader
ISBN: 978 1 84694 672 1

Overview

Reading Between The Lines is a true story about real people. People who have decided to change their lives. Their journey begins with the Palm Reader. Not a fortune teller or charlatan, but an educated, trustworthy person who holds the key to uncover each person's truth.

Truths that are meant to heal, not hurt. Truths to help the client realize his full potential, choose an appropriate career, find a soulmate, avoid potential illness, create an abundant lifestyle.

Author Wendy Willow invites you into her private practice where you will listen to each person's story unfolding. Lines and signs on the hand are interpreted for guidance, for understanding, for healing and personal growth.

Seeing yourself reflected in these pages might just prompt you to sneak a peek at your own palm!

Praise

Reading the palms of the hands is a well-proven way to access the deeper, and ever-evolving patterns in a person's life. *Reading Between The Lines* takes you directly into the experience of entering the wisdom contained in the handprints. You'll feel how different patterns can be interpreted for guidance and growth, and be encouraged to "try your hand" at this wonderful, ancient art.

Penney Peirce, intuition expert and author of *Frequency: The Power of Personal Vibration* and *The Intuitive Way: The Definitive Guide to Increasing Your Awareness*

Wendy Willow is a seasoned palm reader and has been practicing for over 20 years. She is a Montrealer who does not confine her work solely to palm reading (including past life readings for some clients), but also makes use of the healing arts (such as affirmations and creative visualization) and numerology. She seems to be particularly adept at discerning what lines of work a person could successfully and naturally follow. As often noted in her interesting descriptions of her sessions with clients, many experience a "Eureka moment" after being told of their natural bents.

Elaine Campbell, author of *My Friend Nick The Greek*

An enjoyable read, covering the experiences of a traditional, intuitive palm reader.

Johnny Fincham, author of *Palmistry: From Apprentice to Pro in Twenty-Four Hours* and *The Spellbinding Power of Palmistry*

Note to Reader

Thank you for purchasing *Silver Butterfly Wings*. My sincere hope is that you derived as much pleasure from reading this book as I have in creating it. If you have a few moments, please feel free to add your review of the book at your favorite online site for feedback. Also, if you would like to connect with other books that I have coming in the near future, please visit my website for news on upcoming works, recent blog posts and to sign up for my newsletter:

www.wendywillowauthor.com

Sincerely,

Wendy Willow

O-BOOKS

SPIRITUALITY

O is a symbol of the world, of oneness and unity; this eye represents knowledge and insight. We publish titles on general spirituality and living a spiritual life. We aim to inform and help you on your own journey in this life.
If you have enjoyed this book, why not tell other readers by posting a review on your preferred book site?

Recent bestsellers from O-Books are:

Heart of Tantric Sex
Diana Richardson
Revealing Eastern secrets of deep love and intimacy to Western couples.
Paperback: 978-1-90381-637-0 ebook: 978-1-84694-637-0

Crystal Prescriptions
The A-Z guide to over 1,200 symptoms and their healing crystals
Judy Hall
The first in the popular series of eight books, this handy little guide is packed as tight as a pill-bottle with crystal remedies for ailments.
Paperback: 978-1-90504-740-6 ebook: 978-1-84694-629-5

Take Me To Truth
Undoing the Ego
Nouk Sanchez, Tomas Vieira
The best-selling step-by-step book on shedding the Ego, using the
teachings of *A Course In Miracles*.
Paperback: 978-1-84694-050-7 ebook: 978-1-84694-654-7

The 7 Myths about Love...Actually!
The Journey from your HEAD to the HEART of your SOUL
Mike George
Smashes all the myths about LOVE.
Paperback: 978-1-84694-288-4 ebook: 978-1-84694-682-0

The Holy Spirit's Interpretation of the New Testament
A Course in Understanding and Acceptance
Regina Dawn Akers
Following on from the strength of *A Course In Miracles*, NTI
teaches us how to experience the love and oneness of God.
Paperback: 978-1-84694-085-9 ebook: 978-1-78099-083-5

The Message of A Course In Miracles
A translation of the Text in plain language
Elizabeth A. Cronkhite
A translation of *A Course in Miracles* into plain, everyday
language for anyone seeking inner peace. The companion
volume, *Practicing A Course In Miracles*, offers practical lessons
and mentoring.
Paperback: 978-1-84694-319-5 ebook: 978-1-84694-642-4

Your Simple Path
Find Happiness in every step
Ian Tucker
A guide to helping us reconnect with what is really important in
our lives.
Paperback: 978-1-78279-349-6 ebook: 978-1-78279-348-9

365 Days of Wisdom
Daily Messages To Inspire You Through The Year
Dadi Janki
Daily messages which cool the mind, warm the heart and guide
you along your journey.
Paperback: 978-1-84694-863-3 ebook: 978-1-84694-864-0

Body of Wisdom
Women's Spiritual Power and How it Serves
Hilary Hart
Bringing together the dreams and experiences of women across
the world with today's most visionary spiritual teachers.
Paperback: 978-1-78099-696-7 ebook: 978-1-78099-695-0

Dying to Be Free
From Enforced Secrecy to Near Death to True Transformation
Hannah Robinson
After an unexpected accident and near-death experience, Hannah
Robinson found herself radically transforming her life, while a
remarkable new insight altered her relationship with her father, a
practising Catholic priest.
Paperback: 978-1-78535-254-6 ebook: 978-1-78535-255-3

The Ecology of the Soul
A Manual of Peace, Power and Personal Growth for Real People
in the Real World
Aidan Walker
Balance your own inner Ecology of the Soul to regain your
natural state of peace, power and wellbeing.
Paperback: 978-1-78279-850-7 ebook: 978-1-78279-849-1

Not I, Not other than I
The Life and Teachings of Russel Williams
Steve Taylor, Russel Williams
The miraculous life and inspiring teachings of one of the World's
greatest living Sages.
Paperback: 978-1-78279-729-6 ebook: 978-1-78279-728-9

On the Other Side of Love
A woman's unconventional journey towards wisdom
Muriel Maufroy
When life has lost all meaning, what do you do?
Paperback: 978-1-78535-281-2 ebook: 978-1-78535-282-9

Practicing A Course In Miracles
A translation of the Workbook in plain language, with
mentor's notes
Elizabeth A. Cronkhite
The practical second and third volumes of The Plain-Language
A Course In Miracles.
Paperback: 978-1-84694-403-1 ebook: 978-1-78099-072-9

Quantum Bliss
The Quantum Mechanics of Happiness, Abundance, and Health
George S. Mentz
Quantum Bliss is the breakthrough summary of success and spirituality secrets that customers have been waiting for.
Paperback: 978-1-78535-203-4 ebook: 978-1-78535-204-1

The Upside Down Mountain
Mags MacKean
A must-read for anyone weary of chasing success and happiness – one woman's inspirational journey swapping the uphill slog for the downhill slope.
Paperback: 978-1-78535-171-6 ebook: 978-1-78535-172-3

Your Personal Tuning Fork
The Endocrine System
Deborah Bates
Discover your body's health secret, the endocrine system, and 'twang' your way to sustainable health!
Paperback: 978-1-84694-503-8 ebook: 978-1-78099-697-4

Readers of ebooks can buy or view any of these bestsellers by clicking on the live link in the title. Most titles are published in paperback and as an ebook. Paperbacks are available in traditional bookshops. Both print and ebook formats are available online.
Find more titles and sign up to our readers' newsletter at http://www.johnhuntpublishing.com/mind-body-spirit
Follow us on Facebook at https://www.facebook.com/OBooks/ and Twitter at https://twitter.com/obooks